# FROM EMPEROR TO CITIZEN

—The Autobiography of Aisin-Gioro Pu Yi

## VOLUME TWO

FOREIGN LANGUAGES PRESS
BEIJING

First Edition     1965
Second Edition     1979
Third Printing   1986


Translated by
W. J. F. JENNER




ISBN    0-8351-1159-8

Copyright 1986 by Foreign Languages Press

Published by Foreign Languages Press
24 Baiwanzhuang Road, Beijing, China

Printed by Foreign Languages Printing House
19 West Chegongzhuang Road, Beijing, China

Distributed by China International Book Trading Corporation
(Guoji Shudian), P.O. Box 399, Beijing China

*Printed in the People's Republic of China*

# Contents

CHAPTER SIX    FOURTEEN YEARS OF "MANCHUKUO"    251

The Puppet Play Begins                                                    253
Majesty Without Power                                                     258
The Signing of the Secret Treaty and After                               262
The Report of the League of Nations Commission of Enquiry                267
"Emperor" for the Third Time                                             273
The End of Illusion                                                       283
Yoshioka Yasunori                                                         292
"Imperial Rescripts"                                                      295
Home Life                                                                 303
The Collapse                                                             312


CHAPTER SEVEN    IN THE SOVIET UNION    321

Fear and Illusion                                                         323
Still Giving Myself Airs                                                  325
I Refuse to Admit My Guilt                                               327


CHAPTER EIGHT    FROM FEAR TO RECOGNIZING MY
                 GUILT    331

I Expect to Die                                                           333
Arriving in Fushun                                                        339
Separated from My Family                                                  343
Move to Harbin                                                            349
Writing My Autobiography and Presenting My Seals                         354
Changes in My Household                                                   359
Confession and Leniency                                                   365

Making Boxes                                                  371
The Investigators Arrive                                      378
The Sufferings and Hatred of the People of the Northeast      383
"You Can Never Escape the Consequences of Your Sins"          388

CHAPTER NINE    I ACCEPT REMOULDING                           395

How Shall I Be a Man?                                         397
It Is Up to Me                                                403
Why So Magnanimous?                                           408
The Changes Explain Everything                                416
Meeting Relations                                             421
The Japanese War Criminals                                    431
"The World's Glory"                                           437
Another Visit                                                 444
Labour and Optimism                                           453
The Test                                                      458
Special Pardon                                                466
A New Chapter                                                 472

Index                                                         485

CHAPTER SIX

# FOURTEEN YEARS OF "MANCHUKUO"

# The Puppet Play Begins

My feelings were confused and contradictory at the private banquet Colonel Itagaki gave for me on the evening of February 24, 1932 to celebrate my consenting to become "Chief Executive" of the new Japanese puppet state of "Manchukuo". Itagaki had provided Japanese prostitutes for the guests, and he fondled and embraced them without bothering about the conventions of polite behaviour. As he drank freely and roared with laughter he made no attempt to conceal his pleasure at his success in forcing me to accept his terms. While he still had some control over himself he toasted me most respectfully, wishing me a successful future and the fulfilment of my ambitions, and I was very pleased to hear this. But as the evening wore on and he drank more and more his face became increasingly livid and things started to go wrong. One Japanese prostitute asked me in forced Chinese, "Are you in trade?" When Itagaki heard he burst into a strange laugh, and I realized that I had little to be pleased about.

On February 28 the "All-Manchurian Assembly" in Shenyang passed a resolution at the bidding of the Kwantung Army proclaiming the independence of the Northeast and appointing me "Chief Executive of the new state". Kaeisumi and Cheng Hsiao-hsu told me that as delegates from this "assembly" were going to come to Lushun to invite me to accept the office, we would need to prepare a reply in advance, or rather two replies. The first would be a refusal and the second an acceptance, to be produced when the delegates pressed me a second time. On March 1 the nine-man delegation arrived in Lushun, and Cheng Hsiao-hsu, who met them on my behalf, handed them the first reply. Afterwards I met them myself, and both sides made the set speeches they had been told to make; they "earnestly beseeched" me, I "modestly refused", and before twenty minutes had passed the meeting finished. On March 5 the "delegation" was increased to twenty-nine members at the bidding of the Fourth Section[1] of the Kwantung Army and came once more to "plead earnestly" with me. This time they accomplished their mission, and my final answer ran as follows:

> As you entrust me with this great responsibility, how could I venture to refuse for the sake of idleness and leisure? But, after careful reflection, I feel that I should disappoint the hopes of the masses. . . . I shall exert my feeble abilities to the utmost and act as a temporary Chief Executive for one year; and if my shortcomings are too many I shall respectfully retire after that year. If within the year a constitution is created and the form of the state settled in accordance with my original intention I shall then carefully reconsider my virtue and my strength and decide what to do.

This interlude over, I left for Changchun the following day with Wan Jung, Cheng Hsiao-hsu, Chang Ching-hui and others. As my train pulled into Changchun station at 3 p.m. on March 8, I heard the sound of military bands and cheering crowds. When I stepped on the platform surrounded by Chang Ching-hui, Hsi Hsia, Amakasu, Kaeisumi and others I saw Japanese gendarmes and rows of people wearing all sorts of clothes; some were in Chinese jackets and gowns, some in Western suits and some in traditional Japanese clothes, and they were all holding small flags in their hands. I was thrilled, and I reflected that I was now seeing the scene I had missed at the harbour. As I walked past them Hsi Hsia pointed out a line of dragon flags between Japanese ones and said that the men holding them were all Manchu bannermen who had been waiting for me to come for twenty years. These words brought tears to my eyes, and I was more strongly convinced than ever that my future was very hopeful.

When I climbed into my car my thoughts were on my Forbidden City, my expulsion from it, the robbery of the Eastern Mausolea,

---

[1] This section dealt with political and military affairs in the Northeast.

and the oath I swore as a result. I was too preoccupied with my hopes and hates to notice the streets I was driving through, or to observe the cold welcome that the citizens of Changchun, silent from terror and hatred, were giving me. After a short journey the car drove into the courtyard of an old building. This was to be the "Residence of the Chief Executive", although it was far from being the grandest house in the city.

I took office ceremonially the next day in a large reception room that had been put hurriedly in order. Uchida, the director of the Japanese South Manchuria Railway, Honjo, the commander of the Kwantung Army, Miyake, its chief of staff, and the staff officer Itagaki were among those present. Many of my "old ministers" attended: in addition to Cheng Hsiao-hsu, Lo Chen-yu, Hu Sze-yuan and Chen Tseng-shou they included other former Ching officials and a number of Mongol princes. There were also former members of the Fengtien clique, such as Chang Ching-hui, Tsang Shih-yi, Hsi Hsia and Chang Hai-peng; and there was a former staff officer of the Dog-meat General Chang Tsung-chang.

I wore Western evening dress. Under the gaze of the Japanese dignitaries the "founders of the nation" bowed to me three times and I bowed once to them. Then Tsang Shih-yi and Chang Ching-hui, acting on behalf of "the people of Manchuria", presented me with the "seal of the Chief Executive" wrapped in yellow silk. After this Cheng Hsiao-hsu read out the "Proclamation of the Chief Executive" on my behalf.

Mankind should respect morality, but as racial discrimination exists people oppress others to exalt themselves, thus weakening morality. Mankind should respect benevolence, but because of international strife some try to injure others for their own advantage, thus weakening benevolence. Morality and benevolence are the principles on which our country is founded, and with the removal of racial discrimination and international strife it will inevitably become a paradise of the Kingly Way. I hope that all my people will endeavour to achieve this.

When I met the foreign guests after the ceremony the director of the South Manchuria Railway made a congratulatory address and Lo Chen-yu read out my reply. Then we went into the courtyard for the raising of the new flag and for photographs. The proceedings ended with a banquet.

That afternoon Cheng Hsiao-hsu came with some "official business" to the "Office of the Chief Executive".

"General Honjo has recommended that your servant become prime minister and organize a cabinet." He bowed as he spoke, his voice smooth and his bald pate glistening. "This is a list of special appointments and of ministers.[1] Will Your Majesty please sign it."

As the Japanese agent Amakasu had already discussed this with me in Lushun I took my brush and signed. I had transacted my first item of "Manchukuo" state business.

---

[1] Here is a list of the chief traitors who held office in the "Manchukuo" regime.
*Prime Minister and Minister of Education:* Cheng Hsiao-hsu
*Minister of Civil Affairs and Governor of Fengtien Province:* Tsang Shih-yi
*Foreign Minister:* Hsieh Chieh-shih
*Minister of Defence and President of the Privy Council:* Chang Ching-hui
*Minister of Finance and Governor of Kirin Province:* Hsi Hsia
*Minister of Industry:* Chang Yen-ching
*Minister of Communications:* Ting Chien-hsiu
*Minister of Justice:* Feng Han-ching
*Governor of Heilungkiang Province:* Cheng Chih-yuan
*President of the Legislative Council:* Chao Hsin-po
*President of the Supervisory Council:* Yu Chung-han
*President of the Supreme Court:* Lin Chi
*President of the Supreme Procurator's Office:* Li Pan
*Deputy President of the Privy Council:* Tang Yu-lin
*Privy Councillors:* Chang Hai-peng, Yuan Chin-kai, Lo Chen-yu, Kuei Fu
*Chief Secretary of the Office of the Chief Executive:* Hu Sze-yuan
*Members of the Secretariat of the Office of the Chief Executive:* Wan Sheng-shih, Shang Yen-ying, Lo Fu-pao, Hsu Pao-heng, Lin Ting-shen
*Head of the Bureau of Internal Affairs:* Pao Hsi
*Special Officials of the Bureau of Internal Affairs:* Chang Yen-ching, Chin Pi-tung, Wang Chi-lieh, Tung Chi-hsu, Wang Ta-chung, Shang Yen-ying
*Head of the Security Bureau:* Tung Chi-hsu
*Commander of the Guard:* Chang Hai-peng
*Secretaries to the State Council:* Cheng Chui, Cheng Yu

I had been deeply impressed by the bands and the dragon flags on Changchun station, the ceremony of taking office and the speech of praise made when I met the foreign guests, and as a result I was feeling light-headed. But by taking office openly I had put myself into a position from which there was no retreat. Moreover, if I got along with the Japanese they might even help me to recover my imperial title. When I looked on the bright side, being "Chief Executive" seemed to be not a humiliation but a step towards the imperial throne. The problem to which I now gave my attention was how best to use this position. After thinking it over for several days I announced my conclusions to Chen Tseng-shou and Hu Sze-yuan, who were both now in my secretariat:

"I have made two vows and a wish, and I want to tell you about them. First, I am going to overcome all my old faults, and I vow that I will never again be lazy or frivolous as Chen Pao-shen said I was ten years ago. Secondly, I vow that I shall not rest until I have overcome all obstacles and restored my ancestral heritage. Thirdly, I beg that heaven will send me an heir to continue the line of the Great Ching. If these three things are accomplished I can die happy."

About a month after I took office the "Residence of the Chief Executive" was changed to a redecorated building that had previously been the Kirin-Heilungkiang Salt Tax Office. At first I rose early every morning and went straight to my office, not going back to my living quarters until evening. Hoping to carry out my vows and return to the throne, I followed the instructions of the Kwantung Army while working long hours under the illusion that I would be able to use my power as head of state. But this diligence did not last long as there was no state business to transact and I soon found out that the powers of the "Chief Executive" existed on paper only.

# Majesty Without Power

The thirteen clauses of the first section of the "Organizational Law of Manchukuo" laid down my powers in black and white. The first clause stated that "the Chief Executive rules Manchukuo", and the second to the fourth stipulated that I had legislative, executive and judiciary power. Other clauses laid it down that my proclamations would be as binding as laws; that I determined the official structure and made official appointments; that I was the supreme commander of the army, navy and air force; that I had the power to issue pardons and amnesties, to lighten punishments and to restore rights to men who had been deprived of them; and so on.

In fact I did not even have the power to decide when I would go out of my own front gates. One day I thought of going for a stroll and took my wife Wan Jung and two of my sisters for a walk in the "Tatung Park". Before I had been in the park for many minutes Japanese gendarmes and men of the "Security Bureau of the Residence of the Chief Executive" drove up and asked me to go back. Apparently my absence from my residence had been reported to the Japanese gendarmerie, and large numbers of troops and police had been mobilized to search for me, causing a great commotion throughout the city. After the affair my adviser Kaeisumi told me that for the sake of my dignity and my security I should not go out again by myself. From then on I never went out of the front gate except on expeditions arranged by the Kwantung Army.

At first I believed the explanation about why I should not go out by myself, but after a few days of working on "state business" in my office I began to have doubts. Although I seemed to be very busy and had many visitors, mostly government ministers and high-ranking advisers, they only expressed their loyalty to me and gave me presents, never discussing official business. If I asked them about such subjects their reply was either, "The vice-minister is looking after that", or, "I must ask the vice-minister about it". The vice-ministers were Japanese, and they never came to see me.

Hsu Sze-yuan was the first to lose patience. He pointed out to Cheng Hsiao-hsu, now premier of the puppet regime, that the ministers should have control of their ministries and that important decisions should first be made by the Chief Executive and then carried out by the ministries. It was quite wrong that the vice-ministers should settle everything. "We are carrying out responsible cabinet government," was Cheng's reply, "and affairs of state must first be decided at the meetings of the State Council. The cabinet is responsible to the Chief Executive, and every week the premier refers the proposals it has adopted at its meetings to the Chief Executive for decision. This is the way it is done in Japan." Cheng agreed that the minister should control his own ministry and said that he was going to bring up this point with the commander of the Kwantung Army. He had, in fact, met the same problem in his relationship with the Japanese head of the General Affairs Office of the State Council.

I do not know how Cheng Hsiao-hsu's conversation with the Kwantung Army commander on this subject went, but I learnt what was really meant by "responsible cabinet government" and the relationship between ministers and vice-ministers from the account Hu Sze-yuan gave me of a meeting of the State Council.

The subject under discussion was official salaries. As usual, the draft bill was prepared by the General Affairs Office of the State Council and a printed copy was handed to each of the ministers. They had agreed quickly enough to previous bills, which had been on such subjects as the take-over of the property of the previous Northeastern government, the provision of grain and fodder to the Japanese army and the confiscation of four major Northeastern banks. But they were not so casual now that their own interests were directly involved. They went into the bill thoroughly, and when they found that the pay scales for Japanese officials were about 40 per cent higher than those for "Manchurian" ones, they made their dissatisfaction clear in the angry discussion that followed. Hsi Hsia, the Minister of Finance, protested that the higher salaries for Japanese were incompatible with the racial equality and friendship on which the state was supposed to be founded. Seeing the awkward turn the meeting was taking, the head of the General

Affairs Office of the State Council, Komai Tokuzo, stopped the discussion and sent for the drafter of the bill, the Japanese head of the personnel department, to answer their questions. The personnel department head calmly explained that before one could consider equality one had first to see whether people were equal in ability. As the Japanese were very able it was only natural that they should be paid more; they were also used to a higher standard of living, and were accustomed to eating rice, not *kaoliang* like the "Manchurians". As for friendship, would not that call for higher salaries for Japanese? This speech, however, failed to appease the ministers, and Komai had to adjourn the meeting until the next day.

The following day Komai reopened the meeting by saying that he had gone into the matter with the vice-ministers, and the Kwantung Army had agreed that the salaries of ministers would be raised to the same level as those of vice-ministers. "But as the Japanese officials will be living far from home," he added, "and are going to build a paradise of the Kingly Way for the Manchurians we should be grateful to them. We are therefore going to give them special supplementary payments. This decision is final and there can be no further discussion on it." Most of the ministers felt that they had got their money and that making more trouble would get them nowhere, but Hsi Hsia, who thought that he was on especially good terms with the commander of the Kwantung Army, was not going to be put off by Komai. "I'm not going to argue over a few cents," he put in, "but I would like to ask where the Japanese are going to establish this paradise of the Kingly Way if not in Manchuria. Could they establish it without the Manchurians?"

Komai was incensed, and he thumped the table. "Do you know the history of Manchuria?" he bellowed. "Don't you realize that the Japanese paid for it with their blood and sweat when they took it from the Russians?"

"Will you let me talk?" retorted Hsi Hsia, his face white. "General Honjo has never shouted at me."

"I'm telling you," roared Komai. "This has been decided by the Army." There was nothing more that Hsi Hsia could say, and the whole room was silent.

From then onwards "responsible cabinet government" and "the meetings of the State Council" fooled no one. The real prime minister was not Cheng Hsiao-hsu but Komai, the head of the General Affairs Office of the State Council. Even the Japanese did not conceal this, and the Japanese magazine *Reform* openly referred to him as the "premier of Manchukuo". And the real premier regarded the commander of the Kwantung Army as his superior, not the nominal chief executive. Similarly, the bills discussed at the meetings of the State Council had already been decided at the weekly discussions of the vice-ministers who formed the real cabinet of "Manchukuo", responsible to "His Imperial Majesty" the commander of the Kwantung Army. The Fourth Section of the Kwantung Army always participated in these discussions, and many of the bills were drafted to meet its requirements.

All this soon became obvious to anybody and should have shattered my illusions, but that was not in my character. The talkative Hu Sze-yuan was always reminding me of my unique position, and I recalled a view that I had held in my Tientsin days: "Without me, the true emperor, the Japanese will be in a very difficult position." The outwardly respectful way in which the Japanese behaved towards me misled me into believing that I was entirely different from Hsi Hsia and that the Japanese were obliged to treat me with respect. This was what I thought at the time of the foundation of the "Concordia Association".

One day about a month after I had taken office, Cheng Hsiao-hsu told me in the course of one of his regular reports that the Kwantung Army wanted to form a political party and call it the "Concordia Party". The purpose of the party was to "organize the masses to co-operate in building the nation" and to cultivate a spirit of "respect for the rites and glad acceptance of the heavenly commands". The word "party" always terrified me, and hearing this news made me even more alarmed than I had been when I was told about Komai thumping the table. I cut Cheng's remarks short and waved my hand in disapproval. "What do they want a party for? What good can a party do? Wasn't the fall of the dynasty the work of a party? Have you forgotten that Confucius said that a gentleman should have nothing to do with parties?" Cheng Hsiao-hsu's face fell. "Your Majesty is quite right, but the Army has already made up its mind." He had hoped that this would silence me, but to his surprise I regarded this as a matter of life and death and refused to agree to it. I was sick of hearing that everything had been decided by the Army. "Either go and inform the Japanese," I said angrily, "or tell them to come and see me."

Two days later Itagaki and two other officers from the Fourth Section of the Kwantung Army came to offer me explanations, but they all failed to convince me, so that the matter dragged on unresolved.

In July, three months later, I thought that I had won. The Kwantung Army decided to form not a "Concordia Party" but a "Concordia Association". Its function would be to support the government, and the association and its affiliated organizations were meant to include the whole population of "Manchukuo" above the age of ten.

The real reason why the Kwantung Army changed it from a "party" to an "association" was nothing to do with me. They thought that the latter would be more effective than a political party for propagandizing, spying on and enslaving the people. I, of course, did not realize this and thought that they were complying with my wishes. As I was under this illusion it was not surprising that I got nowhere after the signing of the secret treaty between "Manchukuo" and Japan.

# The Signing of the Secret Treaty and After

Cheng Hsiao-hsu had settled with Honjo the conditions on which I would take office as Chief Executive and he would become premier back at the time when we were staying in Lushun. Cheng told me about this on the eve of Honjo's resignation.

On August 18, 1932 Cheng Hsiao-hsu came to my office with a pile of documents. "This is an agreement your subject has made with General Honjo," he said. "Will Your Majesty please approve it."

I looked at the agreement. "Who told you to sign this?" I was furious.

"These are all the conditions that Itagaki laid down in Lushun," he replied with icy calm. "Itagaki told Your Majesty about them a long time ago."

"Nonsense. He never told me, and even if he had done so you still have no right to sign before consulting me."

"I did it on Itagaki's instructions. He said that he was afraid that it would only cause trouble if Hu Sze-yuan and the others saw it beforehand as they don't understand the situation."

"Who is in charge here? You or I?"

"Your subject would not dare to presume. This agreement is a temporary measure. How can Your Majesty refuse to sign it if you want the help of the Japanese? All that is conceded in it is what the Japanese already have in fact, and we can sign another agreement in future stating that after a few years you will resume these powers."

He was right in saying that the Japanese already had the powers that were conceded in the agreement. The essence of the agreement was that Japan would have complete control over the "defence and security" of "Manchukuo"; that Japan would administer the railways, harbours, waterways, and airways of "Manchukuo" and could carry out further construction; that the supplies and equipment needed by the Japanese troops would be provided by "Manchukuo"; that the Japanese would have the right to open mines and exploit natural resources; that the Japanese would be allowed to hold office in "Manchukuo"; that Japan would have the right to move immigrants into "Manchukuo"; and many other items. The agreement ended by stating that it would be the basis for a formal treaty between the two countries. Cheng Hsiao-hsu was right in saying that we would have to pay a price for the "support" of Japan. But all the same, I could not help feeling angry. I felt that Cheng Hsiao-hsu had gone too far on his own initiative in selling "my" country to the Japanese. I was also angry with Japan for deceiving me. Although it had refused to give me an imperial throne, it still wanted to take so much from me.

Although I was furious, there was nothing I could do as the matter was already settled. I signed the secret agreement and Cheng took it away with him. Hu Sze-yuan came in, and was indignant when I told him what had happened.

"Cheng Hsiao-hsu is disgraceful. Chen Pao-shen said a long time ago that he is generous with other people's property, and now he has dared to take it on himself to do this."

"It's too late to do anything about it now," I said dejectedly.

"It may not be. We must see what news we get from Tokyo."

Some time previously we had learnt that Honjo, the commander of the Kwantung Army, was going to be replaced and that Japan was going to recognize "Manchukuo". Hu Sze-yuan attached great importance to this news as he thought that the change of command probably indicated a slight difference in Tokyo's attitude, and reckoned that we should send somebody to Japan to make the most of this opportunity. In his view it was impossible to avoid giving Japan some privileges, such as the control of the country's mining, railways, natural resources and defence, but it was essential that I keep the appointment of officials in my hands. On Hu's recommendation I sent two emissaries to Tokyo to see some senior military men, and they put my demands to the chief of the Japanese army staff, to Kashii, the former Japanese commander in Tientsin, and to Muto Nobuyoshi, the incoming Kwantung Army commander. On Hu Sze-yuan's advice I overstated my demands to allow room for concession without giving way on the vital point of control of official appointments. These additional demands were that the ministers have real control of their ministries, that the system of Japanese-run general affairs offices be abolished, that new troops be trained, that the Legislative Council settle the form of the state, and that I be allowed to reorganize the cabinet.

Two days later an excited Hu Sze-yuan told me that a letter had come from my emissaries in Tokyo in which they said that some Japanese elder statesmen and military men who sympathized with me and disapproved of Honjo's attitude towards me were willing to support all my demands. Hu went on to say that this showed that things would change with the arrival of the new Kwantung Army commander, and that I would be able to choose my own officials and rule my own country. But to rule it successfully I would need an obedient prime minister. I agreed, and decided to dismiss Cheng Hsiao-hsu and replace him with Tsang Shih-yi, who would feel grateful to me and obey my directions. I sent for Tsang Shih-yi, but instead Cheng Chui came to see me and protest at the reports that I wanted to reorganize the cabinet. A little later Tsang Shih-yi refused to become prime minister. He knew that he would only be asking for trouble if he accepted without the permission of the Kwantung Army.

When Cheng Hsiao-hsu heard that Tsang Shih-yi had refused he decided to adopt the tactic of asking for leave on grounds of ill health. I had been emboldened by the encouraging news from Tokyo and to his surprise I seized this chance to be rid of him. "It is time you retired," I said, not making the least effort to persuade him to stay on. "I shan't keep you. Please nominate a successor."

The shine disappeared from his bald pate. "Your servant only wanted a few days' sick leave."

"Very well."

As soon as Cheng Hsiao-hsu had gone I sent for Tsang Shih-yi and asked him to be acting prime minister, thinking that I could find a way of getting rid of Cheng Hsiao-hsu later. But before Tsang Shih-yi had committed himself one way or the other Cheng was back at his post.

I decided that when the new Kwantung Army commander arrived I would raise my demands in person. Hu Sze-yuan backed me on this and reminded me to insist on the removal of Cheng Hsiao-hsu.

All this happened at the beginning of September. In the middle of the month Muto Nobuyoshi, the new commander of the Kwantung Army and the first Japanese "Ambassador to Manchukuo", arrived in Changchun. On the 15th Muto and Cheng Hsiao-hsu signed the "Japan-Manchukuo Protocol". This was the public treaty envisaged by the secret agreement.

When the ceremony was over and we had drunk champagne I was most impatient to have a private talk with Muto. I was confident about its outcome as my emissaries in Tokyo had reported that Muto sympathized with my demands and was even willing to consider restoring my imperial title. Muto had commanded the Japanese forces that occupied Siberia during the First World War. He came to the Northeast this time in three concurrent capacities — commander of the Kwantung Army, governor of the "Kwantung Leased Territory", and "Ambassador to Manchukuo". He was the real ruler of the Northeast, the true emperor of "Manchukuo". The Japanese press called him the "guardian deity of Manchuria", and in my eyes this white-haired old fellow of sixty-five really was as powerful as a god. When he bowed to me for the first time, with the greatest politeness, I was overwhelmed with a feeling of being specially favoured by heaven. Having heard me out he replied courteously, "I shall go into Your Excellency's suggestions most carefully."

He took away the list of demands that Hu Sze-yuan had written out for me, but days passed without my hearing the results of his deliberation. As I normally saw the commander of the Kwantung Army three times a month I met him again ten days later. I asked him what his conclusions were, and he replied that he was still considering the demands.

Every time I saw him he was unfailingly courteous, bowing deeply, smiling, always saying "Your Excellency", and talking of each of my ancestors with the greatest respect; but he never once referred to my demands. If I tried to steer the conversation that way he would change the subject. Having been deflected like this a couple of times I did not have the nerve to ask him about them again. Right up to the time of Muto's death in July 1933 we only talked about Buddhism, Confucianism and "friendship". While there was no growth in my power his authority seemed to me to increase every day.

# The Report of the League of Nations Commission of Enquiry

In May 1932 the Commission of Enquiry of the League of Nations arrived in the Northeast. Cheng Hsiao-hsu and Cheng Chui had placed high hopes in the Commission, and when its report was published in October of that year they were sure that their dream of international administration was going to be realized within the foreseeable future. I did not share their passion, but I learnt quite a lot about international affairs from their discussions. Unlike them, I only got an even stronger belief in the might of Japan from the Commission.

The Chengs often spoke about the attitude of the Western powers to the "Manchurian question", and what they said was usually something like this: "Don't pay any attention to the noisy meetings (of the League of Nations) in Geneva and Paris. None of those countries is in fact prepared for a head-on clash with Japan; and America, the one really powerful country since the World War, does not want to take a tough line with Japan either." Cheng Chui, who was highly proficient in English and Japanese, often told me what the foreign press was saying. He reported that quite a few American papers were pro-Japanese, and he once revealed to me that there was a secret agreement between the United States and Japan, one of the terms of which was that America would be understanding about Japan's actions in the Northeast. He also told me in great detail that even before the events of September 18, 1931 an important American personage had advised Chiang Kai-shek to sell Manchuria to Japan and thus bring Japan into direct conflict with the Soviet Union.

"The Commission of Enquiry has come," said Cheng Hsiao-hsu, "at the invitation of the Kuomintang. The Kuomintang hopes that the Commission will help them to deal with Japan, but they are going to be disappointed, as the Commission is interested in the open door, equality of opportunity, and resisting Soviet Russia.

That was what they discussed with Uchida[1] in Tokyo. There is no need to worry; when the time comes you will only have to say a few words to them. In your subject's view the Kuomintang knows that the Commission is not going to achieve anything, and may well see the advantages of international administration of Manchuria." Later events showed that the Chengs were not far wrong.

After the outbreak of fighting in the Northeast on September 18, 1931 Chiang Kai-shek had repeatedly instructed Chang Hsueh-liang to order his troops in the Northeast "not to resist under any circumstances, in order to avoid the spreading of the incident". Four days later, on September 22, Chiang Kai-shek proclaimed at a Kuomintang rally in Nanking that China should "meet might with right, meet savagery with peace, bear her humiliation, restrain her wrath, and temporarily accept the unacceptable until international justice gives its verdict". Yet at the same time he was pursuing the civil war with the utmost barbarity at home, casting "peace" and "right" to the winds.

On September 30 the Kuomintang asked the League of Nations to send a neutral investigating commission to the Northeast. After protracted discussions, Japan agreed to this on December 10, and the motion calling for the setting up of a Commission of Enquiry was passed. It was made up of the nationals of five countries — Lord Lytton of Britain (chairman), Major-General Frank Ross McCoy of the U.S.A., Lieutenant-General Henri Claudel of France, Count Aldrovani of Italy and Dr. Heinrich Schnee of Germany. The group set out on February 3, 1932, and after visiting other parts of China and Tokyo they arrived in the Northeast in May. During this time the Japanese had been expanding the scope of their aggression while the Nanking government made further concessions.

On May 3 I had a meeting with the Commission of Enquiry that lasted about a quarter of an hour. They asked me two questions: how had I come to the Northeast and how had "Manchukuo" been founded?

---

[1] The former director of the South Manchuria Railway who was now Japan's Foreign Minister.

Before I answered them a thought flashed through my brain. I remembered that in the past Johnston had told me that the gates of London were open to me, and wondered whether they would agree to take me to London if I told them that I had only become the "Chief Executive of Manchukuo" as a result of the trickery of Doihara and the threats of Itagaki. But then I remembered that Itagaki and the Kwantung Army chief of staff Hashimoto Toranosuke were sitting beside me. With a glance at the pallid face of Itagaki I obediently started to say what I had been told to say beforehand: "I came to Manchuria after being chosen by the Manchurian masses. My country is completely independent. . . ."

The members of the Commission of Enquiry all nodded and smiled, and they asked no more questions. Then we were photographed together and drank toasts to each other in champagne. After the commission left Itagaki's cold, white face was wreathed in smiles as he praised my performance. "Your Excellency's manner was perfect; you spoke beautifully." Cheng Hsiao-hsu also congratulated me.

I was shown a translation of an article by Komai that was published by the Japanese magazine *Chuokoron* in October, and soon after that the Report of the Commission of Enquiry also came into my hands. Both these documents confirmed the view of the Chengs that the questions that really interested the Commission were "equality of opportunity" and the "open door".

The title of Komai's article was "Manchukuo Speaks to the World", and it contained an account of his conversations with Lord Lytton and others. Komai said that the first question Lytton asked him was, "Was not the founding of Manchukuo a little premature?" His answer had been some nonsense about its foundation being not too early but too late. The talks continued as follows:

General McCoy then asked me, "Is Manchukuo's proclamation of the principle of the open door being carried out?" I replied at once that the open door and equality of opportunity were two of the corner-stones of the country. "Of all the countries that formerly had dealings with China, America was the guiding spirit in initiating this policy. But while this principle is now universally accepted, China has closed her doors. Where in China can open doors now be found? Now we have opened the doors of Manchukuo with a very powerful key, and for this we deserve the thanks and not the protests of you gentlemen. . . . I must add, however, that there is no open door when it comes to national defence, any more than there is in any other country in the world."

Lytton then asked, "Is Manchukuo putting equality of opportunity into practice?"

"Equality of opportunity," I replied without hesitation, "is a subject on which your country has set a precedent. At the end of the former Ching Dynasty, a time when China's political decay had brought her to the brink of partition, Robert Hart warned the Ching court that if China continued the way she was going, she would cease to play any role in international affairs. She would do better to rely on Westerners, and a customs administration was absolutely essential. Thereupon the Ching government appointed Hart as Inspector-General of the Imperial Maritime Customs, and the Imperial Maritime Customs was established. As the customs employed many Englishmen, Frenchmen and Japanese it was known as the most reliable government organization in China, and because of it the powers made loans to China that afforded her great financial assistance. The British regarded the customs as affording equality of opportunity, but if we Japanese wanted to work for the customs we had to pass an almost impossibly stiff test in English.

". . . Manchukuo is a state founded through the co-operation of Manchukuoans and Japanese, which is why all documents of the new state are published in Manchukuoan and Japanese. We will warmly welcome any person of any nationality who is fluent in the Manchukuoan and Japanese languages and would be satisfied with the terms that Manchukuo has to offer. This is what we mean by equality of opportunity."

I asked them if they had any other questions, and they all replied, "There is no need to ask anything else as we fully understand the position of Manchukuo. We are completely satisfied."

When I was seeing the members of the League of Nations Commission of Enquiry off from Hsinking (Changchun) station, Lytton shook me firmly by the hand and said quietly, "I wish the new state of Manchukuo a healthy development."

This conversation made Cheng Hsiao-hsu and his son most excited, and Cheng Chui even reckoned that the League might pass a resolution bringing about the international administration of Manchuria. They were even surer that this was going to happen when the Report of the Commission of Enquiry was published. This document stated openly that China should accept international control. It described Japan's wish for "stable government" as not "unreasonable", but added that "it is only in an atmosphere of external confidence and internal peace . . . that the capital which is necessary for the rapid economic development of Manchuria will be forthcoming". It looked as though the Chengs had been right in expecting that the Commission would advocate international management with pickings for all the foreign powers.

Cheng Hsiao-hsu's forecast of anti-Sovietism was also borne out. The Commission expressed sympathy with Japan regarding Manchuria as her "lifeline". It acknowledged "the interest of Japan in preventing Manchuria from serving as a base of operations directed against her own territory, and even her wish to be able to take all appropriate measures if in certain circumstances the frontiers of Manchuria should be crossed by a foreign power". But, the Commission went on to say, "it may be questioned whether the military occupation of Manchuria for an indefinite period, involving, as it must, a heavy financial burden, is really the most effective way of ensuring against this external danger; and whether . . . the Japanese troops would not be seriously embarrassed if they were surrounded by a restive or rebellious population backed by a hostile China." Japan "might even find it possible, with the sympathy and goodwill of the rest of the world and at no cost to herself, to obtain better security than she will obtain by the costly method she is at present adopting" if she thought of some solution "analogous to arrangements concluded by other Great Powers in various parts of the world".

The Commission opposed the restoration of the *status quo ante* and suggested that "a satisfactory regime for the future might be evolved out of the present one [i.e. the "Manchukuo" regime] without any violent change". It could be given a high degree of autonomy and have foreigners from all countries serving as advisers. As the interests of Japan in the Northeast were much the greatest there would be a high proportion of Japanese, but there would also be set quotas for the nationals of other countries. To put this new form of government into effect the Commission suggested as the first step the setting up of an Advisory Conference composed of the representatives of the Chinese and Japanese Governments and "neutral observers". This conference would refer to the Council of the League of Nations if it failed to agree. The Commission was of the opinion that the method of "international co-operation" was suitable for the rest of China as well as for "Manchuria". The reason they gave for this was the one that the Chengs were constantly giving: China only had labour power, and if she did not draw her capital, technology and talent from abroad she would be unable to build herself up.

In the first few days after seeing the Commission's report, Cheng Hsiao-hsu told me with great glee that things were "very hopeful". He said that Hu Shih had published an article in which he proclaimed the report as the "world's verdict".

But the Chengs were cast into deep depression by the Japanese reaction. Although the Commission had repeatedly stressed that it respected Japan's rights and interests in the Northeast and even described the "September 18th Incident" as an act of self-defence by Japan, the Japanese Foreign Ministry spokesman had only agreed with them on one point: "The proposals on Manchuria of the Commission of Enquiry could probably be applied with profit to the relations between China and the powers, as for example the plan for international control." But Japan was not in the least interested in the plans for international administration of the Northeast. As I have mentioned above, Cheng Hsiao-hsu's enthusiasm for the "open door" and "equality of opportunity" was the reason why he later lost favour with the Japanese and was finally discarded by them.

Before the publication of the Commission's report I had imagined that if the Northeast was put under international control, as the Chengs hoped, I might be much better off than with only the Japanese. But I also had two worries. One was that the Nanking government of Chiang Kai-shek might take part in the "international control", which would put me in a very difficult position; and the other was that even if Nanking left me alone, the international control committee would not want me as emperor if the "autonomous government" were not a monarchy. More important than these worries, however, was the deep impression I had of the savagery of Japan, which had not been restrained in the least by any international action. When I remembered the thought that had flashed through my mind at the time I met the Commission I reflected that it was lucky that I had done nothing foolish, as otherwise my fate would have been sealed. The most important thing now was not to provoke the Japanese, as I would be unable to reascend the throne without their help.

## "Emperor" for the Third Time

It had been agreed that if the Kwantung Army did not institute a monarchy after I had been Chief Executive for a year I could resign. I did not do so, however, as I had not got the necessary courage, and even if the Kwantung Army had allowed it I would have had nowhere to go.

A few days after the anniversary of my taking office, the Kwantung Army commander Muto raised the question, to my great surprise, during one of our regular meetings. He said that Japan was considering the form of the state of "Manchukuo", and that when the time was ripe this problem would be solved.

Soon afterwards, on March 27, 1933, Japan left the League of Nations to increase her freedom of movement. At the same time she stepped up her military attacks on China, pushing south of the Great Wall and encircling Peking and Tientsin. At the end of May the Nanking government, preoccupied with the civil war against the Communists, made further concessions to Japan in signing the "Tangku Agreement". Under this agreement Chinese troops were withdrawn from a large area south of the Great Wall and Japan's control over north China was strengthened. These events were a strong stimulus to the advocates of my restoration, who became active again in the Northeast and north China. In July, Komai, the head of the General Affairs Office of the "State Council of Manchukuo", resigned his post to go and work secretly for the "independence" of north China. He told Cheng Hsiao-hsu that he was going to work for the restoration of my rule throughout the country. All these reports made me and my associates most excited.

My dreams of empire became more vivid. I followed the news with the closest attention, and placed even higher hopes on the Japanese soldiers who were slaughtering my compatriots. After the Japanese occupation of Jehol[1] in 1933 I gave a banquet to congratulate Muto and other officers who had taken part in the fighting, and to wish them ever greater victories. When a Japanese column halted after occupying Miyun, only about fifty kilometres from Peking, I was deeply disappointed. Cheng Hsiao-hsu told me that the Japanese military occupation of north China and even of south China was only a matter of time, and the urgent question of the moment was to settle the form of the "Manchukuo" state. He said that this would be decided not by the Kwantung Army but by Tokyo; he had heard that many of the elder Japanese statesmen were in favour of my return to the throne. I therefore felt that I had to have someone to lobby for me in Tokyo, or at least let me know the latest news.

The man I chose for this job was my guard Kudo Tetsusaburo, a Japanese who had accompanied me from Tientsin to the Northeast. He had given me the impression of being dissatisfied with the attitude of the Kwantung Army, and was the only Japanese who addressed me as "Your Imperial Majesty" after I became Chief Executive. He once demonstrated his loyalty to me by tasting a cup of tea that I suspected of containing poison. I gave him the Chinese name of Chung ("Loyal") and treated him as a member of

---

[1] This province was abolished in 1955 and its territory divided between Hopei, Inner Mongolia and Liaoning.

my own household. When he returned from his short stay in Japan he told me that he had seen Minami Jiro and some leading figures in the Black Dragon Society. He had heard that the military authorities were in favour of a monarchy. This news made me believe that my chance was just about to come.

Kudo's reports were confirmed in October 1933. Hishikari Takashi, the new commander of the Kwantung Army, informed me officially that the Japanese Government was about to recognize me as the "Emperor of Manchukuo".

I went wild with joy, and my first thought was that I would have to get a set of imperial dragon robes.

These were brought from Peking, where they had been in the keeping of one of the High Consorts, but I was unable to wear them as the Kwantung Army pointed out to me that Japan recognized me not as the Great Ching Emperor but as the "Emperor of Manchukuo". Instead I had to wear the "dress uniform of the Generalissimo of the Land, Sea and Air Forces of Manchukuo".

"This won't do at all," I said to Cheng Hsiao-hsu. "I am the descendant of the Aisin-Gioro, so I have to continue the imperial system. Besides, what will the members of the Aisin-Gioro clan think if they see me ascend the throne in foreign-style uniform?"

"Your Majesty is quite right," said Cheng Hsiao-hsu, nodding as he looked at my dragon robes laid out on the table. "Your Majesty is quite right, but what will the Kwantung Army say?"

"Go and see them for me."

After he had gone I gazed with emotion at the dragon robes that the High Consort Jung Hui had preserved for twenty-two years. They were real imperial dragon robes that had been worn by the emperor Kuang Hsu, the robes I had been dreaming of for twenty-two years. I would wear them to reascend the throne, and that would mark the restoration of the Ching Dynasty.

Cheng Hsiao-hsu came back before I had calmed down and told me that the Kwantung Army insisted that I wear military uniform for the enthronement. I was not satisfied, so I sent Cheng to negotiate with them again. They later agreed to allow me to wear the dragon robes to perform the ceremony of "announcing the accession to heaven" and this satisfied me.

On March 1, 1934 I performed the ancient ritual of announcing my accession on an earthen "Altar of Heaven" that had been erected in the eastern suburbs of Changchun, and after this I returned to my residence to change from the dragon robes into the "generalissimo" uniform to enact the enthronement ceremony. The "Office of the Chief Executive" was renamed the "Palace Office" and the place where I lived was now called the "Emperor's Palace". (The term "Imperial Palace" could not be used as that was the name of the palace of the Japanese emperor.) Apart from one new building, the palace was just the "Residence of the Chief Executive" redecorated and given a new name, and it was in one of its halls that the enthronement was held.

The floor was covered with a crimson carpet. A part of the north wall was hung with silk curtains in front of which was a high-backed chair carved with the "imperial emblem" of orchids. I stood before this, flanked on both sides by palace officials. The civil and military officials, headed by "Premier" Cheng Hsiao-hsu, stood in line before me and bowed low three times. I bowed in reply, then Hishikari, the commander of the Kwantung Army, presented me with his credentials as Japanese "Ambassador" and congratulated me. The ceremony over, the members of the Aisin-Gioro clan, who had come from Peking in all but full strength, and some former members of the Household Department performed the ninefold kotow to me as I sat on the chair.

Congratulatory memorials were sent by Ching veterans from China south of the Great Wall, and the Shanghai underworld boss Chang Yu-ching was among those who proclaimed themselves my subjects.

On June 6 Prince Chichibu (Chichibu-no-Miya Yasuhito) came to congratulate me on behalf of his brother the emperor of Japan and give the Japanese Grand Cordon of the Chrysanthemum to me and the Order of the Crown to Wan Jung.

I had not yet got the rights that Hu Sze-yuan repeatedly reminded me to ask for, but I was oblivious to that. The way I received my father at Changchun station when he came up from Peking with my

Going to take office as the "Chief Executive of Manchukuo" on March 9, 1932

Setting out to sacrifice to heaven before the ceremony of
my "accession" to the "Manchukuo" throne: March 1, 1934

The headquarters of the Japanese Kwantung Army

My "palace" in Changchun

Cheng Hsiao-hsu meets the Lytton Commission. *Second from right*: Lord Lytton. *Seventh from right*: Cheng Hsiao-hsu. *Tenth from right*: Komai Tokuzo

After the signing of the "Japan-Manchukuo Protocol". *Front row, fourth from right*: Muto Nobuyoshi, commander of the Kwantung Army. *Seventh from right*: Chang Ching-hui. *Second row, seventh from right*: Itagaki Seishiro

A group photograph including my "supreme emperor", the Kwantung Army commander Hishikari Takashi (*fifth from left*), taken after my enthronement as puppet emperor

Meeting the Japanese Emperor Hirohito during my visit to Japan in 1935

Worshipping at the "National Foundation Shrine"

The Fushun War Criminals Prison

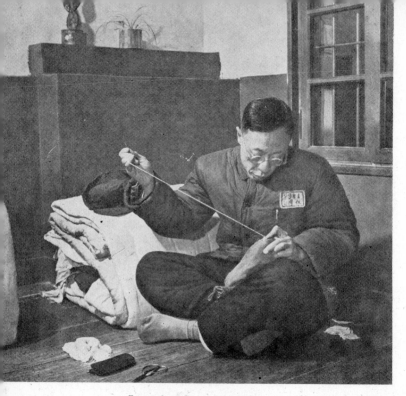

**Learning from Scratch**

Watering plants
in the hothouse

**Labour**

Improving the yard

The underground shop

**Our visit to the Fushun mines**

The workers' old-age home

The sun-lamp room

## Study and daily life

*Top*: consulting reference books

*Middle*: looking at the latest issue of the wall newspaper

*Bottom*: studying Chinese medicine

Morning exercises

Playing *weichi* with Pu Chieh

Appearing as a witness at the military tribunal of the Supreme People's Court. Standing on the right is Furumi Tadayuki

The family heirloom I handed over: the imperial seals in *tienhuang* stone

Receiving my special pardon on December 4, 1959

The official notification of my special pardon (see page 472)

Working at the Peking Botanical Gardens

With my colleagues Yang Po-tao (*first from left*) and Wang Yao-wu (*second from left*) after starting to do literary and historical research at the C.P.P.C.C.

Three generations of the Aisin-Gioro clan spending the 1961 Spring Festival at Tsai Tao's home. Tsai Tao next to me on the right, and Pu Chieh behind me

My voter's card

Taken on the occasion of the fiftieth anniversary of the Revolution of 1911.
*Left*: Lu Chung-lin. *Right*: Hsiung Ping-kun

A corner at the wedding — May Day, 1962. Li Shu-hsien and myself are
second and third from the right, middle row

Setting out to work in the morning with my wife Li Shu-hsien

brothers and sisters a month later is a good illustration of how deeply intoxicated with myself I was.

I sent a group of palace officials and a guard to line up on the platform to receive him, while I and Wan Jung waited outside the palace gate. She wore court dress, while I was in military uniform, my chest covered in Japanese and "Manchukuoan" decorations, as well as ones of the "Great Ching Empire" that I had sent for from south of the Great Wall. As I did not dare to wear these Ching decorations in front of the Kwantung Army I was glad of this chance to show them off.

When my father's car arrived at the palace I saluted and Wan Jung knelt, then I accompanied him into a drawing-room where nobody else was present. I knelt to him and greeted him in the old style.

A great banquet was held that evening. The cuisine and the etiquette were Western. Wan Jung and I sat at the head of the table as host and hostess. I had arranged that an orchestra would play from the moment we entered the banqueting hall; I cannot remember what they played, and I probably had not chosen any particular pieces as I liked anything with trumpets in it.

When we reached the stage of drinking champagne my brother Pu Chieh raised a glass, as I had arranged beforehand, and shouted, "Long live His Majesty the Emperor". My family all joined in the call, and the sound of it made me reel with self-satisfaction.

The next day the senior palace official, Pao Hsi, told me that the Kwantung Army Headquarters had sent someone along to protest in the name of the Japanese Ambassador that in sending an armed guard along to the station I had infringed an agreement between the former Northeastern authorities and Japan that "Manchukuo" had undertaken to observe. Under this agreement a strip of land on either side of the railway lines was to be the territory of the South Manchuria Railway, and no armed men were to be allowed into it except those of the Japanese Army. The Kwantung Army Head-quarters — no, the Japanese Ambassador — wanted an assurance that no such incident would recur.

This should have been enough to bring me to my senses, but the Japanese still allowed me plenty of face. They did not make any public protest, and they said no more about the incident after I had sent someone to apologize and promise that it would not happen again. What was more important was that they arranged that I should have plenty of pomp and circumstance to satisfy my vanity and blind me to reality.

What I found most intoxicating were "imperial" visits and "progresses".

The Kwantung Army arranged that I should make one or two trips outside Changchun every year, and they called these "imperial progresses". I also had to take part in four ceremonies every year in Changchun. Of these one was the sacrifice at the "Pagoda of the Loyal Souls" to the Japanese killed in the aggressive war; another was the sacrifice to the dead soldiers of the "Manchukuo" puppet army at the "Temple of the Loyal Souls Who Founded the Country"; another was the visit to the Kwantung Army Headquarters to offer congratulations on the birthday of the Japanese emperor; and the fourth was the annual meeting of the "Concordia Association". A description of my visit to the "Concordia Association" meeting can illustrate the absurd fuss that accompanied these occasions.

I drove there in a motorcade worthy of an emperor. First went gendarmerie cars, and these were followed at a distance by an open red car in which was seated the Chief of Police. Behind this came my car, also red, with two motor-cyclists on each side. At the end of the procession came the cars of my attendants and of more police.

The day before I went out the Changchun police and gendarmes would arrest "suspicious characters" and unsightly "vagabonds", and on the day itself gendarmes would be posted along my route to stop people from moving along it. Nobody was allowed to enter or leave the shops or houses beside the road or even to put their heads out of the window, and sand was spread on the drive of the "Concordia Association". Before my car left the palace the radio station would broadcast to the whole city in Chinese and Japanese that "the carriage of His Majesty the Emperor is leaving the palace". At this announcement the officials of the "Concordia Association" all had to go out to meet me, and when my car arrived they bowed low to the strains of the "national anthem". After a short rest I met my "ministers". This interlude over, I went into the main hall and climbed on to the platform while a band played and the whole assembly bowed low. The Kwantung Army commander bowed slightly to greet me and I nodded to him in reply. I then read an address to the assembly, who all stood there with their heads lowered and were not allowed to look up, then they all bowed low once more as I left the hall. When I started my journey back to the palace there was another announcement on loudspeakers throughout the city, and a third one was broadcast on my return.

It was said that all this was borrowed from Japan. The words printed on my photograph were also taken from Japanese. Originally it was called "Imperial Countenance", but when the Japanese-style Chinese that the Japanese tended to use was being promoted under the name of "Concordese" the photographs were renamed "True Imperial Images". These pictures had to be displayed in offices, schools, army units and all public organizations. For example, a kind of shrine had to be set up in the conference rooms of offices and the head teacher's study in schools; on the outside was a curtain, and behind this hung my picture and a copy of my "Imperial Rescripts". Anyone who entered the room first had to bow towards the curtain. Although there was no law saying that ordinary citizens had to have a "True Imperial Image" in their houses, the "Concordia Association" often forced people to buy photos of myself and Wan Jung to hang in their main rooms.

The focal points from which this idolatry was spread were the schools and the armed forces. A meeting was held in all schools and military units every morning at which the participants had to bow low, first in the direction of the imperial palace in Tokyo and then towards my palace in Changchun; and whenever the anniversary of the issue of one of my "rescripts" came round, it would be read aloud. I shall have more to say about these "rescripts" later.

I will not go into the "imperial progresses" with which the Japanese built up my majesty. They did it all most conscientiously, and in my experience this was not only to make the Chinese accustomed to

279

blind obedience and feudal, superstitious beliefs, but also to have the same effect on Japanese people. I remember that on a visit to a coal-mine a Japanese foreman was so moved by the "signal honour" of a few words from me that he wept. This, of course, made me feel that I was really somebody.

The time when I was under the gravest misconceptions and thought that I had reached the very pinnacle of authority was after my visit to Japan in April 1935.

All the arrangements for this visit were made by the Kwantung Army. They said that it would be necessary both as a sign of my gratitude to the Japanese emperor for sending Prince Chichibu to congratulate me on my accession and in order that I might give a personal demonstration of "Japan-Manchukuo friendship".

The Japanese government organized a reception committee of fourteen headed by Baron Hayashi Gonsuke, a Privy Councillor. The battleship *Hie Maru* was sent to take me, and other warships provided an escort. When I set sail from Talien I inspected the destroyers *Tamama* No. 12 and No. 15, and there was a fly-past of a hundred aircraft to greet me at Yokohama. I remember that I wrote a toadying poem while I was suffering from seasickness and overwhelmed with the honours that had been paid me on that voyage.

> The sea as flat as a mirror,
> I make a long voyage.
> The two countries hold hands
> To consolidate the East.

On the fourth day of the voyage I watched manoeuvres by seventy warships, and penned some more verses:

> The boats that sail ten thousand *li*
>     cut through the flying waves,
> While heaven and earth
>     commingle in one azure blue.
> This journey is not only
>     to admire mountains and waters,
> But to make our alliance shine
>     like the sun and moon.

Thus even before landing in Japan I had already been deeply struck by her might, and regarded all the honours that had been paid me on the voyage as proof that Japan sincerely respected me and was genuinely helping me. All my misgivings of the past now seemed to have been groundless.

When I arrived in Tokyo the emperor Hirohito himself came to meet me at the station, and then he gave a banquet for me. When I went to visit him, he returned my call. I received Japanese elder statesmen who offered me their congratulations; I inspected a military parade with Hirohito; I went to visit the shrine to the emperor Meiji and a military hospital where there were some soldiers who had been wounded in the invasion of China. I also went to pay my respects to Hirohito's mother. The Japanese press described a walk we took together, saying that the spirit in which I helped the empress dowager of Japan up a slope was the same as that in which I helped my father up steps in the palace in Changchun. In fact I had never once helped my father up a single step, and it was only to ingratiate myself that I supported Hirohito's mother. On the last day of my visit Yasuhito (Prince Chichibu) was at the station to see me off on behalf of his brother the emperor.

"This visit of Your Imperial Majesty to Japan," he said in his farewell speech, "is a great contribution to the close friendship between Japan and Manchukuo. It is my hope that Your Imperial Majesty will return to your country rightly convinced that friendship between our two countries can certainly be achieved."

My reply was as fawning as ever. "I have been most deeply moved by the magnificent reception given me by the Japanese Imperial Family and the warm welcome I have received from the Japanese people. I am determined to do all that is in my power to strive for eternal friendship between Japan and Manchukuo."

When I went on board my ship I was actually in tears as I asked Baron Hayashi to convey my thanks to the emperor and his mother, and this moved him to cry as well. There was nothing Chinese about me at all.

The treatment I had received from the Japanese imperial house really went to my head, and the air seemed to have a different tang to it now that I was emperor. According to my logic I was the equal of the Japanese emperor, and consequently I occupied the same position in "Manchukuo" that he did in Japan; the Japanese should therefore treat me in the same way that they treated their own monarch.

My head full of these illusions, I returned to Changchun and issued the "Admonitory Rescript on the Occasion of the Emperor's Return" that was packed with toadying expressions. I invited the new commander of the Kwantung Army, General Minami Jiro, to come and see me so that I could express my gratitude to him; the next day (April 29) I was an enthusiastic participant in the celebration of Hirohito's birthday. The following day I issued an order that all senior officials in the capital, whether they were Chinese or Japanese, were to come and hear me talk about my visit to Japan. I did not discuss this in advance with the Japanese, nor did I prepare any notes from which to speak. When the time came I gushed away about my visit, describing in detail how the Japanese emperor had met me and elaborating on the respect with which his subjects had treated me. My speech ended:

The friendship between Japan and Manchukuo has led me to hold the firm belief that if any Japanese acts against the interests of Manchukuo he is guilty of disloyalty to His Majesty the Emperor of Japan, and that if any Manchurian acts against the interests of Japan he is being disloyal to the Emperor of Manchukuo. Disloyalty to the Emperor of Manchukuo is the same as disloyalty to the Emperor of Japan, and disloyalty to the Emperor of Japan amounts to disloyalty to the Emperor of Manchukuo.

Within a month of my return to Changchun the Kwantung Army commander Minami told me during one of our regular meetings that "Premier Cheng Hsiao-hsu wishes to retire as he is exhausted by his efforts". He advised me to grant the request and replace Cheng with a new prime minister. I had already heard that Japan was dissatisfied with Cheng and was myself looking for some excuse to get rid of him, so that when Minami raised the matter I agreed at once and suggested Tsang Shih-yi as his successor. I thought that Minami, who had heard my views on Japan-Manchukuo friendship twice in recent days, would be bound to comply with my order; but to my surprise I found that I had run straight into a brick wall. "No," he replied, shaking his head. "The Kwantung Army has already considered the question and chosen a suitable man. There is no need for Your Majesty to worry; all will be well if you choose Chang Ching-hui for the job."

Not long before this Cheng Hsiao-hsu had annoyed his Japanese masters by saying that as "Manchukuo" had now grown up there was no longer any need for them to exercise such tight control; they had therefore kicked him aside. His bank account was frozen, and he was forbidden to move out of Changchun. He lived at home, a disappointed man, under the surveillance of the Japanese gendarmerie until he died a sudden death three years later. His son had also died suddenly, three years before him. It was rumoured that both deaths were the work of the Japanese. Even if this was untrue, Cheng Hsiao-hsu's fall should have been enough to smash my illusions; but it was another year before I began to see what my real position was.


## The End of Illusion


From Japan's withdrawal from the League of Nations at the beginning of 1933 onwards she threw herself with less inhibition than ever into expanding her armed forces and preparing for war. She devoted special attention to speeding up her arrangements for the invasion of the whole of China. Even before the Lukouchiao Incident of July 7, 1937, Japan continued to use armed force and to make coups in north China, while the Kuomintang government in Nanking made concession after concession. It signed the "Ho-Umezu Agreement" in 1935, the "Chin-Doihara Agreement" and other secret treaties which gave the Japanese control of north China. It permitted the functioning of the "Autonomous Military Government of Inner Mongolia", the "Anti-Communist Autonomous Government of

283

Eastern Hopei", and other puppet bodies. It repeatedly assured the Japanese that "not only do we engage in no anti-Japanese activities or thoughts, but we do not even have any cause for being anti-Japanese". It promulgated to the people of China the "Harmony with Our Neighbour Order" and issued many bans on anti-Japanese activities on pain of heavy penalties. All this greatly strengthened Japan's position in north China, and made it clear that it would only be a matter of time before the five provinces of the North were completely lost to China. This was the time when restoration fanatics were active in the Northeast and in north China and I was intoxicated with my third enthronement. But as Japan sunk her claws deeper into north China she tightened her grip on "Manchukuo", and in the end I felt it too.

The process of colonization in the Northeast was very profitable for the Chinese traitors. When the monarchy was introduced, for example, the restorationists gained more than psychological satisfaction. The leading traitors from Cheng Hsiao-hsu downwards were given "rewards for efforts in establishing the country" that ranged from 50,000 to 600,000 dollars each and totalled 8,600,000 dollars; and whenever there was a major act of plunder, such as a "provision of grain" or "patriotic donations", all officials from the prime minister downwards would receive their rewards. Rather than go into the details of all the Japanese measures I will describe how my dreams of restoration gave way to terror.

The Kwantung Army had officially told me at the time they decided to install a monarchy that this was not a restoration of the Ching Dynasty. They had not allowed me to wear the dragon robes for my enthronement and had ignored my opinion in choosing a prime minister. I should have realized how hollow was my majesty, but I was too intoxicated to come to my senses. The first time I knew the taste of disillusion was over the affair of Ling Sheng.

Ling Sheng was the son of Kuei Fu, a former Ching military governor in Mongolia, and had been an adviser in the headquarters of Chang Tso-lin's Peace Preservation Army. He had been one of the members of the delegation that had come to Lushun to invite me to become "Chief Executive", and on the strength of this had been included in the ranks of the "Founders of the Nation". At the time of his sudden arrest in the spring of 1936 by the Kwantung Army he was the governor of the "Manchukuo" province of Hsingan.

The Kwantung Army sent Colonel Yoshioka Yasunori, the "Attaché to the Imperial Household", to tell me that Ling Sheng had been engaged in anti-Manchukuo and anti-Japanese activities. According to information I was given by Tung Chi-hsu, he had voiced his complaints at the last joint meeting of the provincial governors, to the irritation of the Japanese. Apparently Ling Sheng had accused the Japanese of failing to keep their word; Itagaki had originally told him in Lushun that Japan was going to recognize "Manchukuo" as an independent country, but later the Japanese had interfered everywhere. Ling Sheng was powerless in Hsingan as the Japanese controlled everything. After returning from this meeting to Hsingan he was arrested.

I found this news most disquieting as it was only six months back that his son had become engaged to my fourth sister. Just as I was wondering whether I should go and tell the Kwantung Army about this, Ueda Kenkichi, the latest Kwantung Army commander and Japanese "Ambassador", came to see me.

"A few days ago we solved a case in which the criminal was an acquaintance of Your Majesty's — Ling Sheng, the governor of Hsingan province. He had been plotting rebellion and resistance to Japan with the collusion of foreign countries. A military tribunal has found him guilty of crimes against Japan and Manchukuo, and has sentenced him to death."

"Death?" I was shocked.

"Death." He nodded to his interpreter as he repeated the word, wanting to be sure that I understood. "This will be a warning, Your Majesty," he went on to say. "It is essential that he should be killed as a warning to others."

After Ueda's departure Colonel Yoshioka told me that I had better break off the engagement between my sister and Ling Sheng's son at once, and I hurriedly complied.

Ling Sheng's sentence was carried out by decapitation, and several members of his family were killed at the same time. This was the

285

first case of the Japanese killing a high "Manchukuo" official that had come to my knowledge, and the man had only recently wanted to become a relation of mine. I had thought that Ling Sheng must be very loyal to me if he wanted this matrimonial link; but the only criterion by which the Kwantung Army had judged him was his attitude to Japan. Doubtless they used the same criterion with me too. Ueda's statement about killing him as a warning to others now seemed even more ominous.

I remembered that the Kwantung Army had questioned me at the time of some Ching restoration activities at the end of the previous year, and I had decided that I must be more careful in future. How then did the Japanese like people to behave? I thought of a man whose fate had been in direct contrast to that of Ling Sheng's. He was Chang Ching-hui, the "premier", and clearly the Japanese intended me to see two examples in him and Ling Sheng. One can get an idea of the character of this bandit turned "prime minister" and of the appreciation that the Japanese had of him from the way they repeated a saying of his: "Japan and Manchukuo are like two dragonflies tied on a single string." The Japanese used this saying to "educate" the officials of "Manchukuoan" nationality.

When the Japanese were carrying out their policy of settling their own people in the Northeast they wanted to get a bill passed by a "cabinet meeting" to enable them to expropriate agricultural land in the Northeast at a quarter or a fifth of its market price. Some of the "ministers" protested as they were frightened that this might lead to rebellion or that they might lose heavily on their own large landholdings. Chang Ching-hui made this comment: "Manchukuo has masses of land, and the Manchurians are so crude and ignorant. If the Japanese come to open virgin land and teach them modern techniques, both sides will benefit." The bill was passed. "Both sides will benefit" became another favourite Japanese quotation.

Chang Ching-hui uttered a third saying when the Japanese were making so many compulsory grain purchases that the peasants of the Northeast had none left. Some of the "ministers" whose own interests were affected by the low prices protested at a "cabinet meeting" that the peasants were starving, and clamoured for higher prices. This was, of course, something that the Japanese were not prepared to concede. Chang Ching-hui said, "Soldiers of the Imperial Japanese Army are giving their lives, and for us in Manchuria to send some grain to them is nothing in comparison. The people who are hungry will be all right if they tighten their belts." "Tightening belts" became a popular expression with the Japanese, though they did not, of course, apply it to themselves.

The Kwantung Army commander was always praising Chang Ching-hui to me as a good prime minister and "a man who puts Japan-Manchukuo friendship into practice". I had not previously thought what significance all this had for me, but now that I knew the fate of Ling Sheng I understood well enough.

After the Ling Sheng affair I was even more deeply disturbed by a meeting I had with Prince Te.

Prince Te, or Demchukdongrub, was a Mongol prince whom the Japanese had used to set up the "Inner Mongolian Autonomous Military Government". He had sent me money in my Tientsin days, given thoroughbred Mongol horses to Pu Chieh, and shown his loyalty to me in many other ways. He had come to see the Kwantung Army on business and had obtained its permission to come and visit me. He told me about his experiences over the past few years and about the founding of the "autonomous military government". Before long he was grumbling and complaining that the Japanese in Inner Mongolia were too domineering and that the Kwantung Army had not kept a single one of the long string of promises it had made to him before the founding of the Inner Mongolian "government". What made him most angry was his complete lack of power. I found myself echoing his complaints and trying to console him. The next day the Kwantung Army sent Yoshioka, the "Attaché to the Imperial Household", to ask me with a grim expression on his face: "What did Your Majesty discuss with Prince Te yesterday?"

Realizing that something was wrong I said that we had only been chatting.

He pursued his questioning relentlessly: "Did he express dissatisfaction with Japan?"

My heart was pounding. I knew that I could either make a firm denial, or, better, "retreat by advancing". "Prince Te must have been telling a pack of lies."

Although Yoshioka did not go into the matter any further with me I was in a state of terror for several days. My mind seethed with suspicions, and I decided that there were two possibilities. One was that the Japanese had installed some kind of listening device in my room, and the other was that Prince Te had told them everything. I spent a long time trying to solve this mystery, searching the room for a listening device. When I did not find one I suspected that Prince Te had deliberately betrayed me, but I had no proof of that either. I was completely bewildered.

This incident taught me more than the Ling Sheng business. From then on I did not talk frankly to any outsider and behaved cautiously towards all visitors. People who came of their own accord to see me had become fewer and fewer since the speech I made after my return from Japan, and they almost stopped coming altogether after Prince Te's visit. The Kwantung Army thought up a new rule in 1937 and insisted that the "Attaché to the Imperial Household" should be present whenever I saw a stranger.

I felt more and more tense from 1937 onward. The Japanese stepped up their preparations for the full-scale invasion of China during the first six months of that year and carried out whole-scale repression of the anti-Japanese patriots in the Northeast. They issued a penal code in my name, started the *pao-chia* system of mutual surveillance, forced everybody to join the "Concordia Association", repaired roads, built fortifications, and combined villages and hamlets. They used about twenty divisions to try to deal with the 45,000 men of the Anti-Japanese Allied Army that was operating in the Northeast, while at the same time they arrested many members of the Anti-Japanese National Salvation Society and other "unstable" people. These operations were so unsuccessful that they had to be repeated on an even larger scale the following year, when a million Japanese and puppet troops were used. But, according to Tung Chi-hsu, people disappeared all over the Northeast, while the arrests never came to an end.

I never heard any real news from my talks with the Kwantung Army commander or from the reports of the "prime minister". Tung Chi-hsu was the only person who kept me in touch with what was really happening. He told me that the reports of victories in the "punitive" campaigns that the Kwantung Army commander gave me were not reliable, and that it was hard to say who the "bandits" the Japanese wiped out really were. He said that a relation of his had been taken off to do forced labour on some secret project, and that after the job was completed all the labourers had been slaughtered except for him and a few others who had been lucky enough to escape. In his view, one of the gangs of "bandits" whose destruction had been reported with a great fanfare in the press was this group of labourers.

Soon after I heard about this a former English interpreter of mine disappeared. One day my brother Pu Chieh told me that after being arrested because he had been in contact with Americans while attached to our "embassy" in Tokyo he had been killed by the Japanese gendarmerie. Pu Chieh also said that this interpreter had sent him a letter via his warder begging him to ask me to speak for him, but he had not dared to tell me about it at the time. I told Pu Chieh to say not another word about the matter.

Many of the policies and laws to which I gave my assent in those days were connected with Japan's war preparations and the strengthening of her rule over her Northeastern colony. They included the "First Five-Year Plan for Developing Production", the "Property Control Law", the "Reorganization of the Government" to strengthen Japanese rule, and the adoption of Japanese as a "national language"; but none of them made such an impact on me as Pu Chieh's marriage.

After finishing at the school for the children of the Japanese nobility, Pu Chieh had gone on to the Japanese Army Cadet School. He returned to Changchun in the winter of 1935 and was made a lieutenant in the Imperial Guard. From then on his associates in the Kwantung Army were always bringing up the subject of marriage and extolling the virtues of Japanese wives. Yoshioka, the Japanese officer who was always at my side, told me that the Kwantung Army hoped that Pu Chieh would marry a Japanese girl for the sake of friendship between the two countries.

I was very alarmed to hear this and decided to get Pu Chieh a wife from Peking to forestall this Japanese plot. Clearly they intended to bring Pu Chieh completely under their control and, what was more important, to get a child of Japanese descent who could replace me in future. Pu Chieh agreed to my plan, but when Yoshioka put pressure on him by telling him that General Honjo was acting as matchmaker on his behalf in Tokyo, he obeyed the Kwantung Army, and on April 3, 1937 married Saga Hiro, daughter of the marquis Saga. Less than a month later the "State Council", prompted by the Kwantung Army, passed a bill by which Pu Chieh and his son would be the successors to the throne if I had no male offspring.

After Pu Chieh's return from Tokyo I decided that I could no longer speak frankly in front of him or eat food that his wife sent me. If Pu Chieh was eating with me I would make an exception to this latter rule only if he tasted his wife's cooking first. When Pu Chieh was about to become a father I was deeply concerned for my own safety and even for his, as the Kwantung Army seemed quite capable of killing both of us for the sake of getting an emperor of Japanese descent. I breathed a deep sigh of relief when the child turned out to be a girl.

I was even worried about what would happen if I had a son, as the Kwantung Army had made me sign a document saying that I would send any son of mine to Japan when he was five to be brought up by a nominee of theirs.

On June 28, nine days before the July 7 fighting at Lukouchiao, I was frightened once more, this time by the affair of my Palace Guard.

This force was distinct from the "Imperial Guard" that came under the control of the "Ministry of Defence", and I paid for it out of my own pocket. My object in founding it had been not only to protect myself but also to have a skeleton military force under my personal control. All its 300 men were given officer training. Tung Chi-hsu, who was in charge of them, had told me long ago that the Kwantung Army was not happy about their existence, but before now I had been unable to understand Tung's forebodings.

On June 28 some members of my Palace Guard went to amuse themselves in a park and were arguing with some Japanese in civilian clothes about hiring boats when a crowd of Japanese surrounded them and started hitting them. The guards, forced to defend themselves, beat off the Japanese, whereupon the latter set dogs on them. My guards kicked the dogs to death, broke through the encirclement and returned to their barracks. Little did they know that this had caused a disaster. Soon afterwards some Japanese gendarmes appeared outside the palace office demanding that Tung Chi-hsu hand over all the guards who had gone to the park, and the terrified Tung complied. The Japanese gendarmes took them away and tried to force them to admit that they had been engaged in "anti-Manchukuo and anti-Japanese" activities. When the guards refused, the Japanese inflicted a variety of tortures on them, and the guards now realized that the incident had been a deliberate plot by the Kwantung Army. The Japanese in civilian clothes had been sent there by the Kwantung Army, two Kwantung Army staff officers had been injured in the brawl, and the dogs that had been kicked to death were Kwantung Army dogs.

When I heard of their arrest I assumed that they must have started some trouble accidentally, and so I asked Yoshioka to go straight to the Kwantung Army Headquarters and speak for them. He came back with three conditions on which they would be released: Tung Chi-hsu must apologize to the wounded officers; the members of the Palace Guard who had "caused the trouble" must be expelled from the country; and I must guarantee that such an incident would never recur. When I had complied with these conditions I was forced to dismiss Tung Chi-hsu from his post as Commander of the Palace Guard and to appoint a Japanese to succeed him. I also had to cut down the size of the Palace Guard and change their rifles for pistols.

I had previously sent a number of young men to military academies in Japan with the intention of building up my own military power, but when they came back their postings, even that of Pu Chieh, were all made by the "Ministry of Defence", and I had no say in the matter.

So my plans for an army under my own control now turned out to have been nothing but a dream.

When the July 7 fighting broke out and led to the Japanese occupation of Peking, some princes and old-timers in Peking were eager for a revival of the old order, but by now I knew that this was impossible. My only remaining concerns were how to preserve my own safety in the face of the Japanese and how to deal with Yoshioka, the "Attaché to the Imperial Household" and embodiment of the Kwantung Army.

# Yoshioka Yasunori

If one compares the Kwantung Army to a source of high-tension electric current and myself to an electric motor, then Yoshioka was a wire of high conductivity.

He was a short man with a small moustache and high cheek-bones, and he never left me during the ten years from the time he first came to the palace in 1935 to the Japanese surrender in 1945, when he was captured by the Soviet Army at the same time as I was. In those years he rose from lieutenant-colonel to lieutenant-general. He had two posts: one was as a senior staff officer in the Kwantung Army and the other was "Attaché to the Manchukuo Imperial Household". This latter was a Japanese term, but it does not make much difference how one translates it as the words did not describe his real function. He was the wire through which the Kwantung Army transmitted its intentions to me. The excursions I made, the visitors I received, the protocol I observed, my admonitions to my subjects, the toasts I proposed, and even my nods and smiles were all under Yoshioka's direction. He decided what meetings I was to attend and wrote out my speeches in his own Japanese-style Chinese.

After the Japanese unleashed their full-scale invasion of China in July 1937 they wanted grain, men and supplies from "Manchukuo". I ordered Chang Ching-hui to read out an exhortation written by

Yoshioka at a meeting of the puppet provincial governors. In this document I urged them to "carry out their duties diligently to support the holy war". The Pacific War faced Japan with a shortage of soldiers, and they wanted "Manchukuo" troops to replace some of the Japanese units engaged in China. I read out another of Yoshioka's scripts, this time at a banquet given for the commanders of the various military zones, in which I expressed my determination to "live or die with Japan, and, united in heart and virtue, smash the power of Britain and America".

Every time Yoshioka reported to me that the Japanese had occupied a major Chinese city he would make me get up with him and bow low in the direction of the battlefield as a mark of mourning for the Japanese soldiers killed in the fighting. After he had made me do this a number of times I needed no prompting to make my bow when he told me of the capture of Wuhan.

As I made more progress he would increase the number of my lessons. After the fall of Wuhan, for example, he suggested to me that I should write a congratulatory letter to the butcher Okamura who had taken the city and send a telegram to the Japanese emperor.

When the "National Foundation Shrine" was built I used to go there every month to pray for the victory of the Japanese troops, and this too was after receiving an impulse along the same electric wire.

The Kwantung Army did not interfere much in my private and domestic affairs before the July 7 Incident, but things changed after that. Before the incident some of my relations would come up from south of the Great Wall every year to see me on my birthday and at other times. But after July 7 the Kwantung Army only allowed a few of them to come to Changchun at specified times. The Japanese army also insisted that, with the exception of my closest relations, they should only bow to me and not talk. All my mail was read by Yoshioka's Japanese underlings in the palace office, and he decided whether or not I was to see it. The Kwantung Army was of course perfectly well aware that I was not anti-"Manchukuo" or anti-Japanese, but they were worried that I might become involved in plans to revive the Ching Dynasty south of the Great Wall, which would have been a nuisance to them.

It would have been completely impossible in those days for me to meet an outsider or receive a letter without the knowledge of Yoshioka. There was a gendarmerie office in the palace staffed by dark-green uniformed Japanese gendarmes; no one could come or go without being seen by them, and they heard everything that went on in the courtyard. All this, and the fact that the Japanese in the Palace Office were Yoshioka's tools, meant that I was under very strict control.

Yoshioka had shown considerable cunning in getting his post in the palace, making friends with Pu Chieh when he was one of his instructors at the Army Cadet School in Japan. Some accounts say that he was also a friend of mine before I went to the Northeast, but in fact he had only given me a few talks on current affairs in Tientsin. All the same, he managed to use his friendship with Pu Chieh to convince the Kwantung Army that he was a personal friend of mine, and it was on the strength of this that he got the twin appointments as "Attaché to the Manchukuo Imperial Household" and as a senior staff officer with the Kwantung Army.

During his time with me he made frequent visits to Japan, and often carried little presents between me and the Japanese empress dowager. Once he persuaded me to record some greetings in Japanese to the Japanese emperor.

When Yoshioka spoke he would often grunt "uh" and "ha" while twitching his eyebrows, a habit that got worse with time and which I found increasingly irritating. As this tic grew more pronounced his attitude to our relationship changed.

After my visit to Japan in 1934 the Japanese empress dowager wrote me some *waka* poems, and what Yoshioka said then was music in my ears:

"Her Majesty the Empress Dowager is the equivalent of Your Majesty's mother, and as I am almost a relation of yours I feel very honoured at this."

At that time he said to Pu Chieh, "You and I are related like hand and foot, and although I cannot claim such a relationship with

His Majesty the Emperor, I can feel that I am to him as a toe to a finger. We are almost kinsmen."

In about 1936 he said to me:

"Japan is the equivalent of Your Majesty's father, uh, and the Kwantung Army represents Japan, uh, so the commander of the Kwantung Army is the equivalent of Your Majesty's father, ha."

As the Japanese army ran into more and more trouble at the front my standing went down in the eyes of the Kwantung Army. Yoshioka finally went so far as to say, "The Kwantung Army is your father, and I am the representative of the Kwantung Army, uh."

Yoshioka used to make frequent visits to the palace throughout the day. Sometimes he would stay for ten minutes then leave, only to return five minutes later. He would give ridiculous reasons for these frequent comings and goings, such as that he had forgotten to say something, or not remembered to ask me if there was anything I wanted him to do for me the following day. I naturally feared that he was using these lightning attacks as a way of spying on me; and I thought that the only way I could avoid suspicion was to agree at once to everything he suggested and never keep him waiting. I would even see him in the middle of a meal if he came while I was eating.

## "Imperial Rescripts"

All who studied in "Manchukuo" schools were compelled to learn my "Imperial Rescripts" by heart. On the anniversary of the issue of each rescript all schools, government offices and units of the armed forces would assemble to hear the rescript read out. In schools, for example, all the staff and pupils in their dark-green "Concordia" uniforms would stand solemnly in front of the platform. The school official responsible for ideology and discipline would enter wearing white gloves and holding a yellow cloth bundle above his head. The whole assembly would bow while he carried the bundle up to the platform, put it on the table, and opened it. He would take out the rescript and pass it with both hands to the head of the school who would accept it with gloved hands, unroll it, and then read it aloud. If the date happened to be May 2 he would read out the "Admonitory Rescript on the Occasion of the Emperor's Return":

Ever since we ascended the Throne we have been eager to pay a personal visit to the Imperial House of Japan, in order that by cultivating our friendship and enjoying their company we might show our great admiration for them. By making this voyage to the East we were able to fulfil our long-cherished ambition.

The Japanese Imperial House was most hospitable to us and made magnificent preparations, while their subjects welcomed us and saw us off with sincere enthusiasm, being without exception extremely courteous and respectful. This is engraved on our heart, and we shall never forget it.

We are deeply aware that from the foundation of our State to the present day we have relied throughout on the devotion to righteousness and the great efforts of this Friendly Country in strengthening the Great Foundation; and on this occasion we were fortunate enough to be able to express our heartfelt gratitude. Moreover, we ascertained through careful observation that the government in that country is based on benevolence and love, while the emphasis of education is on loyalty and filial piety; the people respect their Emperor and love their superiors as they do heaven and earth; and every one of them is loyal, brave, public-spirited, and sincerely devoted to his motherland. This is why they are able to enjoy domestic peace, resist foreign powers, and take pity on their neighbours, in order to maintain the Imperial line that shall continue unbroken for ten thousand generations. We have personally come in contact with high and low in that country, and they are united with the greatest sincerity in a common temperament and a shared morality; their mutual reliance is unshakable.

We and His Majesty the Emperor of Japan are of one spirit. All ye our subjects should therefore be mindful of this and be one in heart and virtue with our ally, in order to lay a firm and everlasting foundation for our two countries and display the true meaning of Oriental morality. Then will it be possible for the world to be at peace and mankind to be happy.

Let all our subjects strive to observe this our Rescript for ever and ever.

By the Command of the Emperor.

There were six "Imperial Rescripts" altogether:

The "Accessional Rescript" of March 1, 1934;

The "Admonitory Rescript on the Occasion of the Emperor's Return" of May 2, 1935;

The "Rescript on the Consolidation of the Basis of the Nation" of July 15, 1940;

The "Rescript on the Current Situation" of December 8, 1941;

The "Rescript on the Tenth Anniversary of the Founding of the Nation" of March 1, 1942;

The "Abdication Rescript" of August 15, 1945.

The "Accessional Rescript" was later replaced by the "Rescript on the Tenth Anniversary of the Founding of the Nation"; and the "Abdication Rescript" of August 15, 1945 was never read aloud by anybody. Thus four rescripts were the important ones. Schoolchildren, students and soldiers had to be able to recite them fluently, and anyone who forgot them or repeated them inaccurately would be punished. In addition to being part of the slave propaganda put out by the Japanese in the Northeast, they were also used as the ultimate legal justification for the repression of all forms of resistance. Any Northeasterner who revealed the slightest trace of dissatisfaction with his colonial rulers could be punished for infringing this or that clause of a rescript.

The origin of each of these rescripts illustrates how low a man can sink. As I have already mentioned the way the first two were issued, I will now talk about how the third, the "Rescript on the Consolidation of the Basis of the Nation", came to be published.

One day I was sitting in my room with Yoshioka. Neither of us was talking as he had said what he came to say, but as he had not gone I guessed that he had some other important business on his mind. He stood up and walked over to the part of the room where there was a statue of the Buddha. He stopped there and grunted.

297

"Buddhism came from abroad," he said, turning towards me. "Uh, a foreign religion. As Japan and Manchuria share the same spirit they should have the same beliefs, ha?"

Then he explained to me that the Japanese emperor was the divine descendant of the Heaven Shining Bright Deity,[1] that every emperor was a reincarnation of the great god, and that all Japanese who died for the emperor would become gods themselves. From my experience I knew that the Kwantung Army was transmitting current along the high-tension wire, but after this statement of Yoshioka's the current was cut off. I spent many days thinking about these myths but I reached no conclusion about what they meant.

The Kwantung Army had in fact thought of something it wanted me to do, but its commander, Ueda, was preoccupied with the defeats his troops had suffered in the border fighting they had provoked with the Soviet Union and the Mongolian People's Republic. Before returning to Japan stripped of his office for this failure he indicated that, for the sake of "Manchukuo-Japanese friendship" and their unity in spirit, there should be religious identity between the two countries; he hoped that I would think the matter over.

I had always obediently followed the instructions of my "supreme emperor", but this time I did not know what to do. All my old advisers had either left or been thrown out by the Japanese, and my young brothers-in-law and nephews were too inexperienced to be of any use to me. I had to think this problem out for myself, but before I could reach any conclusion the new Kwantung Army commander and fifth "Ambassador to Manchukuo", Umezu Yoshijiro, arrived. He told me through Yoshioka that Japan's religion was "Manchukuo's" religion, and that I should welcome the "Heaven Shining Bright Deity", the divine ancestor of the Japanese imperial family, and make this cult into the religion of "Manchukuo". He added that as this year was the two thousand six hundredth anniversary of Emperor Jimmu it was a highly suitable time to introduce the

---

[1] The Japanese Sun Goddess Ama-terasu-o-mi-Kami. Her worship forms part of the Japanese Shinto religion.

great goddess into this country. He suggested that I should go to Japan to offer my congratulations and arrange the matter.

I later heard that there had been disagreements over this within the Kwantung Army as some of the officers who knew China better thought that it would arouse fierce opposition among the people of the Northeast and increase Japan's isolation. Later it was decided that with the passage of time the Shinto religion would take root among the young while the older generation would get used to it. The decision to go ahead with this policy was unpopular with most of the Chinese collaborators, to say nothing of ordinary people, and I found it even more difficult to stomach than the robbery of the Eastern Mausolea. I had previously been prevented by Yoshioka from sacrificing publicly at the graves of my imperial ancestors, and now I was being called upon to acknowledge myself as the descendant of a foreign line. This was very hard to bear.

Although my every action since the time I yielded to Itagaki's pressure in Lushun had been an open betrayal of my nation and my ancestors, I had managed to justify my doings to myself. I had represented them as filial deeds done for the sake of reviving the ancestral cause, and pretended that the concessions I made were only for the sake of future gains. I had hoped that the spirits of my ancestors in heaven would understand this and protect me. But now the Japanese were forcing me to exchange my ancestors for a new set. Surely my forbears would never forgive me for this.

But I remembered that I had to agree to this proposal if I wanted to preserve my life and safety. Even in reaching this conclusion I was able to justify myself: I would continue to sacrifice to my own ancestors at home while publicly acknowledging the new ones. My mind made up, I sacrificed to the tablets of my forefathers and set off for Japan.

I made this second trip to Japan in May 1940, and I stayed there for eight days.

When I met Hirohito I read out an address that had been written out for me by Yoshioka. The gist of it was that I hoped that for the sake of the "indivisible unity in heart and virtue" between the two countries I would be allowed to worship the Heaven Shining Bright Deity in "Manchukuo".

The Japanese emperor's reply was very short: "If that is Your Majesty's will, I must comply with your wishes." He then rose to his feet and pointed to three objects lying on a table: a sword, a bronze mirror, and a curved piece of jade, three sacred objects which were supposed to represent the Heaven Shining Bright Deity. As he explained them to me I thought that the antique shops of Liulichang in Peking were full of things like that. Were these a great god? Were these my ancestors?

I burst into tears on the drive back.

On returning to Changchun I built a "National Foundation Shrine" beside my palace and founded a "Bureau of Worship" under the former chief of staff of the Kwantung Army Hashimoto Toranosuke. On the first and fifteenth of every month I would lead the Kwantung Army commander and the puppet officials to go and make offerings at the shrine. Later on such shrines had to be built all over the Northeast, and offerings were made there at set times. Everyone who walked past one of these shrines had to do a ninety-degree bow on pain of being punished for "disrespect". The result of this was that the places where the shrines were built became deserted.

The Kwantung Army tried to induce me to wear the strangest clothes to perform these rituals, but I countered this proposal by saying that as this was wartime it would be best if I wore military uniform with my Japanese decorations to show my determination to support my ally Japan.

I would always kotow to my own ancestors at home before going to the shrine, and when I was bowing to the altar of the Heaven Shining Bright Deity at the shrine I would say to myself, "I am bowing not to that but to the Palace of Earthly Peace (Kun Ning Kung) in Peking."

Despised and cursed by the entire people of the Northeast, I issued the "Rescript on the Consolidation of the Basis of the Nation". This was written not by Cheng Hsiao-hsu (who had been dead for two years) but by a Japanese sinologue called Sato Tomoyasu who had been commissioned by the "General Affairs Office of the State Council". The text was as follows:

Whereas we are respectfully establishing the NATIONAL FOUNDATION SHRINE in order to consolidate the basis of the Nation in perpetuity and spread the principles of the Nation to infinity, we issue this rescript to you, our subjects.

Since the inception of our State the foundation of our Country has grown stronger and its destiny has been glorious. It enjoys sound government that improves with every passing day. When we reflected upon this great achievement and looked to its source, we saw that it was all thanks to the divine blessing of the HEAVEN SHINING BRIGHT DEITY and the protection of His Majesty THE EMPEROR OF JAPAN. Therefore did we visit in person the JAPANESE IMPERIAL HOUSE and in order to express our heartfelt thanks and deep gratitude we issued a Rescript to our subjects instructing you in the duty of being one in virtue and in mind with Japan. Profound was the meaning of this.

The purpose of our recent voyage to the East was to celebrate the two thousand six hundredth anniversary of Emperor Jimmu and to worship the AUGUST DEITY in person. On the occasion of our happy return to our own country we have respectfully established the NATIONAL FOUNDATION SHRINE in which to make offerings to the HEAVEN SHINING BRIGHT DEITY. We shall pray in our own person, and with the deepest reverence, for the prosperity of the Nation; and we shall make this an eternal example that our sons and grandsons for ten thousand generations shall follow without end. Thus may the basis of the Nation be consolidated by venerating the Way of the Gods,[1] and the principles of the Nation be founded in the teaching of Loyalty and Filial Piety. Pacified through Benevolence and Love and civilized through Concord, this land will be pure and illustrious, and will be assured of the divine blessing.

Let all our subjects understand our meaning. Strengthen the basis and extend our principles; strive to carry this out unremittingly, and do not pause in your efforts to make the country strong.

By the Command of the Emperor.

---

[1] The Japanese Shinto religion.

The toadying expressions "the divine blessing of the Heaven Shining Bright Deity" and "the protection of His Majesty the Emperor of Japan" were from then onwards an essential part of all rescripts.

The Kwantung Army went to great efforts to prepare me and the puppet ministers to receive the "Way of the Gods" (Shinto), and provided me with a famous Shinto expert to instruct me. The teaching materials he used were decidedly odd. One was a scroll picture of a tree. He explained that the root of the tree was Shinto, while the branches were all the other religions of the world; in other words, all the other religions had sprung from Shinto. I and the puppet ministers found it hard not to laugh or sleep during these lectures.

When Japan declared war on the U.S.A. and Britain on December 8, 1941, the Kwantung Army made "Manchukuo" issue the "Rescript on the Current Situation" in which I announced my support for the Japanese declaration of war and enjoined my "subjects" to do their utmost to help the Japanese war effort. Previous rescripts had been issued by the "State Council", but this time a special "Imperial Council" meeting was called on the evening of December 8 at which Yoshioka made me read the rescript out myself.

Whenever the Kwantung Army commander came to visit me I would open my mouth and pour out such remarks as "Japan and Manchukuo are one and indivisible, and they live or die together; I am determined to devote the whole strength of this nation to the struggle for victory in the Great East Asian holy war, and for the Greater East Asian Co-Prosperity Sphere headed by Japan."

Tojo Hidemichi, the Japanese premier and former Kwantung Army chief of staff, paid a lightning visit to "Manchukuo" in 1942. When I met him I burst straight into "Your Excellency may rest assured that I shall devote the full resources of Manchukuo to supporting the holy war of our parental country Japan."

At the time of Tojo's visit Japan had been already changed from "ally" into a "Parental Country". This new humiliation had been introduced in the "Rescript on the Tenth Anniversary of the Founding of the Nation". On the eve of this anniversary, which fell in March 1942, Yoshioka had said to me, "There could have been no Manchukuo without Japan, uh, so Japan should be regarded as Manchukuo's father. So, uh, Manchukuo should not call Japan an ally or friend as other countries do; it should refer to Japan as its Parental Country. Meanwhile the Japanese head of the "General Affairs Office of the State Council" was giving a similar talk to the puppet ministers. After this the "Rescript on the Tenth Anniversary of the Founding of the Nation" was issued.

From the publication of this "rescript" on, Japan was always referred to as the "Parental Country".

In 1944, when it was becoming increasingly obvious that Japan was losing the war and even I could see that her armies would soon be finished, Yoshioka came to beg me to make a donation of materials, particularly metal, for the war effort as an example for others. In addition to doing this I spontaneously gave a lot of gold, silver and jewellery to the Kwantung Army. Later I presented them with the carpets from the palace floors and hundreds of items of clothing. All these actions of mine were widely publicized and made the task of looting easier for the Japanese officials, who sent vast quantities of goods, including 300,000 tons of rice, to Japan in the closing months of the war.

## Home Life

As I was not allowed to play any part in politics, or to go out as I pleased, or to send for my "ministers" for consultations, I had nothing to do when the Kwantung Army was not transmitting current to me. I developed the habit of getting up at eleven and going to bed after midnight, sometimes as late as 3 a.m. I ate two meals a day: breakfast between noon and one, and supper between nine and eleven at night, or even later. I would take a nap from 4 p.m. to 5 or 6 p.m. Apart from eating and sleeping, my life could be summarized as consisting of floggings, curses, divination, medicine, and fear.

All these elements were interconnected. As the signs of the Japanese collapse became clearer, I became more and more frightened that the Japanese would kill me to stop me talking afterwards. So I was fawning and affable with them, while I flogged and cursed as my temper became increasingly violent at home. I became more and more superstitious, eating vegetarian food, reciting sutras, consulting oracles, and seeking the protection of Buddha and the gods. My health, which had already been ruined, became even poorer as I lived this neurotic and unstable life, so I desperately took medicine and had injections.

My tendency to cruelty and suspicion went back to my years in the Forbidden City, and had been strengthened in Tientsin, where I had made this set of Household Rules for the servants:

1. Irresponsible conversations are prohibited to prevent underhand dealings.
2. You are not allowed to shield each other or cover up for each other.
3. Embezzlement and profiteering are forbidden.
4. When your colleagues do something wrong you must report it at once.
5. Senior staff must beat their juniors immediately they discover that they have done wrong.

The severity of the punishment will be increased by one grade if there is any slackness in the enforcement of these rules.

After the move to the Northeast I made my staff swear, "If I break these rules may heaven punish me and strike me with a thunderbolt."

I became so savage that I would have my staff beaten incessantly and even use instruments of torture on them. There were many different kinds of beatings, and I always got other people to administer them for me. This job would be entrusted to any of the members of my household present. They had to flog very hard, or else I would suspect that they had conspired with each other, and if this happened they would find themselves the victims of the rod.

My victims included almost everyone in my household except my wife, my brothers, and my sisters. In those days a number of my nephews were studying in the palace. They used to keep me company, talk to me and wait on me. I was bringing them up to be my trusted relatives, but that did not save them from scoldings and beatings. The words they most dreaded hearing me say were "Take him downstairs", as this meant that they were to be taken down for a flogging.

These actions of mine go to show how cruel, mad, violent and unstable I was.

I suffered from piles while in Changchun. When a young nephew saw the medicine I used he thoughtlessly remarked that it looked like bullets. This infringed one of my taboos: did he mean that he wanted me to be shot? At my suggestion another cousin belaboured him with the rod.

The most wretched victims of my rule were the pages. There were about a dozen of them, and they came from a Changchun orphanage. Most of their parents had been killed by the Japanese. For fear they would grow up with a longing for revenge the Japanese had made the puppet government bring them up in an orphanage, change their names, teach them to be slaves, and wear them out through heavy labour. Some of them had been very hopeful when they were told that they were being sent to the palace, thinking that life would be much better there than in the orphanage. It turned out to be even worse. They ate *kaoliang* of the lowest grade, dressed in rags, had to work fifteen or sixteen hours a day, and sometimes had to sit up on duty all night as well. In winter they were so tired, cold and hungry that they would sometimes fall asleep leaning on the radiators while they were working and wake up covered with burns. They were always being beaten — for falling asleep on the job, for not sweeping clean enough, or for talking too loud. When my personal assistants were in a bad temper they took it out on the pages, who were in their charge, putting them in a solitary confinement cell. So wretched was their life that at the age of seventeen or eighteen they were as small as ten-year-olds.

One page called Sun Po-yuan died of his sufferings. Finding life in the palace intolerable he had tried to escape. After being recaptured on his first attempt he was given a savage beating. The next time he tried to get out through the tunnel for the central heating, but after crawling round for two days he found no way out. Suffering from hunger and thirst, he came out for a drink of water and was captured. When I was informed of this by my assistants I ordered, "Let him have something to eat and then give him a good lesson." But before he could be given a "good lesson" he was beaten till he was almost dead. The news that he was nearly dead gave me a terrible fright, as I was afraid that he might turn into a ghost and take my life in revenge, so I gave orders that a doctor was to be sent for to save him. It was too late.

I spent several days after this kotowing and reciting scriptures in front of a Buddhist altar, praying for his soul to cross safely to the next world, in the hope that I could thus avoid retribution. I ordered that the assistants who had beaten him were to strike the palms of their own hands with bamboo rods every day for six months as a penance. It was as if these measures would absolve me of all responsibility for the killing. My cruelty to the pages later developed to an extreme because of my neurotic state.

I took the most careful precautions to make sure that I was not swindled of a cent when the kitchen staff bought vegetables, sending spies to tail them when they did their shopping, and questioning my sisters about the prices of pork and chicken. The cooks would be fined if the food was not to my liking or if I found anything dirty in it. Of course, they were sometimes rewarded if I was pleased. While I was powerless outside, I was the absolute ruler in my own house.

At the close of the "Manchukuo" period the coming defeat of Japan became more and more obvious. The news from Allied radio broadcasts and Yoshioka's low spirits strengthened my feeling that this was the end of an era. My temper became worse than ever, and I behaved even more viciously at home than before. One of the elders of my clan who came to greet me on my birthday in early 1944 became the innocent victim of my love of throwing my weight around.

A skating display had been arranged in the palace to celebrate my birthday, and he had politely greeted some Japanese officers in my presence. This apparently harmless act was reported to me by one of my nephews at the banquet after the show, as to pay respects to anyone else in the presence of the "Son of Heaven" was forbidden in the palace, and he had been taught that it was his duty to report such occurrences. As I was in a good temper at the time and the offender was of an older generation I let the matter drop. But the old man was inquisitive enough to ask the nephew what he had whispered in my ear. This second act of "gross disrespect" was too much for me, and I flared into a rage, shouting at him and thumping the table. He went white with terror, and knelt on the floor and kotowed to me. I was not to be pacified, and I left my seat to accuse him of disloyalty not only to myself but to our imperial ancestors as well. The whole assembly was silent. In my vanity I thought that this old fellow was worse than the Japanese, who at least were never rude to me in public.

While in Changchun I read huge quantities of superstitious books, and became addicted to them. When I read that all living things had a Buddha-nature I became afraid that the meat I ate was the reincarnation of some relation of mine. So in addition to the Buddhist scriptures that I read morning and evening I would say a prayer before every meal for the better reincarnation of the soul of the animal whose meat I was going to eat. At first I recited it silently to myself in front of everyone else, but later I made all other people leave the room until I had finished reciting it and only then allowed them back in again. I remember that I once kotowed to an egg three times before eating it in the palace's air-raid shelter. By that time I was eating vegetarian food only.

I did not allow my staff to kill flies, insisting that they drive them away instead. I knew that flies could carry disease, so I never ate food that a fly had touched. If one landed on my lip I would dab the spot with cotton-wool soaked in surgical spirit from a tin I always carried about with me, and if I found a fly's leg in my food I would fine the cook; but despite all this I did not allow anyone to kill a single fly. And when I saw a cat catching a mouse I had the whole staff chase the cat away to save the mouse's life.

The more I read Buddhist books the more I believed them, and this belief was strengthened by dreams of visiting Hell. I once read that if you recited scriptures for many days the Buddha would appear and would want something to eat. So I prepared a room, and after reading scriptures I proclaimed to everyone that "Buddha has come" and crawled into the room on my knees. The room was, of course, empty, but I was trembling with fear as I kotowed to nothing.

Under my influence the whole household started intoning Buddhist chants, while the air echoed with the sound of the wooden drum and brass gong. The palace seemed to have become a temple.

I continued with my old practice of consulting oracles, and I would repeat my divinations until I got a good omen. When I was frightened that the Kwantung Army was going to murder me I used to consult the oracle every time Yoshioka came to see me. Avoiding calamity and bringing on good fortune became the guiding thought behind my every action. I ended up by asking myself what place, what garment, or what food was propitious and what was unlucky. There were no fixed criteria by which to answer these questions. If I was walking along a path and I saw a brick in front of me I would make a ruling: "If I pass it on the left it is lucky, and if I pass it on the right it is unlucky." Then I would pass it to the left. I could cite numerous other examples, like whether to cross a threshold with one's right or one's left foot first, and whether to eat something white before something green or *vice versa*. Wan Jung was as engrossed in this as I was, and she made a rule that whenever she encountered anything unlucky she would blink or spit. This became such a habit with her that she would blink and spit incessantly as if she were suffering from some mental illness. My nephews, young men of about twenty, all turned into ascetics under my guidance. Some of them would meditate every day, some would not go home in the evening although they were newly married, some would hang pictures of skeletons above their beds, and some would intone spells and prayers all day as if they had just seen ghosts.

I used to "meditate" every day. All sounds were forbidden while I did this, even that of heavy breathing. I kept a large crane in the courtyard, and it ignored this rule, calling whenever it happened to feel in high spirits. I made the pages responsible for it, and fined them fifty cents whenever it made a noise. After losing many dollars this way the pages found a way of dealing with the bird: whenever it stretched out its neck they would hit it, and then the crane kept quiet.

Because I was terrified of death I was frightened of illness. I became a medicine addict, giving a lot of trouble to myself as well as to my household. I used to collect the stuff as well as take it: I had a store of Chinese-style medicine and a dispensary for Western drugs, and I spent thousands or even tens of thousands of dollars importing drugs from abroad that I never used. Several of my nephews had to spend the time when they were not studying looking after all this medicine, and they and my personal doctor gave me injections for several hours every day.

When I lived in the Forbidden City I had often suffered from imaginary illnesses, but now I was really sick. I once made a "royal progress" to Antung to inspect a hydro-electric generating station that the Japanese had recently built. When I got there I had to hold myself up stiff and straight in front of the Japanese as I was in military uniform. Before I had walked very far I was fighting for breath, and on my return journey I nearly blacked out. My physical weakness and mental anxiety made me fear that I was on the brink of the grave.

One day I saw "Haven't you had enough humiliation from the Japanese?" written in chalk on a palace wall. I forgot all about the game of tennis that I was going to play and gave orders for it to be erased at once. I went back to my bedroom, my heart pounding, feeling too weak to last much longer. I was terrified that the Japanese would find out about it and hold a full-scale investigation of my household, and I did not know what that might lead to. I was even more frightened by the discovery that there was an "anti-Manchukuo, anti-Japanese element" in my own court. If he dared write that on the wall, what would stop him from killing me?

As I was so confused and terrified all day I had even less interest than ever in my family life. I had married a total of four wives, or, to use the terms employed then, one empress, one consort, and two minor consorts. But in fact they were not real wives, and were only there for show. Although I treated them differently they were all my victims.

The experiences of Wan Jung, who had been neglected for so long, would be incomprehensible to a modern Chinese girl. If her fate was not determined at her birth, her end was inevitable from the moment she married me. I have often thought that if she had divorced me in Tientsin as Wen Hsiu did she might have escaped it. But then she was quite different from Wen Hsiu. To Wen Hsiu an ordinary family life was more important than a high status and feudal morality. Wan Jung, however, attached great significance to her position as "empress", and was prepared to be a wife in name only for the sake of it.

After she had driven out Wen Hsiu I felt a revulsion for her, hardly ever talking to her or paying her any attention. So she never told me of her feelings, her hopes and her sorrows; and all I knew was that she had become addicted to opium and behaved in a way that I could not tolerate. When our ways parted after the Japanese surrender her opium addiction was very serious and she was extremely weak; she died the following year in Kirin.

In 1937 I chose a new victim called Tan Yu-ling as a punishment for Wan Jung and because a second wife was an essential piece of palace furniture. She had been recommended by a relation in Peking, and she became a Minor Consort. She was of the old Tatala Manchu clan, and was a schoolgirl when I married her at the age of sixteen. She too was a wife in name only, and I kept her in the palace as I might have kept a bird until her death in 1942. The cause of her death is still a mystery to me. She was suffering from an attack of typhoid that should not have been fatal according to the Chinese doctor who saw her. Then Yoshioka said that he wanted to "look after" her, and moved into the palace office. Under the supervision of Yoshioka and the ministrations of a Japanese doctor she died suddenly the next day.

What seemed odd to me was that the Japanese doctor was most diligent in his care of her at first, but that after going into another room for a long talk with Yoshioka he lost his enthusiasm and stopped giving her injections and blood transfusions. Yoshioka made the Japanese gendarmes keep ringing up the nurses in the sickroom all that night for information, and the following morning Tan Yu-ling died.

As soon as I had been informed of her death Yoshioka came to express the condolences of the Kwantung Army commander, and immediately produced a wreath. This amazing speed naturally strengthened my suspicions. I remembered that Tan Yu-ling often used to talk to me about the Japanese and knew a lot about the way they had behaved south of the Great Wall from the books she had read in Peking. I had suspected that the Japanese had listened in to my conversation with Prince Te, and Tan Yu-ling's death naturally reminded me of my old fears.

Soon afterwards I suspected more strongly than ever that the Kwantung Army must have been connected with her death when Yoshioka brought me a sheaf of photographs of Japanese girls for me to choose from.

I refused to consider such a matter while Tan Yu-ling's corpse was still warm. He, however, insisted that he wanted to arrange this for me to console me in my grief. I then said that it should not be done in haste, and pointed out that there was, besides, the language barrier.

"You will be able to understand each other, uh. She will be able to speak Manchukuoan."

I hastened to explain that while this was not a question of race, I had to have someone who was suited to me in her tastes and living habits. I dared not refuse in as many words to have a Japanese wife.

The "Attaché to the Imperial Household" really seemed to attach himself to me, and he kept bothering me about this day after day. Finally he realized that I was adamant — or perhaps the Kwantung Army changed its mind — and he produced some pictures of Chinese girls from a Japanese school in Lushun. Although my second sister warned me that they would all have been so indoctrinated as to be virtually Japanese, I felt that I could not put the Kwantung Army off for ever. I chose a girl who was young and not very highly educated, thinking that I would be able to deal with her even if she had been trained by the Japanese.

Thus it was that a fifteen-year-old schoolgirl became my fourth victim as a Minor Consort. Within two years of her arrival "Manchukuo" collapsed and she was sent back to her home.


# The Collapse


While I was in the prison for war criminals a former "Manchukuo" brigade commander told me a story. In the winter in which the Pacific War broke out he led a body of puppet troops to attack some anti-Japanese forces on Kwantung Army orders. His men drew a blank in the forests, and could only find one injured anti-Japanese fighter hiding in a dugout. This man's clothes were so ragged and his hair so unkempt that he looked as if he had been in prison for years. At the sight of this captive the officer had jeered at him:

"From the state you're in, it's obvious that your lot can't achieve anything. Don't you know that the Imperial Japanese Army has occupied Hongkong and Singapore?"

The captive burst out laughing. The "Manchukuo" major-general banged the table. "What are you laughing at? Don't you realize that you're on trial?"

"Who is on trial? Your end is near, and it won't be long before you are tried by the people."

All the puppet officers and civilian officials knew that the people of the Northeast loathed them and the Japanese, but they could not understand why the people had such courage and so much self-confidence, or why they were so sure that their powerful rulers were doomed. I had always regarded the might of Japanese imperialism as both matchless and unshakable. I did not think that even the Great Ching Empire or the Republic of China, whether ruled by he Peiyang warlords or the Kuomintang, was a match for Japan; and the common people never entered my calculations.

Although countless facts should have taught me who was really strong and who was weak, I remained completely in the dark until Yoshioka revealed it to me. Even then I only understood vaguely.

One year the annual "imperial progress" arranged for me by the Kwantung Army was to the Yenchi area, which is mainly inhabited by people of the Korean nationality. When my train arrived I saw that I was surrounded by huge numbers of Japanese gendarmes and six battalions of puppet troops. When I asked Yoshioka why they were there, he replied, "To guard against bandits." "Why are so many soldiers needed to guard against bandits?" "These bandits aren't the old sort; they are the Communist army." "How is it that Manchukuo has Communist forces too? Aren't the Communist armies in the Republic of China?" "Yes, there are some here . . . but very few." Yoshioka then changed the subject.

On another occasion when a Kwantung Army staff officer was making one of his regular reports on the military situation he made a special announcement of a victory. In this campaign the anti-Japanese leader General Yang Ching-yu had sacrificed his life. The staff officer told me with great glee that the death of General Yang had eliminated "a great threat to Manchukuo". The words "great threat" prompted me to ask how many bandits there were in "Manchukuo". He gave the same reply as Yoshioka had: "Very few, very few."

In 1942 the Japanese troops launched their big mopping-up campaign in north and central China. In some places they carried out the "Three All" policy of burn all, kill all and loot all, thus totally devastating some areas. Yoshioka once told me how the Japanese Army used all sorts of tactics against the "Communist armies" of north China, such as "iron encirclements" and "using a fine comb". "The fighting history of the Imperial Japanese Army has been immeasurably enriched." Hearing this bombastic account I asked, "The Communist armies are tiny, so why does His Majesty the Emperor of Japan need to use all these new tactics?"

To my surprise he mocked at me. "If Your Imperial Majesty had battle experience you would not say that."

"May I ask why?"

"The Communist army is different from the Kuomintang army. There is no division between soldiers and people, uh. It's like, uh, for example, red beans mixed up with red pebbles." Seeing my incomprehension he used the Chinese saying "fish eyes mixed with pearls" to make me understand. He said that when the Japanese Army was fighting the Eighth Route Army or New Fourth Army[1] it often found itself completely surrounded. Later he explained to me that no matter where the "Communist armies" went the common people were not afraid of them. Moreover once men had been in their ranks for a year they would not desert, something which made their army unprecedented in the history of China. These armies were getting bigger and bigger, and would be quite impossible to cope with in future. "Terrifying, quite terrifying," he sighed and shook his head. The sight of an officer of the "Imperial Japanese Army" rating the "tiny" enemy in these terms made me so uneasy that I did not know what to say. I screwed myself up to remark, "They really are dreadful, the way they burn and kill, and communize property and wives."

"Only an idiot could believe that," he interrupted me rudely. A moment later he looked at me with a mocking expression and said, "This was not an official comment; I must now ask Your Majesty to listen to the report of the chief of staff of the Kwantung Army."

I gradually came to realize that Yoshioka's unofficial comments were closer to reality than the official briefings of the Kwantung Army commander and chief of staff. When the Kwantung Army started the Nomanhan campaign in 1939 its commander Ueda invited me and some other puppet officials to see a demonstration of how much faster the Japanese aircraft were than the Soviet ones. But the Japanese were disastrously defeated in that campaign, losing over 50,000 men, and Ueda was cashiered. Yoshioka's unofficial

---

[1] Both led by the Communist Party.

comment was that "the Soviet heavy artillery has a far longer range than ours".

As I listened to the radio I gradually understood more of Yoshioka's hidden anxieties. There were more reports of Japanese military defeats on all fronts, and these were confirmed by reports of "smashed jade" ("heroic sacrifices") in the "Manchukuo" press. Even in my isolation I could see that there was a shortage of material supplies. Old brass and iron, such as door-knockers and spittoons, disappeared from the palace, while court officials were so short of food that they had to ask me to help them out. For fear that I knew how poor the food of the soldiers was, the Kwantung Army invited me to see a special exhibition of military rations; and to counteract the influence of foreign radio broadcasts they sent films propagandizing Japanese victories for me to see. Neither I nor the youngest of my nephews was taken in.

What made the deepest impression on me was the fear that the Japanese revealed. Yamashita Tomoyuki, who had been so proud when he had been transferred to the Kwantung Army after capturing Singapore, was a changed man when he came to take his leave of me on being posted back to Southeast Asia in 1945. Covering his nose and weeping, he said, "This is our final parting. I shall never come back again."

I saw even more tears at a farewell ceremony for "human bullets". Human bullets were soldiers selected from the Japanese Army who had been poisoned with a belief in *Bushido* and loyalty to the Japanese emperor and chosen for the task of stopping aircraft and tanks with their own bodies. Yoshioka always spoke of such deeds with the greatest respect, but they horrified me. This ceremony had been devised by the Kwantung Army for me to encourage the men who had been chosen as human bullets and wish them success. It was a cloudy day, and there was a big dust-storm blowing. The courtyard in the palace was made even more depressing by the sandbags that were piled up as an air-raid precaution. The dozen or so victims were drawn up in a line in front of me; and I read out the speech of good wishes that Yoshioka had written out, then toasted them. Only then did I see the ashen grey of their faces and the tears flowing down their cheeks, and hear that some of them were sobbing.

The ceremony came to a scrappy end in the swirling dust, and as I hurried back to my rooms to wash, my mind was in turmoil. Yoshioka followed close behind, so I knew that he must have something to say to me and waited for him to catch me up. He cleared his throat, hummed and hawed, and said, "Your Majesty spoke very well and moved them deeply, which was why they shed manly Japanese tears."

"You really are frightened," I thought. "You're frightened that I've seen through the human bullets. Well, if you're frightened, I'm even more scared."

The German surrender in May 1945 made Japan's position more desperate than ever, and it was now only a matter of time before the Soviet Army entered the war. Even I realized that Japan's plight was hopeless.

The final collapse came at last. On the morning of August 9, 1945 the last commander of the Kwantung Army, Yamata Otozo, and his chief of staff came to the palace to report to me that the Soviet Union had declared war on Japan.

Yamata was a short, thin old man who was normally grave in manner and slow in speech. But today he was completely different; he gave me a rushed account of how well prepared the Japanese troops were and told me that they were fully confident of victory. Before he could finish speaking an air-raid siren sounded and we all hid in a shelter. Before long we heard bombs exploding nearby, and while I quietly invoked the Buddha he was silent. He did not refer again to his confidence in victory before we parted after the all-clear.

From that night onwards I slept in my clothes, kept a pistol in my pocket, and ordered martial law in the palace.

Yamata and the chief of staff came again the next day to tell me that the Japanese Army was going to withdraw and hold southern Manchuria, so that the "capital" would be moved to Tunghua. I would have to be ready to move the same day. Realizing that it would be impossible to move my large household and all my property so soon, I pleaded for and won a delay of two days.

I now started to undergo new mental torments. These were partly caused by the further change in the attitude of Yoshioka and partly because of my morbid suspicion. I noticed the change in Yoshioka's attitude from a remark he made after Yamata had gone: "If Your Majesty does not go, you will be the first to be murdered by the Soviet troops." He spoke in a very sinister way, and what made me even more frightened was the obvious implication that the Japanese suspected that I did not want to go and was planning to betray them.

"If they think that I might be captured by the allied armies, might they not want to kill me to keep me quiet?" This thought made my hair stand on end.

I remembered a trick I had used over ten years previously to demonstrate my "loyalty and sincerity" in front of Yoshioka. I sent for the "premier" Chang Ching-hui and Takebe Rokuzo, the director of the General Affairs Office of the State Council, and ordered them: "We must support the holy war of our Parental Country with all our strength, and must resist the Soviet Army to the end, to the very end."

I turned to look at Yoshioka's expression, only to find that the "attaché" who normally stayed with me like a shadow had gone. Full of terrible forebodings, I paced up and down the room. I looked out of the window and saw some Japanese soldiers advancing towards the building with their rifles at the ready. My heart almost jumped out of my mouth, and I thought my hour had come. Realizing that I had nowhere to hide, I went to the top of the stairs to meet them. When they saw me the soldiers went away.

I thought that they must have come to test whether I would run away or not. The more I thought about it the more frightened I felt, so I picked up the telephone to ring Yoshioka. I could not get through. It looked as though the Japanese had gone without me, and that terrified me too.

Later I managed to get through to Yoshioka. His voice was very faint, and he said that he was ill. I expressed my concern, said some

317

kind words, heard him say, "Thank you, Your Majesty", and rang off. I heaved a sigh of relief, and realized that I had not eaten all day and was very hungry. I asked my last personal attendant, Big Li, to bring me some food, but he told me that the cooks had all gone. I had to make do with biscuits.

A little after nine in the evening of the 11th Yoshioka arrived. My brother, sisters, brothers-in-law, and nephews were already at the railway station, and of my family only myself and my two wives were left in the palace. Yoshioka addressed me and the servants who were still with me in a peremptory tone:

"Whether we are walking or in cars, the sacred objects carried by Hashimoto Toranosuke will go in front. If anyone passes the sacred vessels they must make a ninety-degree bow."

I realized that we must now be going to set out. I stood respectfully and watched Hashimoto, the President of the Bureau of Worship, carry the bundle containing the sacred Shinto objects and enter the first car. I got into the second, and as we left the palace I looked round and saw flames rising above the "National Foundation Shrine".

The train took three days and two nights to reach Talitzukou. The original plan had been for it to go via Shenyang, but it was re-routed along the Kirin-Meihokuo line to avoid air-raids. Throughout the journey we only ate two proper meals and some biscuits. We saw Japanese military vehicles all along the route, and the men in them looked like a cross between soldiers and refugees. The train stopped at Meihokuo for Yamata, the commander of the Kwantung Army, to come aboard. He reported to me that the Japanese Army was winning and had destroyed numbers of Soviet tanks and aircraft. But his story was belied by what I saw at Kirin station. Crowds of Japanese women and children, screaming and shouting, were pushing towards the train as they wept and begged the gendarmes to let them pass. At one end of the platform Japanese gendarmes and soldiers were brawling.

On August 13 I arrived at Talitzukou, a coal-mine set amid mountains whose beauty I was too terrified to appreciate, and two days later the Japanese surrender was proclaimed.

When Yoshioka said, "His Imperial Majesty has proclaimed our surrender, and the American government has given guarantees about his position and safety", I fell on my knees and kotowed to heaven, intoning, "I thank heaven for protecting His Imperial Majesty." Yoshioka also knelt down and kotowed.

Yoshioka then said with a dejected expression that the Kwantung Army had been in touch with Tokyo. It had been decided to send me to Japan. "But," he added, "His Imperial Majesty cannot assume unconditional responsibility for Your Majesty's safety. This will be in the hands of the Allies."

I felt that death was beckoning to me.

Chang Ching-hui and Takebe Rokuzo came with a group of "ministers" and "privy councillors". As there was one more farce to be played out they had brought with them a new composition of the Japanese sinologue Sato — my "Abdication Rescript". They looked like so many lost dogs as I stood before them and read it out. I have forgotten the wording of this sixth rescript, but I do remember that the indispensable references to the "Divine Blessing of the Heaven Shining Bright Deity and the Protection of His Imperial Majesty the Emperor of Japan" were struck out by Hashimoto with a wry smile. Hashimoto had formerly been a commander of the Japanese Imperial Guard Division, and he had later been made president of the "Manchukuo" Board of Ritual with the responsibility for guarding the Heaven Shining Bright Deity: as such he could be regarded as an expert on the emperor and the goddess.

Had I known at the time that the status I enjoyed was even lower than that of Chang Ching-hui and his group I would have been even more depressed. When the Japanese decided that I was to go to Tokyo they arranged for the secret return of Chang Ching-hui and Takebe to Changchun to make arrangements for the future. When Chang Ching-hui got back to Changchun he made radio contact with Chiang Kai-shek in Chungking and announced the establishment of a "Committee for the Preservation of Public Order" that was preparing to receive the Kuomintang troops. He and his group hoped that they would be able to make a lightning change into representatives of the Republic of China before the Soviet troops arrived, but the Soviet advance was much quicker than they had expected, and the Communist-led Anti-Japanese Allied Armies were sweeping aside the resistance of the Japanese soldiers as they approached the capital. The day after the Soviet Army reached Changchun Chang Ching-hui's dreams were shattered when he and his fellow-ministers were put into an aircraft and flown off to captivity in the U.S.S.R.

On August 16 the Japanese learnt that there had been clashes between the palace guards and the Japanese army in Changchun, so they disarmed the guard company that had come with me. At the same time Yoshioka told me that I was to go to Japan the next day. I nodded rapidly in agreement and pretended to be very pleased.

Yoshioka told me to decide who I would take with me. As we would be flying in a small aircraft I only chose my brother Pu Chieh, two brothers-in-law, three nephews, a doctor and my personal attendant Big Li. My concubine asked me amid sobs what she was to do. "The plane is too small," I replied, "so you will have to go by train."

"Will the train get to Japan?"

"Of course it will," I answered without a moment's thought. "In three days at the most you and the Empress will see me again."

"What will happen if the train doesn't come for me? I haven't got a single relation here."

"We'll meet again in a couple of days. You'll be all right."

I was far too preoccupied with saving my own life to care whether there would be a train for her or not.

We landed at Shenyang, where we were to change to a large aircraft at eleven in the morning, and sat in the airport rest-room waiting for the second aeroplane.

Before we had been waiting for long the airfield reverberated to the sound of aircraft engines as Soviet aircraft landed. Soviet troops holding submachine-guns poured out of the planes and immediately disarmed all the Japanese soldiers on the airfield, which was soon covered with Soviet troops.

The next day I was put on a Soviet aircraft and flown to the U.S.S.R.

CHAPTER SEVEN

# IN THE SOVIET UNION

# Fear and Illusion

When we landed in Chita it was all but dark. My party, the first batch of "Manchukuo" war criminals to arrive in the Soviet Union, was driven away from the airfield in a Soviet Army car. As I looked out of the windows it appeared that we were driving across a plain that stretched out black and immense on either side. After a while we went through woods and started climbing. The road became narrow and bending, and the car slowed down considerably. Suddenly it stopped, and a voice shouted in Chinese from the darkness, "Get out if you want a pee".

I was terrified, thinking that the Chinese had come to take me back; but the speaker turned out to be a Soviet officer of Chinese descent. As happened so often in the first part of my life, I had suffered quite unnecessary mental agony because of my morbid suspicion. I was terrified of falling into Chinese hands, as I thought that while in the power of foreigners I had a chance of staying alive, but was bound to be killed by the Chinese. It was, of course, absurd to imagine that I would be sent back to China just after arriving in the Soviet Union.

After we had relieved ourselves we got back into the car, and two hours later we stopped at a large, lighted building in a mountain valley. We got out of our car and looked at this handsome building; someone muttered, "This is a hotel." Everyone's spirits rose.

When we entered the hotel we were greeted by a man in his forties wearing civilian clothes, and behind him was a group of Soviet officers. He announced solemnly that the Soviet Government had ordered that we were to be detained here. This man later turned out to be the major-general in command of the Chita garrison. After making his announcement he told us kindly that we were to wait here calmly until a decision was made on how we were to be dealt with. Then

323

he pointed at a bottle of water on the table and told us that the place was famous for its health-giving mineral springs.

At first I did not like the mineral water, but later I became very fond of it. We spent a privileged detention in this sanatorium. with three large Russian meals a day and afternoon tea as well. There were attendants to wait on us, doctors and nurses to look after our health, radios, books, papers, and facilities for other kinds of recreation. There were even people to take us on frequent walks. I was satisfied with this life from the first.

Before I had been there long I had the wild hope that as Britain and America were allies of the Soviet Union I might be allowed to go and live in one of those two countries as a refugee; I had brought enough jewellery with me to last me for the rest of my life. To achieve this ambition I had first to make sure that I would be allowed to stay in the U.S.S.R., and apart from verbal requests I made three written applications to the Soviet authorities during those five years asking to be allowed to stay permanently in the Soviet Union. All three went unanswered.

The other "Manchukuo" detainees[1] took a completely different attitude. Chang Ching-hui, Tsang Shih-yi, Hsi Hsia and some others arrived at the sanatorium a few days after I did, and the next day they came to see me. I thought that this must be a courtesy call until Chang Ching-hui said:

"We hear that you want to stay in the Soviet Union, but our families are in the Northeast and need us to look after them. Besides, we have some official business to do there. We would like you to ask the Soviet authorities to let us go back soon. Do you think that would be possible?"

What the "official business" might be I did not know or care, and I did not take the slightest interest in their request. But when they pleaded with me I told the Soviet officer in charge of us about it. He gave the same reply as he did to my own requests — "Very well, I shall pass it on." Nothing came of it.

---

[1] The civilian "Manchukuo" officials enjoyed the status of detainees, while the military officers were war criminals.

The reason they wanted to go back was that they understood the Kuomintang better than I did. They knew that the Kuomintang needed them, and believed that they would be able to do well for themselves. Some of them almost went mad in their longing to return.

While we were in the Soviet Union we were told about the news by the Soviet interpreters, and we often saw the Chinese-language paper *Shih Hua Pao* that was published by the Soviet Army in Lushun. The former puppet ministers followed the development of the Chinese civil war closely, and their sympathies were naturally with the American-backed Kuomintang, which they expected to win. When the war ended with the defeat of the Kuomintang, however, they wanted to send a telegram of congratulations on the founding of the People's Republic of China. But I took no interest in the war as I felt that it made no difference to me who won — the Communists and the Kuomintang would both want my life. My only hope was that I would never return to my country.

## Still Giving Myself Airs

I never stopped giving myself airs during my five years in the Soviet Union. Although there were no more attendants when we were moved to the reception centre at Khabarovsk, there were still people to wait on me. Members of my family would fold up my quilt, tidy the room, bring me food and wash my clothes. As they did not dare to address me as "Your Majesty", they called me "Above"; and they would come into my room every morning to pay me their respects just as in the old days.

One day soon after my arrival in Khabarovsk I decided to go for a stroll. As I started downstairs I noticed a former minister sitting in a chair at the bottom of the staircase, and when he saw me he ignored my presence completely. I was so angry that I never thought of going downstairs again, and spent most of my time reciting scriptures. Most of the ex-"ministers", however, still behaved respectfully towards me. When we ate *jiaozi*[1] at the Chinese New Year, for example, they would always give me the first bowl.

On top of doing no work myself, I was not pleased if the members of my family worked for anyone else. When my brother and brothers-in-law were laying the table for everyone at one meal, I stopped them. I was not going to have my relations waiting on anyone but myself.

For some time in 1947 and 1948 the members of my household were moved to another reception centre in the same city, and I found this most inconvenient, as I had never been separated from my family before. The Soviet authorities were very kind to me and allowed me to eat by myself, but who was to bring me my food? Fortunately my father-in-law volunteered to do this and my washing into the bargain.

In order to make us parasites do a little light labour we were given a corner of the yard of the reception centre where we could grow vegetables. I and my household members were given a small plot where we grew green peppers, tomatoes, aubergines, beans and other things. I watched with fascination as the green shoots grew day by day, and I greatly enjoyed filling the watering can and watering them. This was a new experience for me. But the main reason why I was interested was because I liked eating peppers and tomatoes; I often thought that it would be far more convenient to buy them from a greengrocer's.

The authorities of the reception centre gave us some books in Chinese for us to study, and there were set times when my brother and brothers-in-law would read out *Problems of Leninism* and the *History of the Communist Party of the Soviet Union (Bolsheviks)* to everyone. But the books did not mean anything to the readers or the audience. I found them depressing and irrelevant. If they were not going to let me stay in the Soviet Union but were sending

---

[1] A traditional north Chinese New Year dish. *Jiaozi* are made by putting finely-chopped meat and vegetable fillings into flour "skins". They are then boiled.

me back to China, what good would it do me even if I learnt the two books by heart?

The word "study" seemed less real to me in those days than peppers and tomatoes. As I sat in my special place I would listen to the "teacher" mumbling away about words like "Menshevik" and "State Duma" that I neither understood nor wanted to understand; meanwhile I would be wondering how long the jewellery I had brought with me could last me in Moscow or London, or asking myself, "If the Russians don't eat aubergines, how am I going to eat the ones we've picked?"

After supper came the time for free activities. At one end of the corridor would be some mah-jong tables, while at the other end people would be looking out at the sky with their hands joined as they invoked Amitabha Buddha and the Bodhisattva Kuanyin. From upstairs, where the Japanese war criminals were kept, drifted the sounds of Japanese opera. The strangest sight was that of men crowded round a divination stand trying to find out when they would be allowed home and what had happened to their families. Some would consult the planchette secretly in their bedrooms, always asking about their return home. For the first few days the sentries would be startled by the shouting and come and peer at these strange men and shake their heads; later they got used to it.

I spent most of my time during this period in my own room, shaking my coin-oracle and reciting the *Diamond Sutra*.

# I Refuse to Admit My Guilt

As I did not stop behaving like a superior being and refused to study, there was no fundamental change in my thinking and I naturally did not admit my guilt.

I knew that legally I was guilty of treason, but I thought that this was just a quirk of fate. "Might is right" and "The victor becomes a king and the loser a bandit" was my attitude in those days. I did not think that I bore any responsibility, I did not wonder what kind of ideology it was that caused my crimes, and I had never heard of the necessity of thought reform.

In order to avoid punishment I resorted to my old tricks and tried to curry favour with the Soviet authorities who were now the controllers of my destiny. So I offered my jewellery as a contribution to the Soviet Union's post-war reconstruction.

I did not offer all of it, keeping the best for myself. I gave the jewels I kept to a nephew to hide under the false bottom of a suitcase. Unfortunately he could not conceal them all in this space, so I had to try and put the rest of them in every hiding place I could think of. But when even my soap could hold no more I had to throw away what was left.

One day a Soviet officer came into the main hall with an interpreter. Holding a bright object in his hand he asked everybody, "Whose is this? Who put it in the old radiators in the yard?"

The prisoners in the hall all crowded round and saw that the officer was holding a piece of jewellery. "It's got the hallmark of a Peking silversmith," someone observed. "I wonder who put it there."

I recognized it at once as one of the pieces I had told my nephews to get rid of, but as they were now separated from me I could not have this out with them. I hastily shook my head and said, "Very odd, very odd. I wonder who put it there."

To my surprise the interpreter walked over to me with a wooden comb in his hand. "This was found with it, and I remember that it was yours."

I was desperate. "No, no, it isn't mine."

The two men hesitated for a while, astounded at the naivety of my denial and then went away.

Apart from throwing away jewellery, I burnt some pearls in a stove and told Big Li to hide some remaining ones in the chimney just before we left the Soviet Union.

Because of my hatred for the Japanese I enthusiastically gave the Soviet authorities a lot of information when they questioned me about Japanese crimes in the Northeast. When I was summoned to appear as a witness at the International Military Tribunal for the Far East in August 1946 I denounced Japanese war crimes with the greatest vehemence. But I never spoke of my own crimes, for fear that I would be condemned myself. My testimony lasted eight days, and was the longest one in the trial. It gave first-rate news to those papers throughout the world that deal in sensation.

The reason why I was asked to give evidence was to expose the truth about the Japanese invasion of China, and to demonstrate how Japan had used me as a puppet to help them rule the Northeast. I now feel very ashamed of my testimony, as I withheld some of what I knew to protect myself from being punished by my country. I said nothing about my secret collaboration with the Japanese imperialists over a long period, an association to which my open capitulation after September 18, 1931 was but the conclusion. Instead I spoke only of the way the Japanese had put pressure on me and forced me to do their will.

I made several displays of emotion at the tribunal. When I spoke about introducing the cult of the Heaven Shining Bright Deity into the Northeast a Japanese lawyer asked me whether my attack on the ancestor of the Emperor of Japan conformed with Oriental morality. "I never forced him to adopt my ancestor as his ancestor," I shouted in reply. The whole room burst out laughing, but I was most indignant. When the death of my wife Tan Yu-ling was brought up I spoke as if my suspicions about her death were established facts, and said tragically: "Even she was murdered by the Japanese." I was, of course, worked up emotionally, but I was also deliberately portraying myself as the victim of the Japanese.

The defence counsel tried all sorts of devices against me in the hope of discrediting my evidence, and even suggested that I was not qualified to be a witness. These attempts naturally failed, and even had they been successful it would have made no difference to the fate of the accused. When they deliberately played on my fear of punishment to make me keep quiet, however, they were partially successful. I remember that after I had enumerated a list of Japanese war crimes an American lawyer shouted: "You put all the blame on the Japanese, but sooner or later the Chinese government will condemn you for your crimes." His shot hit the mark. It was precisely because I was afraid of this that I maintained that I had not betrayed my country but had been kidnapped; denied all my collaboration with the Japanese; and even claimed that the letter I had written to Minami Jiro was a fake. I covered up my crimes in order to protect myself. This meant that I did not make a full exposure of the crimes of the Japanese imperialists. Thus I was really doing them a good turn.

# CHAPTER EIGHT

# FROM FEAR TO RECOGNIZING MY GUILT

# I Expect to Die

On July 31, 1950 the Soviet train carrying the "Manchukuo" war criminals arrived at the station of Suifenho on the Sino-Soviet frontier. The Captain Asnis who was responsible for escorting us told us that we would be handed over to the Chinese authorities the following morning, and advised us to sleep peacefully.

After boarding the train at Khabarovsk I had been separated from the members of my household and put in the same carriage as the Soviet officers. They had beer and sweets for me, and told me funny stories during the journey; but for all this I felt that they were taking me to my death. I thought that I would be doomed from the moment I set foot on Chinese soil.

From the opposite berth came the even breathing of Captain Asnis. I lay with my eyes wide open, kept awake by the fear of death. I sat up and silently recited some Buddhist scriptures, and was just going to lie down again when I heard the tramp of soldiers coming along the platform. I looked out of the window, but I could not see anyone. The marching boots were growing fainter, and all I could make out were some ominously flashing lights in the distance. I sighed, hunched myself up in the corner of my berth, and gazed at the empty bottles on the table. I remembered something Asnis had said while we were drinking the beer that had been in them: "At dawn you will see your motherland, and returning to one's motherland is an occasion for congratulations. Don't worry, Communist political power is the most civilized on earth, and the Chinese Party and people have great generosity."

"Liar," I thought as I looked across at Asnis, who was now snoring. "Your words, your beer, your sweets — they're all a trick. My life will last no longer than the dew on the outside of the windowpane, but there you are sleeping like a log."

333

I did not believe that Communists could be "civilized". To me they were still the "raging floods and wild beasts" that I had been told they were for decades while I was living in Peking, Tientsin and Changchun. I attributed the humane treatment I had received from the Soviet Union, a Communist state, to the fact that it was one of the Allies and thus restricted by international agreements. I thought that China would be quite different. There the Communists had overthrown Chiang Kai-shek, and would presumably hate me a hundred times more bitterly than he had done. I thought that once I was in the clutches of these notoriously cruel men I could not even hope for a comfortable death.

I spent the night thinking such terrifying thoughts. When Captain Asnis told me the next morning to come with him to see the representative of the Chinese Government my only thought was whether I would have the courage to shout "Long live Emperor Tai Tsu" before I died.

With my mind numb I followed Asnis into another compartment where two Chinese were sitting. One was wearing blue civilian clothes and the other was in a khaki military uniform without any badges of rank and with a patch reading "Chinese People's Liberation Army" on his chest. They stood up and exchanged a few words with Asnis, then the one in civilian clothes looked me up and down and said, "I have come to receive you on the orders of Premier Chou En-lai. You have now returned to the motherland."

I lowered my head, waiting for the soldier to handcuff me. But he sat there motionless, just looking at me.

"He knows I can't run away," I thought as I got out of the train and stepped on the platform over an hour later. Two rows of armed soldiers were drawn up there, one of Soviet troops and one of Chinese troops with the same patch on their chests as the officer in the train. I walked between them and boarded the train opposite. I remembered that Chiang Kai-shek's eight million strong armed forces had been wiped out by men wearing this patch, and reflected that in their eyes I must be lower than a worm.

In the carriage I saw a group of former "Manchukuo" officials and the members of my own household. They were all sitting up straight, and none of them were shackled or bound. I was taken to a seat near the end of the carriage, and a soldier put my case in the luggage-rack. I tried to look out of the window but found that it had been papered over, and I saw that at each end of the carriage was a soldier with a submachine-gun. My heart sank. Surely this meant that we were being sent to the execution ground. The faces of all the criminals around me were deathly pale.

A little later an unarmed man who looked like an officer walked into the middle of the carriage. "Good, now you have returned to your motherland," he said as he surveyed us. "The Central People's Government has made arrangements for you, and you have nothing to worry about. There are medical personnel on the train, so if any of you are sick you can ask to see the doctor."

What ever could he mean, talking like that? Presumably he was trying to reassure us and prevent anything untoward happening on the journey. Then some soldiers came in and gave each of us a pair of chopsticks and a bowl, telling us to look after them carefully as they could not be replaced on the journey. This must mean, I thought, that the journey to the execution ground would be a long one.

Breakfast consisted of pickled vegetables, salted eggs, and rice porridge. The flavour of this home cooking after so many years abroad whetted all our appetites, and we soon finished a big bucket of porridge. When the soldiers saw this they gave us the bucket of porridge that they had been going to eat themselves. I could not understand this. I knew that as there were no cooking facilities on the train they would have to wait till the next station before they could cook some more. I reached the same conclusion: they must have some evil intentions towards us.

After breakfast some faces did not look nearly so worried. When my companions discussed this later they said that the generosity of the soldiers showed that they had been very well trained and disciplined and would not mistreat us on the journey. My views were completely different. I thought that the Communist Party hated me bitterly and might well murder me on the journey for the sake of revenge. Indeed, they would be bound to do so, and almost certainly today or tonight. Some of the others went to sleep after breakfast, but

I was feeling most uneasy and had to have someone to talk to. I wanted to make my escorts know that I ought not to be killed.

Sitting opposite me was a young security soldier, and he seemed the most likely person to have a conversation with. I looked at him carefully, and then found a subject of conversation in the patch on his chest. "You are a member of the Chinese People's Liberation Army (this was the first time I had ever used the respectful form of the word 'you'), and the meaning of the word 'liberation' is very good. I am a Buddhist, and in the Buddhist scriptures there is the idea of liberation. Our Buddha is compassionate, and has sworn to liberate all living beings. . . ."

The young soldier stared at me wide-eyed, listening without a sound as I prattled on. When I said that I had never killed any living thing and did not even swat flies, his expression was incomprehensible to me. My spirits sagged and I stopped talking. How was I to know then that the young soldier found me as incomprehensible as I found him?

My despair was now even deeper. The sound of the wheels on the rails made me feel that death was getting ever closer. I got up from my seat and wandered along the passage between the seats to the other end of the carriage. After standing outside the door of the lavatory I turned back. Half-way down the carriage I heard my nephew Little Hsiu talking to someone in a low voice. Hearing the words "democracy" and "monarchy" I stopped and shouted at them, "Still talking about monarchy these days? If anyone thinks that democracy is bad I'll fight him."

Everyone was dumbfounded by this outburst, but I continued to shout hysterically, "What are you all looking at me for? Don't worry, they'll only shoot me."

A soldier came up and pulled me back to my seat, advising me to take it easy. I clung to him as if I had been bewitched and whispered, "That one is my nephew. His ideas are very bad and he is against democracy. The other one is called Chao and used to be an officer. He said many bad things in the Soviet Union."

I went on like this after returning to my seat. When the soldier asked me to lie down I had no choice but to do so, but I still continued to talk as I lay on the seat with my eyes shut. Finally I dozed off, probably because I had not slept for several nights.

When I woke up it was the next morning. I wanted to know the fate of the two men I had reported. I stood up to look, and saw that they were both sitting in their old places. Little Hsiu's expression was normal, but Chao looked a little odd. On closer examination I saw that he looked depressed and was gazing at his hands closely. I concluded that he knew that he was about to die and was pitying himself. Then I remembered the stories about avenging ghosts and was frightened that his ghost would come to settle accounts with me. I went over and kotowed in front of him. Having thus averted disaster I walked back to my seat muttering an incantation for the souls of the dead.

The train slowed down and came to a halt. Someone muttered "Changchun". I jumped up like a spring and searched in vain for a chink in the papered windows through which to look. I could hear a lot of people singing nearby. I thought that this must be the place where I was going to die as I had been emperor here. Everyone was here, waiting for my public trial. While in the Soviet Union I had read about the struggle against local despots and knew about the procedure of the trials: first of all the accused was escorted to the platform by militiamen. Just then two soldiers came in through the carriage door, which gave me an awful fright. In fact they were only bringing the rice porridge for breakfast, and after their arrival the train started to move again.

When the train reached Shenyang I was convinced that I would die here in the place from which my ancestors had arisen. Soon after the train stopped a stranger came into the carriage with a piece of paper in his hands. "As it's so hot today," he announced, "the older ones among you are to follow me and come for a rest." He started reading out names from the list in his hand. It seemed odd to me that the list included not only myself, who at forty-four might just be considered older, but also my nephew Little Hsiu, who was only in his thirties. Clearly this was a trick. I was an emperor, the others were ministers, and Little Hsiu had been reported by me. We all climbed into a large car which was followed by soldiers with guns. "This is it," I said to Little Hsiu. "I'll take you to meet our ancestors." His face suddenly blanched. The man with the list laughed and said, "What are you afraid of? Didn't I tell you that you were coming here for a rest?" I paid no attention, and went on telling myself that this was a trick.

The car stopped in front of a large building with more armed soldiers at the door. A soldier without any weapon came up to greet us, and led us inside. "Upstairs," he said. I now had the courage of desperation and had decided that if I was to die I might as well get it over with quickly. I rolled my coat into a bundle, tucked it under my arm, and went upstairs. I went so fast that I overtook the soldier who was leading the way and forced him to hurry to get in front of me again. He showed me into a large room with chairs and tables on which was spread fruit, cigarettes and cakes. Throwing my coat on a table I grabbed an apple and started eating it, convinced that this was the banquet always laid on for condemned men, and that the sooner I ate it the sooner it would all be over. By the time I was half-way through the apple the room was full.

A man in civilian clothes started speaking near me, but I was too busy with my apple to pay attention to what he was saying. When I had finished the apple I stood up and cut him short.

"Stop talking. Let's go."

Some people in civilian clothes laughed, and the speaker said with a smile, "You're in too much of a hurry. Don't worry, when you get to Fushun you'll have a good rest and then do some proper study."

I was flabbergasted. Weren't they going to kill me? What did this mean? I went up and grabbed the list of names from the man who had brought us here. Although this made people laugh, I was now certain that the list was not an order for execution or anything of the kind. Then Chang Ching-hui's son Little Chang came in. He had returned to China earlier with another group of war criminals, and he told us about how they were now; he also passed on some family news. When we heard that the earlier group were all alive, that our families were all right and that the

338

children were either studying or working our faces all lit up. Tears came into my eyes.

My relief only lasted for the hour or so it took to get from Shenyang to Fushun, but it saved me from going mad, as I had been thinking of nothing but death for the five days since we had left Khabarovsk.

## Arriving in Fushun

Before our train reached Fushun all kinds of views about our rosy prospects were being voiced. The atmosphere had changed completely, and conversation was animated as we smoked the cigarettes we had brought with us from Shenyang. Some said they thought that we would be put up in a luxurious club they knew there; some thought that we would be allowed home after resting there and reading Communist books for a few days; some said that they were going to cable their families to get things ready for their return; and others thought that we might be able to bathe at the Fushun hot springs before we left. We spoke of the fear that we had all shared earlier and roared with laughter. But when we got out of the train and saw that we were surrounded by armed sentries, there was not a smile to be seen on our faces.

We were escorted by the soldiers into some large lorries. My mind went blank, and the next thing I remember was that I was somewhere surrounded by a high, dark brick wall surmounted with barbed wire and with watchtowers in the corners. I followed the others until we stopped in front of a row of single-storeyed buildings. All of the windows were barred. I realized that this was a prison.

The soldiers escorted us along a narrow passage and into a large room where we were searched. Then we were led away by unarmed soldiers. I and a few others followed a soldier some way along the passage until we came to a cell. Before I had taken a look round the room the sound of a heavy iron bolt being pulled across the outside of the door jarred on my ears. The cell contained a long wooden bed, a long table, and two benches. I did not know the former "Manchukuo" officers who were in the cell with me at all well, and I did not talk to them, so I did not know whether they too were frightened or whether they were inhibited by my presence. They stood to one side with their heads lowered and did not make a sound. Then I heard the bolt being pulled. The door opened and a warder came in to take me to another cell, where I was surprised to meet my three nephews, my brother Pu Chieh and my father-in-law Jung Yuan. So we were to be allowed to stay together. They had just been issued with new quilts, mattresses, and washing kit, and they had brought a set for me.

I was reassured by what Jung Yuan told me. "This is a military prison, and everyone here wears army uniform. It doesn't look as though we are . . . in danger for the moment as otherwise they wouldn't have given us towels and tooth-brushes. When we were searched just now they kept our valuables but gave us receipts for them, which isn't like the way . . . ordinary criminals are treated. And the food isn't bad."

"Perhaps the good food is an execution banquet," suggested my nephew Little Ku bluntly.

"No. That sort of meal includes wine and there wasn't any wine here. Let's see if the next meal is as good. If it is, then we know that it's not what you think: I've never heard of a condemned man being given several banquets."

I began to believe my father-in-law the next day, not because the food was still as good but because some army doctors gave me a physical examination. They were very thorough, asking me what illnesses I had previously suffered from, what I normally ate, and what I could not eat. They gave me a pair of new black trousers, a coat, white underclothes, and, what was even more surprising, cigarettes. This was certainly not the way that condemned men were treated.

A few days later a short, squat man of about forty came into our cell. He asked each of us our names, what books we had read in the Soviet Union, and whether we had been sleeping well for the past few nights. When he had heard our answers he nodded and said, "Good. You will be given books and newspapers at once to do some serious studying." They came a few hours later, along with some board games and playing-cards. From that day on we listened to the radio twice a day, once to the news and once to music. We were allowed to walk in the yard for half an hour every afternoon. The first time we went out for a walk Little Ku told us that he had heard that the man who had told us to "do some serious studying" was the governor of this prison for war criminals. We later learnt that the man who had brought us the books was a section head named Li.

In those days we called all the prison staff "Mister" as we knew no other way to address them. Mr. Li brought us three books: *On New Democracy, A History of Modern China,* and *The History of the New-Democratic Revolution.* He said that as there were not enough books at the moment we would either have to take it in turns to read them or have them read aloud for everyone to hear. Many of the terms used in these books were strange to me, but the strangest thing of all was asking us prisoners to read books.

The first of us to take an interest in them was Little Ku. He read them faster than anyone else and immediately asked the rest of us to help him with his problems. When we could not help he asked the prison staff. Jung Yuan mocked him: "Don't think this is a school — it's a prison." "Didn't the governor tell us to study?" asked Little Ku. "Whether you study or not this is a prison," replied Jung Yuan. "It always has been a prison and it still is one, books or no books." Pu Chieh said that he had heard of prisoners being given books to read in Japanese jails, but never of a "civilized prison" like this in China. Jung Yuan shook his head. "A prison is a prison whether it is civilized or not. You would do better to recite Buddhist scriptures than learn that stuff." Little Ku was going to argue with him, but Jung Yuan shut his eyes and started intoning scriptures in a low voice.

When we came in from our exercise that afternoon Little Ku passed on a piece of news that he had heard. Someone had tried to give his warder a watch, and had been told off for it. This started some of the younger men talking. Hadn't the hot water for our last bath been brought by the warders, asked Little Hsiu. "I've never heard of warders carrying water for prisoners before." Little Jui said that the warders here were not at all like the traditional idea of warders: they did not curse or beat us. Jung Yuan, who had finished prayer as a preparation for his supper, murmured:

"You youngsters are too inexperienced; you're making a big fuss over nothing. The fellow who tried to give the watch probably did it when someone else was looking. How could the warder possibly accept it then? Just because they don't curse or beat you, you imagine that they don't hate us. Just you see, we'll get our punishment later."

"Is bringing us our bathwater a punishment?" retorted Little Ku

"Say what you like," murmured Jung Yuan, "the Communists can't like us." He felt in his pocket. "I left my cigarettes on the windowsill outside," he said angrily. "What a pity, it was the last packet I had left from Shenyang." He opened a packet of low-grade cigarettes he had been issued with and grumbled, "The warders here nearly all smoke. I've made them a present of that packet for nothing."

Just when he had finished saying this the cell door opened and in came a warder named Wang with something in his hand. "Has anyone in this room lost some cigarettes?" he asked. We all saw that what he was holding was Jung Yuan's packet of cigarettes from Shenyang.

Jung Yuan took the cigarettes and thanked him profusely. When he had gone he lit up one of them, and after smoking it quietly for a while he struck his thigh as if he had suddenly seen the light. "These warders must have been specially picked. Of course they could choose some comparatively civilized ones to outwit us."

We were all silent, awed by Jung Yuan's judgement of experience

A few days later Jung Yuan's explanation was made to look very unconvincing. Pu Chieh was impatient to see the day's paper after our exercise one afternoon. He told us with excitement that he had heard there was an article in it which revealed why New China wanted us to study. We crowded round him, eager to see the

342

article. He read it out to us, and it included a passage which said that as New China needed talent of all sorts it was necessary to train and select large numbers of new cadres. He had heard that in the opinion of the other cells the government was letting us study and giving us favourable treatment because it intended to use us to help make up for the lack of talent in New China. Ridiculous as it sounds today, we were nearly all convinced that this was the case. Only Jung Yuan expressed his doubts.

We began to study seriously. Previously all of us except Little Ku had found the books uninteresting and had only read them for the sake of the warders in the passage. But even now our study only amounted to learning the new terms. Jung Yuan, of course, did not take part, and recited his scriptures with his eyes closed while the rest of us studied.

My blind optimism did not last long. Soon afterwards the prison authorities reorganized the cells and separated me from my family.

# Separated from My Family

Why was I separated from my family? It took me a long time to realize that this was a most important step in my remoulding. When it happened I thought that it was because the Communist Party was implacably hostile towards me, and reckoned that they intended to question the members of my household about my past activities so that they could condemn me later.

While in the Soviet Union I had said that all my traitorous actions were carried out under compulsion, completely concealing my collaboration with the Japanese imperialists and my attempts to win their favour. My relations had helped me in this and covered up for me. Now that we had returned to China I needed them to keep my secrets more than ever. I felt that I had to keep a good eye on them and make sure that they did not let slip any careless words. I had to be particularly careful with Little Hsiu.

During the first day at Fushun I had noticed that Little Hsiu'
attitude had changed as a result of the incident on the train.  I ha
felt an insect crawling up my neck and asked him to look at it.  I
the past he would have come at once, but this time he pretended nc
to hear and did not move.  On top of this, when Little Jui cam
and took the caterpillar off my neck and threw it on the floor, Littl
Hsiu snorted and said, "He's still saving life, saving that insect s
that it can harm someone else."  I felt weak all over.

When Little Jui was folding my bedding for me a few days late
I asked him to shake out my quilt.  This was an unpopular thin
to do as it made the atmosphere in the cell unpleasant.  Little Hsi
grabbed the quilt and threw it down on my bed.  "You two aren
the only people in this room," he said.  "Your lack of consideratio
for others won't do at all."  "What do you mean by 'you' and 'us'?
I asked.  "Have you no sense of manners?"  He turned away witt
out answering, sat down by the table and started writing, his lip
pursed.  I went over to look, but he snatched the paper away an
tore it up, only leaving me time to see the words "we shall see".

I bitterly regretted what I had done on the train.  Ever sinc
then I had done my utmost to be friendly to him, and had eve
explained that I had meant no harm by it and had always been ver
fond of him.  I took every opportunity to explain to my three nepl
ews that the principles governing human relationships could nc
be cast aside, and that in times of difficulties it was essential tha
we should be loyal to each other and stand together.  When Litt
Hsiu was not present I warned the others to be very careful wit
him, to make sure he did not do anything wrong, and to try an
win him over.

As a result of our efforts Little Hsiu did nothing dangerous an
I felt that there could be nothing wrong with him after all.  Bu
just when I had stopped worrying about him a warder told me t
move to another cell.

The others packed for me and moved my bedding and case to tl
other cell.  When they went away, I was left by myself amid a crow
of strangers.  I felt so awkward that I did not know whether to s

344

stand, and the eight people who were already in the cell were early inhibited by my arrival and said nothing. After a while, probably as a result of some agreement, my bedding was put on a bed by the wall. Later I realized that this was a good place as it was near the heating in winter, while being cool in summer because was by the window. But at the time I was too worried about the dangers involved in separation from my family to notice this or their respectful expressions. I sat down, but the wooden bed seemed extraordinarily hard, so I got up and started walking to and fro. Then I had an idea and went and knocked on the cell door.

"What is it?" asked the stocky warder as he opened the door.

"May I ask, sir, if I can have a talk with the governor?"

"What about?"

"I want to explain that I have never been separated from my relations before, and I'm not at all used to it."

He nodded and told me to wait. Soon afterwards he came back to tell me that the governor had given permission for me to move back. I was delighted, and gathered up my bedding while the warder took my suitcase. In the corridor I met the governor.

"Out of consideration for you older men the authorities have decided to give you food of a higher standard," the governor said. "We thought that if you were living with your relations but eating different food it might have a bad effect on them, so we. . . ."

I saw what he was getting at, so without waiting for him to finish interrupted, "That doesn't matter. I can guarantee that it won't have any bad effect on them." I almost added, "They have always had to be used to that."

The governor smiled. "Your ideas are too simple. Have you never thought that you must learn to look after yourself?"

"Yes, yes. But I should learn gradually, step by step."

"Very well," said the governor with a nod, "start learning then." When I went back to my old cell I felt that I had been away for a year. They were all pleased to see me, and I told them what the governor had said about learning to look after myself. Everyone

345

was happy to infer from this that the government was in no hurry to deal with us.

They did not let me practise looking after myself, and I had no inclination at all to do so. I was preoccupied with the governor's implication that we would be separated later and was trying to think of some way of preventing it. But ten days later, before I had found a solution to this problem, a warder told me to pack.

While Little Jui got my things together I took the chance to give some instructions to my relations. I could not do this by word of mouth for fear that the warder would hear, so I wrote a note for Pu Chieh to pass round to the others. As there were two outsiders in the cell, former officials in the puppet government of Wang Ching-wei, I had to be rather vague. I wrote that we had got along well, that they should continue to be loyal and stand together after I had gone, and that I felt a deep concern for each of them. I hoped that they would understand that what I really meant was that they should watch their words.

My nephews carried my baggage and took me along to the cell I had been moved to the previous time. Here I was given the same good bed, and once more I could not sit still. I paced up and down, then knocked on the door again.

The same squat warder opened it. I knew now that he was called Liu, and felt friendly towards him because he had brought us some extra *baozi* (steamed dumplings with minced meat filling) when he saw how much we enjoyed them when we ate them for the first time a few days previously.

"Mr. Liu, there's something. . . ."

"Do you want to see the governor?"

"I wanted to discuss it with you first. I . . . I . . . ."

"Aren't you used to it yet?" He laughed, and I seemed to hear other people laughing behind me. Blushing, I tried to explain.

"It's not that I want to move back again, but I wonder if I could be allowed to see my family members once a day. I would feel much happier if I could do this."

"Won't you be able to see them when you take exercise in the yard? There's no problem."

"I'd like to be able to talk to them. Would the governor give permission?" There was a rule then that people in different cells were not allowed to talk to each other.

"I'll ask for you."

Permission was granted, and from then on I was able to talk to the members of my family every day. Some of my nephews told me what happened in their cell and what the authorities had said to them. Little Ku still seemed not to be worried, Little Hsiu was the same as before, and Little Jui continued to wash my clothes and mend my socks for me.

With one worry off my chest new problems arose. For the past forty years I had never folded my own quilt, made my own bed, or poured out my washing water. I had never even washed my own feet or tied my shoes. I had never touched a rice-ladle, a knife, a pair of scissors, or a needle and thread; so now that I had to look after myself I was in a very difficult position. When other people were already washing in the morning I would only just have got into my clothes. When I was getting ready to wash someone would remind me that I should first fold my quilt; and by the time I had rolled up my quilt into an untidy bundle everyone would have finished washing. When I put my tooth-brush into my mouth I would find that there was no tooth-powder on it, and when I had finished cleaning my teeth the others would be almost through with their breakfast. So it went on all day.

Being slower than the others was not nearly as bad as having people laughing at me behind my back. My cellmates were all former "Manchukuo" officers who would never have dared to raise their heads in my presence in the old days; when I first came into the cell they did not venture to address me as "you", so they either called me "sir" or else showed their respect by using no word of address to me. But now I found their sniggers very hard to bear.

But this was not the worst thing. On our first day in Fushun a rota of duties had been made for each cell by which everyone took it in turn to sweep the floor, wipe the table and empty the chamber-pot. I had never had to do any of this when I was in my old cell, but the problem that faced me now was what to do when my turn came. Was I to empty the chamber-pot for others? I felt worse about this than I had about the secret agreement between "Manchukuo" and Japan: I thought that I would be humiliating my ancestors and disgracing the younger members of my clan. Fortunately a member of the prison staff came the next day to say that I was ill and could not take my turn. I was as happy as if I had been saved from certain death, and felt grateful for the first time in my life.

With this danger past another cropped up. The governor appeared as usual when we were taking our afternoon exercise in the yard. He always talked to one of us prisoners while we took our exercise, and this time he seemed to have picked on me. He looked me up and down, and must have seen that I was terrified.

"Pu Yi," he called. I had never been addressed by my personal name before my return to China and was still not at all used to it. I preferred people to call me by my number (981) as the warders had done when we first arrived at Fushun.

"Yes, governor," I said as I went over to him.

"You were issued with the same clothes as the others, so why don't you look like them?" he asked quietly in a friendly voice.

I looked down at my clothes and then looked at the others. Their clothes were neat and clean, whereas mine were creased and filthy. One of my pockets was half torn off; my jacket was missing a button; there was an ink-stain on my knee; my trouser-legs seemed to be different lengths; and my shoes had only one and a half laces between them.

"I'll tidy myself up," I murmured. "When I go back I'll repair my pocket and sew a new button on."

"How did your clothes get so creased?" he asked with a trace of a smile. "You should notice how others do things. If you are able to learn from the good points of others, you will be able to make progress."

Although the governor had spoken very kindly I was furious. This was the first time that my incompetence had been pointed out publicly, and it was the first time I had been in the public eye not as an image of majesty but as "rubbish". I turned away from the gaze of my former "ministers" and "generals", wishing that night

348

would fall. "They want to use me as a specimen for everyone to study," I thought in my misery. I looked at the high, grey wall. All my life I had been surrounded by walls, but in the past I had been treated with respect and enjoyed a special position within them, even in Changchun. But within these walls all that was gone. I was treated the same as anybody else, and even had difficulty in surviving. I was miserable not because of my incompetence but because others regarded me as incompetent, and because I had lost my natural right to have others wait on me. The gratitude I had felt for being let off the cell chores had completely vanished.

That night I discovered that when the others undressed for bed they folded their clothes neatly and put them under their pillows, while I just dropped them in a heap at my feet as I took them off. The governor's remarks seemed to have some sense in them. If I had known about learning from the good points of others I would not have got into the wretched situation I was in now. Why had my fellow prisoners not told me before? What treachery.

In fact those former puppet officers were still too inhibited by my arrogant manner to point any of this out to me.

We spent two months in Fushun, then at the end of October we all moved to Harbin.

## Move to Harbin

Some of the younger men among us felt like chatting on the train to Harbin and were willing to play cards with the warders, while the rest of us said little and spoke very quietly when we did. The atmosphere in the carriage was gloomy most of the time, and quite a few of us could not sleep at night or eat during the day. Although I was not as terrified as I had been when I first returned to China, I was still more worried than any of the others. It was soon after the entry of the Chinese People's Volunteers into Korea, and U.S. forces were close to the Yalu River. One night I and Pu Chieh had been unable to sleep, and I had quietly asked what he thought of the military situation. He answered in a flat voice, "Entering the war is asking for trouble. We'll be finished in no time." I took this as meaning that China would be defeated and the U.S. troops would occupy at least the Northeast; and also that the Communists might finish our group off to prevent us from falling into their hands. I later found out that this was what all we prisoners thought then.

My despair deepened when I saw the jail in Harbin. It was a former "Manchukuo" prison, and the sight of it made me realize what it meant to be paid back in one's own coin. It had been designed by the Japanese specially for imprisoning people who had been found guilty of "anti-Manchukuo and anti-Japanese activities". It consisted of two fan-shaped two-storeyed cell-blocks round a watch-tower in the centre. There was a grille of iron bars an inch thick in front of and behind the cells, which were separated from each other by concrete walls and could hold seven or eight men each. My cell was comparatively uncrowded with only five of us in it, but as it was designed in the Japanese manner we had to sleep on mats on the floor. I spent about two years here, and I have heard that it was later demolished. Although I did not know when I first came that very few of those who had been incarcerated here during the "Man-chukuo" period had survived the experience, the sound of the iron gates being opened or closed was more than enough for me. This noise always made me think of torture and the firing squad.

We were treated as we had been in Fushun. The warders were as kind, the food was as good, and the papers, broadcasts, and recrea-tions continued as before. This reassured me to a certain extent, but it could not calm me completely. I remember how the mournful sound of a practice air-raid warning went on and on in my head one night long after it had really stopped. Before I believed that the Chinese and Korean people's forces were really winning victories in Korea I was convinced that even if the Chinese did not kill me, I would die in an American air raid. I was sure that whatever happened China would be defeated and I would die.

I remember clearly that none of us believed the newspaper re-ports of the first victory of the Chinese People's Volunteers on the

Korean front; and we were very suspicious of the news that in the second successful campaign the Chinese and Korean people's forces had driven the Americans back to near the 38th Parallel. Some time after New Year 1951 one of the administrative cadres read out the announcement that the Chinese and Korean troops had taken Seoul, and clapping burst out from all the cells. Even then I only half believed it. When the "Regulations for the Punishment of Counter-Revolutionaries" were announced in the press that February the prison authorities stopped us from reading the papers for fear that we would be alarmed. We did not know this and thought that the reason must be defeats in Korea. We were more suspicious than ever of the earlier victories, and I was convinced that my doom was at hand.

I was woken up in the middle of one night by iron gates opening and I saw some people taking one of the prisoners out of the next cell. I started to shake all over, convinced that the U.S. forces were approaching Harbin and that the Communists were going to get rid of us at last. After a wretched night I found the next morning that I was completely wrong. In fact one of the men in the next cell had been having trouble with a hernia, and the warder had reported this to the governor, who had brought an army doctor and nurses along to examine the invalid. I had seen them taking him to hospital, but I had been so terrified that I had seen only their army trousers and failed to notice their white coats.

But this did not bring me much relief. I still thought that every motor vehicle I heard was coming to take me to a public trial. All day I watched and listened to everything that went on outside the bars, and I often had nightmares at night. My cellmates were not in a much better state than I was. Their appetites, like mine, were shrinking and their morale sinking. Every time we heard a noise on the stairs we would all turn our heads to look, and at the appearance of a stranger a silence would fall over the cells as if we were all facing our last judgement. When we were all in the depths of despair we were given new hope by a talk a security chief gave us on behalf of the government.

The security chief stood in front of the watch-tower and addressed all the cells for about an hour. He told us that the government had no intention of killing us, but wanted us to examine ourselves and study, and thus remould ourselves. He said that the Communist Party and the People's Government believed that under the people's political power the majority of criminals could remould themselves into new men. He said that the ideal of Communism was to remake the world, and that to do this it was first necessary to remould humanity. When he had finished, the governor spoke. I remember that his speech included a passage that went something like this:

"You are only thinking of death, and imagine that everything is a part of the preparations for your death. Why don't you ask yourselves this: why is the People's Government making you study if it plans to kill you?

"You have a lot of strange ideas about the Korean War. Perhaps some of you think that the People's Volunteers cannot possibly beat the American forces and that the Americans are bound to invade the Northeast, so you are worried that the Communists will kill you first. Some of you may have a blind belief in the might of the U.S.A., and believe that it is invincible. Let me assure you, the Chinese and Korean peoples are certainly capable of defeating U.S. imperialism, and the Chinese Communist Party's policy of remoulding criminals will definitely succeed. Facts have proved that the Communist Party never makes empty claims.

"Perhaps you will say that if we are not going to kill you, it would be a good idea to let you go. No, it wouldn't. If we were to release you before you had been remoulded, you might commit other crimes. Anyhow, the people would not approve and would not forgive you when they saw you. So you must study properly and remould yourselves."

Although I did not understand or believe all of this speech, I did see that there was some justification for claiming that the government did not want to kill us. This was the only possible explanation of why they had extended our bath-house in Fushun, saved the life of the invalid, and given special food to the older men among us.

Later I found out that such things were nothing unusual in the prisons of New China, but at the time they seemed all very strange to us, and we regarded them as marks of special consideration. So when we heard these government officials telling us formally that the government did not want to eliminate us we felt much more relieved at once.

None of us paid much attention to the references to studying and remoulding. I thought that we were given books and papers to pass away our time and keep us from wild thoughts. It seemed absurd to me that reading a few books could change one's thinking. I was even less prepared to believe that the American armed forces could be beaten. The four ex-officers in my cell, who regarded themselves as military experts, maintained unanimously that even if America did not have the nerve to flout world opinion and use atom bombs, she could still dominate the globe with her conventional weapons; her power was unrivalled, and it was nonsense to say that she could be defeated. Later we realized that the Communists were not the sort of people to talk nonsense, and before long we began to notice that the news about Korea did not seem to be faked. My military cellmates told me that while the casualty figures for both sides could be fabricated, it was very hard to keep up lies about territory won or lost. The news that the American commander was willing to hold talks would have been even harder to invent. If the American troops were willing to discuss a ceasefire, how could they be invincible? The ex-officers were mystified, and I was too.

The development of the Korean War showed how wrong our original expectations had been, and proved that America was not a real tiger but a paper one. I now felt much calmer, for if the Communists were not being defeated they would not be in such a hurry to get rid of me.

Our studies, which had previously been haphazard, were now directed by a cadre from the prison authorities. He gave us a talk on feudal society and then let us discuss it. We all had to write notes.

One day this cadre said to us: "I have already said that before you can reform your thought you have to understand what kind of ideology you already have. Your ideology is inseparable from your personal background and history, so you must start by examining them. For the sake of your thought reform, each of you must write an autobiography."

This sounded to me like a trick to make me write a confession. Were the Communists going to finish us off even though the military situation had been stabilized?

# Writing My Autobiography and Presenting My Seals

I regarded writing my autobiography as the prelude to my trial and was determined that I would make the most of this chance to save my life. I knew what line I would take. When we had climbed out of the lorries and were about to enter the Harbin prison Little Ku had whispered in my ear, "If they ask any questions, we'll stick to the story we used in the Soviet Union." I had nodded.

This story covered up my collaboration and represented me as a good, innocent patriot. I realized that I would have to be more careful here than in the Soviet Union and not leave a single loophole in it.

Little Ku had spoken on behalf of all my nephews and my personal attendant Big Li. It meant that they were prepared and were as loyal to me as ever. But loyalty would not be enough to prevent loopholes; I had to give more instructions to them all and to Big Li in particular, as he was the witness of a key part of my story — how I had gone from Tientsin to the Northeast.

I could only talk to him during the rest periods when I was allowed to see members of my family. The younger criminals, including all the members of my household (except Jung Yuan who was dead by now and my "imperial physician" Dr. Huang who was ill) had now started doing such jobs as carrying water, serving food and helping in the kitchen. It was not so easy for me to see them as it had been. But this new development had its advantages in that they could move fairly freely and pass messages for me. I sent for Big Li and reminded him to say that he knew nothing about how I had left Tientsin, and that he had only packed my things on Hu Sze-yuan's instructions after I had gone. Big Li nodded to show that he had understood and went away.

The next day Little Jui passed on a message to me from Big Li. Yesterday evening he had been talking to Section Head Chia of the prison staff and had told him that in the Northeast I had treated those under me with great kindness and had never cursed or beaten anyone; and that when in Lushun I had locked my door and refused to see the Japanese. This alarmed me: why had he mentioned Lushun? I asked Little Jui to tell him not to say too much, and to pretend he knew nothing about what had happened in Lushun.

Having satisfied myself of Big Li's loyalty and given instructions to my nephews I started writing my autobiography. I described my family background and my childhood in the Forbidden City. I said that I had been forced to go to the Japanese Legation and maintained that I had stayed out of politics while in Tientsin; I kept up the fiction that I had been kidnapped and led a wretched existence in Changchun. I ended by saying:

> When I saw the suffering of the people but could do nothing about it I was overwhelmed with grief. I wished that Chinese troops would fight their way into the Northeast, and longed for some international development that could bring about its liberation, a hope that was finally realized in 1945.

After careful revision I wrote out a fair copy and handed it in. I believed it would convince any reader that I had thoroughly repented.

After handing in the autobiography I tried to think of some other way of convincing the government of my "sincerity" and "progress". Clearly it was not enough to have Big Li and the others praising me. I needed some practical achievements. But my achievements since starting to take my turn on prison chores did not even satisfy me, let alone the prison authorities.

After hearing the speeches of the head of the security organization and the prison governor we were nearly all trying to think of ways to show how we had raised our "political consciousness" in the hope that we could save our lives this way. It seems laughable now, but we thought then that efficient hypocrisy would fool the government. My great sorrow during the time I was under this illusion was that I could not make as good a showing as the others.

We all tried to win the confidence of the prison administration through our study, our chores, and our daily life. The member of our group whose "achievements" in study were most outstanding was our group leader, Old Wang, a former "Manchukuo" major-general who had studied law for some years in Peking. As the most educated man among us he picked up the new theoretical terms fast. The other three ex-officers, like myself, found it hard to sort out the difference between "subjective" and "objective", but they made more "progress" than I did. They always had something to say in the discussions. The worst thing was that we each had to write an essay explaining in our own words what we had learnt about the nature of feudal society. I could manage to say something in the discussions, but writing the essay was more difficult. I did not see much point in study, and I was frightened by the explanations of feudalism I read in books. If, for example, the emperor was the chief landlord, then I was doomed because of this as well as for my betrayal of the nation. This thought so terrified me that I had difficulty in writing a single word. When I eventually put a piece together by cribbing passages from here and there I saw that it was not as good as those of the others. My achievements in study were clearly not going to satisfy the authorities.

The only evidence I had given of progress was to take my turn on the rota of cell duties after the move to Harbin. This was made easier because there were water closets in the corner of every cell so that there was no question of emptying chamber-pots. The work was light enough, consisting only of receiving the three meals and the hot water that were sent over every day and wiping the floor mats. This was the first time I had ever served others, and things went wrong when I spilt some vegetable soup on somebody's head. From then on one of the others would always help me when my turn came round, partly from kindness and partly to avoid another scalding.

My clothes were as untidy as ever, and Little Jui continued to wash and mend them for me. This embarrassed me, but when I had tried to do my own washing after the governor spoke to me in Fushun I had soaked myself in water without mastering the art of using soap and wash-board. Soon after handing in my autobiography I resolved to make a second attempt to do my own washing to prevent the authorities from despairing of me. I washed a white shirt, but when it was dry it looked more like a water-colour than anything else, and Little Jui took it away, whispering to me that this was not a thing for "Above" to do. I agreed with him, racking my brains for some other way to impress the authorities.

As I paced up and down thinking, I heard one of my brothers-in-law, Old Wan, and some of his cellmates talking about the donations that were being made by all sections of the Chinese people to buy aircraft and heavy artillery for the Korean War. We were not allowed to talk to prisoners in different cells, but there was nothing to stop us listening to their conversation. One of them was a former "Manchukuo" minister whose son had repudiated him and was now, he thought, fighting in Korea. He said that if his property had not been confiscated he would like to contribute it for Korea. The others laughed at him for thinking that he might still have his property or that his son might be allowed to fight; then one of them said that the only ones among us whose property was really worth anything were the emperor and the former premier.

This woke me up. It was true that I had far more jewellery than any of the others. Apart from the things hidden in the bottom of a suitcase I had some very valuable items that I had not concealed, including a priceless set of three seals exquisitely carved out of three interlocking pieces that had been made for Chien Lung after he retired from the throne. I decided to hand these over as a proof of my "political consciousness".

Some of the prisoners had tried to join the Chinese People's Volunteers to fight in Korea. When their requests were refused I was jealous of the way they had shown their "political consciousness" at no serious risk to themselves. I was not going to lag behind. By a piece of luck a government official was making a tour of inspection that day, and when I saw him coming I recognized him as the man who had told me not to worry in Shenyang. I could see from the manner of the prison governor, who was accompanying him, that this man was his senior. I thought that it would be more effective to make my offering to this high official. When he entered our cell I bowed low and said: "I beg to announce, sir, that I wish to present this object of mine to the People's Government."

He did not take it, but nodded and said, "Aren't you Pu Yi? You'd better discuss this with the prison authorities." He asked a few other questions and went. I told myself that if he had taken a good look at my seals he would not have been so casual about them. I wrote a letter to the prison authorities and handed it over to Warder Liu together with the seals.

I heard nothing more about the seals for many days and began to suspect that the warder had stolen them. One evening when the others were playing chess or cards I was brooding over the seals, convinced that my suspicions were well founded. Just then the stocky Warder Liu stopped outside the cell and asked me why I was not playing cards like the others. When I told him that I could not, which was true, he went off to fetch a pack, then he sat on the other side of the bars and shuffled it. I, meanwhile, was hating him.

"I'm sure you can learn to play," he said as he dealt. "Besides, when you become a new man and start a new life, you won't have much fun if you can't enjoy yourself."

I was amazed at his duplicity. When another warder, who was devoted to his pipe, came along and gave one of my cellmates some of his own tobacco to roll a cigarette, I was convinced that all the warders were trying to deceive us. But I was not going to be taken in.

In fact, of course, the one who was trying to fool others was myself. Soon afterwards the governor said to me in the prison yard:

"I have seen your letter and the seals. We have also got the things you presented in the Soviet Union. But what matters to the people is men, remoulded men."

# Changes in My Household

I did not understand the implication of what the governor said until many years later. At the time I just took it as proving that I must be in no danger for the moment if they wanted me to reform. But just when I was not expecting it, danger came.

One day one of the side-pieces of my spectacles came loose and I asked the warder to take them to Big Li to be repaired. Big Li was skilful at repairing delicate things like spectacles, watches and fountain pens. He often mended them for people, and he had always done my glasses before. This time was different.

In that prison one could hear upstairs what was happening downstairs and *vice versa*. Soon after the warder had gone I could hear Big Li grumbling indistinctly, and I did not like the sound of it. A moment later the warder came back and asked if I could think of some way of doing it myself as Big Li said that he was unable to mend them. I was furious at Big Li's effrontery. "If I could repair them myself I wouldn't have asked him to do it," I replied. "Please speak to him again, Mr. Chiang." Warder Chiang was young, slim and silent, and all my cellmates said that he was a decent fellow. He must have been, because he did as I asked and went down again.

This time Big Li did not refuse and mended them. But he did a rough job, only tying the spectacles together with a thread. The original screw seemed to have disappeared.

I thought the matter over carefully and decided that Big Li had changed. I remembered that a few days ago I had sent Little Jui to fetch him as I had not seen him for some time. Little Jui had come back to tell me, "Big Li says that he's busy and hasn't got time." I could now imagine that he must have said something like, "I haven't got time to be always at his beck and call."

Soon after the affair of the broken spectacles came the new year of 1952. We were allowed to have a New Year party, and we put on a little show, using the empty ground in front of the watch-tower as our stage. One of the acts gave me a warning of disaster.

Little Hsiu, Little Ku and Big Li had written a recitation in dialogue form, and all the men in their cell except Little Jui came on to perform it. They poked fun at the unpopular behaviour of some of the prisoners, such as the former "Manchukuo" minister of justice Chang Huan-hsiang, known as "Big Mouth". Big Mouth had a foul temper. He would disturb all his neighbours when he was quarrelling, and when he was once told that he was dropping rice on the floor he deliberately spilt even more. The satirists then directed their fire at the prisoners who read at the tops of their voices when they saw a warder come past.

I had found all this as funny as the rest of the audience, but then the superstitious prisoners came under attack. The performers jibed that these people did not realize that their divinations and prayers had not saved them before, and were still secretly praying. The targets of this attack clearly included me, as I still recited spells and prayed sometimes. While I was prepared to admit that there was truth in their claim that prayers had done me no good, it was quite intolerable that I should be publicly satirized. This was gross disrespect.

That was not the end of it. The next victim was the type of man who was put in a jail where he learnt what was right and was treated as a human being by the government, but "still acts as the slave of another". Obediently serving that certain "other person" would not help him to reform and would only make the other go on behaving as if he were the lord and master. It was only too clear to me who was being attacked and who was the "other person". I now understood why Little Jui had not taken part in the performance; I felt sorry for him, and was worried that he would not be able to hold out.

In fact, Little Jui had changed as well. Big Li, Little Hsiu and Little Ku had not appeared in the courtyard for some time, and I rarely saw Little Jui, so that my dirty clothes had piled up for days. After the New Year party he did not come for my washing any more, and it was not long before there was another major development.

On a day when it was my turn to do the cell chores, I was squatting by the bars waiting for the food to arrive when Little Jui brought it along. When he had handed it all to me he put a little ball of paper into my hand. I was astonished, but I quickly hid it and turned round to hand out the food, trying hard to act naturally. After the meal I retired to the lavatory that was behind a low wall in the corner of the cell and unfolded the note.

We are all guilty and should confess everything to the government. Have you yet reported the things I hid for you in the bottom of a case? If you take the initiative and hand them over the government will certainly treat you leniently.

Rage welled up within me, but a moment later it gave way to the chilly realization that my subjects were rebelling and my family deserting me. I flushed the note down the lavatory and reflected that these young people had changed. This was beyond my comprehension.

Big Li's father had been a servant of Tzu Hsi's in the Summer Palace, and it was because of this that Big Li had been able to get a job as a page in the Forbidden City after the expulsion of the eunuchs. He was then fourteen. He had followed me to Tientsin, where he studied with some other pages of mine under a teacher of Chinese. He was made a personal attendant of mine, and I regarded him as one of the most reliable of my servants. I chose him to accompany me when I left Talitzukou in my attempt to flee to Japan in 1945, and when we were in the Soviet Union he had once punched a Japanese for not getting out of my way. He had always been respectful and totally obedient to me, and had faithfully carried out my instructions to destroy some of my jewellery without leaving a trace of it. I could not think why such a man as this should have changed and lost his respect for his "superior".

Little Ku was the son of Pu Wei, the second Prince Kung. As the "Great Ching Emperor" I had allowed him to succeed to his father's title and had brought him up to be one of the mainstays of a future restoration. In the Soviet Union he had written poems to express his loyalty to me. My upbringing had made him a devout

Buddhist, and at one stage he spent whole days deep in "White Bone Meditation" before a picture of a skeleton. He had still shown loyalty to me even after our arrival in Harbin. That such a person should have written an attack on me made it clear that this loyalty had disappeared.

The most surprising change was that which had taken place in Little Jui. He came from a fallen princely family, and I had summoned him to Changchun when he was nineteen to study with the sons of other impoverished noble houses. I had regarded him as the most obedient and honest of the court students. He seemed less gifted than the others, but he served me better than his cleverer companions. He showed his loyalty to me throughout our five years in the Soviet Union. I once tested him by asking if he had ever had a disloyal thought, and he confessed that he had once felt that he had been wronged when I made him kneel on the ground for an hour as a punishment. When I told him that I would pardon him he kotowed to me, looking as happy as if he had just gone from hell to paradise. Just before my return to China I nominated him as my "successor" in the event of my death, and his joy at this can be imagined. From then on he did everything for me. But now he of all people was trying to teach me that I was guilty.

If I had been more observant I would have noticed some warning signs of these inconceivable changes. At the New Year party Little Ku had recited a ballad to the accompaniment of clappers describing the way that their thinking had changed. In this he described how having been brought up from childhood in "Manchukuo" they had been indoctrinated with reactionary propaganda. They had been taught to believe that Japan was the most powerful nation on earth; that the Chinese common people were incapable and needed to be governed; that it was natural for men to be divided into different grades; and so on. Their return to China had shown them that these were all lies. On their first day back they had been astonished to see that their engine-driver was Chinese, and similar discoveries had followed almost every day. What had most surprised them had been the attitude of the prison authorities and the victories in the Korean War.

At the time I had thought of this ballad as no more than a curtain-raiser and had paid no attention to it. I was unable to understand that Little Ku was explaining why they had rebelled: they now saw that I had been deceiving them.

I understood least of all that in their contacts with the prison staff since being separated from me they had all been deeply struck by the change in their status. Although they were prisoners, they were treated as individuals with their own characters, whereas before they had been nobles in name but slaves in fact. Now they had heard about different kinds of young people from themselves — about Chao Kuei-lan who had lost a hand to save a factory, and about the exploits of the People's Volunteers in Korea. They had started to ask themselves why they had never heard about such people before. Why had they only known how to meditate and kotow? Why had they been expected to be grateful for curses and beatings while others had covered themselves with glory? Why had they been so ignorant while others had achieved so much?

Thoughts like these had made them change and started them studying seriously and telling the prison authorities all about their pasts.

After destroying the note I sat by the wall gloomily reflecting that the Communists were really dangerous if they could change my nephews and Big Li like that. My only consolation was that my brother and brothers-in-law were still acting normally. But my big worry remained: would Little Jui report on me to the authorities?

I did not know what to do. I had a total of 468 pieces of jewellery hidden in the bottom of the case: platinum, gold, diamonds, pearls and other gems that I had carefully chosen to keep me for the rest of my life. I was sure that without them I would be unable to support myself if I were ever released, as the idea of earning my own living had not occurred to me. If I were to hand them in after hiding them for so long it would prove that I had been deceiving the authorities. But if I did not hand them over, Little Jui was not the only one who knew about them, and the others were even more likely to give me away than he was. If that happened I would really be in a mess.

363

"If you hand them over voluntarily the government will treat you leniently." This sentence floated through my mind and then gradually disappeared. I thought that the words "Communists" and "lenient" were incompatible, despite the way I had been treated in jail and the accounts I had read in the papers of the lenient treatment of offenders exposed in the Five-Anti and Three-Anti movements.[1] Soon after the beginning of these movements I had read of the executions of some monstrously corrupt men. Later I had seen reports of the crimes of capitalists who had been guilty of stealing state property and economic secrets, of graft, and smuggling, and of tax evasion, and had compared them with my own record. I had my own interpretation of the motto, "The ringleaders will always be punished; those who were forced into cooperating will not be punished; and those who perform meritorious deeds will be rewarded." I thought that even if the accounts of leniency were true they could not possibly apply to me: I was a ringleader and therefore bound to be punished.

"If you confess you will be treated leniently." I smiled bitterly to myself. I was convinced that the moment I told the governor about the jewels he would be furious at having been deceived and punish me. He might even go on to find out if I had been engaged in any other kinds of deception. That, after all, was how I had treated those under me in the old days.

No, I could not confess. Surely Little Jui and the others would not be so heartless as to report me. I put the matter aside.

A week later it was again Little Jui's turn to bring food to our cell. I saw that his expression was very serious and that he was not looking at me at all. He stared at my case for a moment and then slipped off. I was worried. What was he up to? Less than two hours later he suddenly appeared again at the beginning of our study period. He paused outside the cell for a moment, looked at my case, and went off again.

---

[1] The Five-Anti (Wu Fan) movement was a campaign against bribery of government workers, tax evasion, theft of state property, cheating on government contracts, and stealing economic information from government sources. The Three-Anti (San Fan) movement was a campaign against corruption, waste and bureaucracy.

I was sure that he had gone to see the prison governor. Torn by worries, I decided to hand the jewels over voluntarily before he reported me.

I took the hand of Old Wang, the head of our group, and told him that I had something to confess to the government.

## Confession and Leniency

"I am no good. The government has treated me so humanely, but I hid all these things in contravention of the prison rules, no, the law of the country. These things do not really belong to me, they belong to the people; I have understood this at last, which is why I have confessed and handed them over."

I was standing in the governor's office with my head bowed before him. My 468 pieces of jewellery lay gleaming on a table by the window. "Let them shine if I can save myself by handing them over, and if the policy of leniency applies to me," I thought.

The governor looked at me carefully and nodded. "Sit down." His tone of voice made me feel that I had grounds for hope. "Did you have much of a mental battle over this?"

I avoided mentioning Little Jui's note. "I was afraid that if I confessed I might not be leniently treated."

"Why?" asked the governor, with a smile on his lips. "Because you were an emperor?"

"Yes," I replied after a moment's hesitation.

"That is not surprising. As you have a peculiar history it is only natural that you should have some peculiar ideas. Let me repeat, then, that the Communist Party and the People's Government are as good as their word. They are lenient to those who confess, they lighten the sentences of those who reform, and reward those who distinguish themselves, irrespective of social status. It all depends on your conduct. You broke the prison regulations by failing to hand these things over at once and by hiding them for so long, but now that you have confessed and admitted your guilt this shows that you have repented. For this reason we shall not punish you."

He told the warder outside the door to fetch the member of the staff responsible for looking after valuables. When he came, the governor told him to take that pile of stuff and give me a receipt for it.

I was astonished. Leaping to my feet I protested: "No, I don't want a receipt. If the government will not confiscate them I want to donate them."

"No, we will look after them for you. Will you please check them through?" The governor got up and was about to go. "I have told you before that remoulded men are far more valuable to us."

I went back to my cell with the receipt. My cellmates were holding a discussion on *How China Became a Colony and a Semi-Colony*, a book we were studying, but when I came in they stopped talking about that and welcomed me with a warmth they had never shown before, congratulating me on my progress.

"Old Pu, we admire you." They had stopped calling me Mr. Pu and changed to this informal way of addressing me. When I had first heard this "Old Pu" I had not liked the sound of it, but today it made me feel good. "Old Pu, your action has shown me the way." "Old Pu, I had never realized you were so brave." "Old Pu, I must thank you for giving me more confidence in the policy of leniency to those who confess."

Here I should add that I was more untidy than ever now that I was washing and mending my own clothes. My cellmates' respect for me had decreased by at least half when they were calling me "Mr. Pu". Some of them had even been calling me "Rag Market" behind my back, and they often laughed at me for my incompetence in study. In contrast to all this, their present praises exhilarated me.

In the rest period that day I heard Old Yuan, the former "Manchukuo" ambassador to Japan, talking about what I had done. Old Yuan was a very intelligent fellow who could think of more in the twinkling of an eye than others do in a day. What he said gave me something to think about.

"Old Pu is a wise man, not a bit stupid. He was absolutely correct in seizing the initiative and admitting that he had those jewels. Of course, he could not have deceived the government, as the government has more information on us than you imagine. Remember the newspaper reports of the Three-Anti and Five-Anti movements. Millions of people gave information to the government. The government even knows about things you forgot years ago."

I realized that I could not get away with the lies I had told in my autobiography. If I were to admit to them, would I go scot-free as I had over the jewels? This would be a political, not an economic question, and I did not know whether it would be dealt with in the same way. The governor had said nothing about this. But then economic crimes were just as criminal as political ones, and the principles that the governor had spoken of should apply to them too.

I could not make up my mind. I started to look more carefully into the examples of leniency in the papers. The Three-Anti and Five-Anti movements were reaching their conclusion, and more and more cases were being dealt with, all of them leniently. I examined them with Old Wang, the former legal official, comparing what I read about with my own record and wondering whether the policy of leniency would help me.

When the government was preparing to deal with the cases of the Japanese war criminals the prison authorities told us to write down what we knew about the crimes of the Japanese in the Northeast. One of the prisoners asked if we were allowed to write about others besides the Japanese. He was told that this was, of course, permissible, but that we should concentrate on the crimes of the Japanese. This worried me. Who else did he want to write about? "Others" clearly referred to Chinese, and the biggest Chinese criminal was undoubtedly myself. Would any of the members of my family write about "others"?

The "Manchukuo" war criminals wrote about the crimes of the Japanese with great enthusiasm. Our group wrote several dozen accusations on the first day alone, and Old Wang said with satisfaction, "We haven't done badly, and I'm sure we can produce as much

367

again tomorrow." "Who knows how much the people of the Northeast could write if they were asked to," put in somebody. "Of course the government will carry out investigations among them," replied Old Wang. "What do you think, Old Pu?" "I'm sure it will," I answered, "but I wonder whether it will ask about others besides the Japanese." "Some people will be bound to write about us even if they are not asked to. The common people hate us just as bitterly as they hate the Japanese."

Big Li brought us our supper that evening. He seemed to be in a very bad temper, putting the food on the floor and going away without waiting for me to take it from him. I remembered at once that he had helped me to get into the luggage compartment of the car when I had left the Quiet Garden.

We spent the next day too writing about the Japanese. As I did not know much I could only write a little, but Old Wang was still satisfied as the others had written a lot. "Just imagine," he said, "how much information the people of the Northeast will be able to give the government. As a former legal official I can tell you that if you have evidence you can get anyone to talk in the end. In the old days we used to think that the most difficult thing was to get evidence, but things are quite different for the People's Government, with the ordinary people all providing information." My heart turned over. I thought of the case I had read about of the man who had executed a leading Communist in 1935 and had recently been caught by the security authorities in his hiding place deep in the mountains. Probably the Communists had been keeping a file on him since 1935.

The next day, when I was writing my last report on the Japanese, I heard a voice on the stairs. I turned to look and saw a stranger near the watch-tower followed by the governor. I guessed that this must be someone from a higher body come to inspect. He looked at each cell in turn, and revealed no emotion as the governor told him the name of each prisoner. Although he was not in uniform I guessed from his stern expression that he must be a military man. He looked as though he was under fifty.

"What are you doing?" he asked me as he looked into our cell. I was surprised by the mildness of his voice and the hint of a smile on his face. I stood up and told him that I was writing about the crimes of the Japanese. He was interested. "What crimes do you know about?"

I told him about the slaughter of the labourers on the construction project, the story that Tung Chi-hsu had told me. Perhaps I imagined it, but the smile seemed to disappear from his face and his expression became very severe. I had not expected that the story would produce so strong a reaction.

"I was shocked by it at the time as I did not realize that the Japanese were so cruel."

"Why didn't you protest to them?"

"I. . . . I didn't dare."

"Because you were frightened?" Without waiting for my answer he went on to say, "Ugh! What disgusting things fear can do to a man." He was speaking calmly again.

"This was all my fault," I said in a low voice. "I must confess my guilt to the people; I could not atone for it even if I were to die ten thousand times."

"Don't put all the blame on yourself. You must take only your share of the responsibility and keep to the facts. You will not be able to evade the guilt that is yours, and you will not be held liable for the crimes of others."

I went on to say that I had been moved by the way the government had treated me, and that I recognized my great guilt and was determined to reform. I do not know whether the official was listening as he examined the cell and asked another prisoner to bring the tooth-mug for him to inspect. When I had finished he shook his head and said, "You must stick to the facts. If you really acknowledge your guilt and show repentance you will certainly be treated leniently. What the Communist Party says counts, and it attaches great importance to facts. The People's Government is responsible to the people. You must show that you are making progress by what you do, not just with your tongue. Try hard." He glanced at what I was writing and then went to the cell next door.

My heart was very heavy. As I looked through the pile of material I had just written, it seemed that only today had I realized how serious were the events described in them. From then on those severe eyes haunted me and his words echoed through my brain. I realized that I was up against an irresistible force, a force that would not rest until it had found out everything. This force had caught the executioner of 1935 although he had been hiding deep in the mountains, and I realized that it would make a full account of the crimes of the Japanese in the Northeast, and that the crimes of the big and little puppets in "Manchukuo" would be unable to escape its attention.

It was a Sunday, and as I was hanging my washing out to dry in the prison yard I saw Big Li, Little Jui and a member of the prison staff approaching from the distance. After standing by the flower beds for a while, the three parted. Little Jui walked over in my direction, but just when I was going to greet him, he went straight past without so much as a look in my direction. I suspected that he had done something irrevocable.

I went back to my cell and re-examined the items about the Three-Anti and Five-Anti movements in the old newspapers. Old Wang came over and said, "What are you doing? Studying the Five-Antis?"

"No." I put the papers down and announced my decision. "I have been thinking about some events of the past. Previously I did not see their true nature, but now I see that they were crimes. Do you think it would be all right if I included them in my study essay?"

"Of course." He lowered his voice and added, "Anyhow, the government has got so much material on us that it is much better to speak up."

I took up my pen. The general outline of my essay was that the feudalists and compradors were indispensable to imperialism in its aggression against China, and that I was a typical example. For the sake of their dreams of restoration the feudal forces had used me as their signboard and collaborated with the Japanese imperialists, while the Japanese had used me as a signboard when they turned the Northeast into their colony. I wrote out the details of my activities in Tientsin and of the relations that I and my clique had with the Japanese, including my meeting with Doihara.

Two days later Old Wang told me that the prison authorities had read my essay and thought that I had made great progress, for which my group ought to praise me.

"A piece of real evidence is worth more than ten thousand empty words," said Old Wang, the former legal official.

## Making Boxes

At the end of 1952 we moved out of the barred building into a new and spacious block. Here there were new beds, tables and benches, as well as windows that let in plenty of light. As what the governor had said about "reform" seemed to be true, and as I had been praised instead of punished for writing that piece of personal history, I began to study seriously. In those days I thought that there was nothing more than reading involved in remoulding oneself, and imagined that once I had mastered the ideas in the books my remoulding would be complete. It never occurred to me that reading was not enough, or that reading alone would not enable me to understand the meaning of the books. In late 1950 and early 1951, for example, I had read *What Is Feudal Society?* but it was only in the spring of 1953 that a period of labour — making boxes — taught me what feudalism really meant.

The prison authorities arranged with a Harbin pencil factory that we prisoners should make some of the cardboard boxes in which the pencils were packed. From then on we spent four hours every day studying and four working. The prison staff told us that this would vary our routine, while a spot of manual work would be good for us as we had never done any before. I did not realize then what special significance these words had for me.

I had, of course, never stuck a pencil box together in my life, and for that matter I had never even sharpened a pencil. All I knew

371

about pencils was what I could remember about the trade-marks on them — Venus pencils had an armless woman on them, and there were German ones with cocks. I had never noticed the boxes they came in, and had no idea that making the boxes was so much trouble. Before I had been pasting for long the novelty had worn off and I felt as if my whole mind was sticky with paste. By the time that the others had all made several I had not finished my first one, and it did not look much like a box or anything else for that matter.

"How on earth did you make that?" asked Old Hsien, a former head of a "Manchukuo" military hospital, taking my creation in his hands. "Why won't it open? What the hell is it?"

Old Hsien had been brought up in Japan, where he studied medicine, and as the brother of the notorious female agent Chin Pi-hui (whose Japanese name was Kawashima Yoshiko) and son of Prince Su he came from a leading family of pro-Japanese traitors. He was a foul-tempered man, and particularly liked to vent his spleen on me as I was too timid to stand up to him.

My feelings were a mixture of jealousy, disappointment, and fear of being mocked at, and that busybody Old Hsien had drawn the others' attention to me. They crowded round my box and laughed unpleasantly. I grabbed the box from Old Hsien and threw it on the waste pile.

"What? Are you deliberately throwing it away?" Old Hsien glared at me, his eyes popping.

"I'm not throwing it away. It's not so bad as to be completely useless," I muttered as I took the box from the rubbish heap and put it on the heap of finished goods. But this was clearly wrong.

"Rejects are rejects wherever they're put."

This ambiguous insult infuriated me. Almost trembling with rage and unable to control myself, I retorted: "You are very brave with me. You bully the weak and are scared of the strong." His face went red and he shouted: "Who do I bully? Who am I scared of? You still think that you're an emperor and that everyone has to wait on you, don't you?" Fortunately the others were ignoring him, and the cell chief came and made him keep quiet.

But this was not the end of the matter. Old Hsien was not prepared to give up that easily, and the next day he chose to sit in the place next to me for pasting. He kept giving my work critical looks, so I turned round and sat with my back to him.

Although I did not do as well as the others I did make some progress that day. In the evening the prison authorities bought some sweets for us with the money that we had earned for our work. This was the first time I had enjoyed the fruits of my own labour, and although my efforts had been the least successful my share of the sweets tasted better than anything I had ever eaten before.

"Pu Yi, you didn't do so badly today, did you?" said Old Hsien.

"No, no rejects today," I said, counter-attacking.

"Hm, you'd do better if you were a bit more humble," replied Old Hsien, smiling coldly.

"What's proud about saying that none of my boxes were rejects?" I was getting angry, and my sweet no longer tasted so good. One of the things about Old Hsien that I found most objectionable was his knack of choosing the moment when I was feeling happy to start picking holes. "If I make any more rejects, you can call me what you like." With that I ignored him. But he went over and picked out one of the boxes I had made and held it up for everyone to see. "Look."

I looked up, and my sweet almost choked me. I had stuck the label on upside-down. I was furious and I wanted to throw the box into his ugly face. Restraining this impulse I muttered, "Think what you like."

"Temper! Still acting the stinking emperor," he raised his voice. "I only criticized you for your own good, but you won't realize it." He heard a warder coming along outside the cell, so he shouted louder still, "You are still dreaming of being emperor again."

"You're talking nonsense," I retorted angrily. "I'm stupider than you, and I'm not as good at talking or doing things, and I was born that way. Will that do for you?"

The others came over to break up the argument. Ours was a big room, and there were eighteen of us in it. Apart from myself there were three former puppet ministers and fourteen ex-officers.

373

One of the ex-ministers was Chang Ching-hui, who was now senile, did not usually study or work and was very silent. That evening all of us except Chang Ching-hui held a discussion on the "boxes affair". Some of them said that even if Old Hsien had meant well in criticizing me he need not have shouted, and some said that I was wrong not to admit that I had made the boxes badly. The Mongol Old Kuo said that it was not surprising that I had lost my temper as Old Hsien had taken such a bad attitude, and a former regimental commander who was a friend of Old Hsien's objected that Old Kuo was looking through tinted spectacles. Another view was that the matter should be discussed at the criticism meeting on Saturday. Everyone was talking at once. Then I saw that the regimental commander was tugging the coat of Old Hsien, who was shouting so much that the corners of his mouth were covered with foam. Everyone fell silent, and when I turned round a prison official called Li who was in charge of study had come in. He asked the cell chief what we were quarrelling about, and Old Wei said: "I report, sir, that this started over a reject cardboard box."

The prison officer picked up the box on which I had stuck the label upside-down and said: "Why quarrel over such a trifle? Why not just stick another label on the right way up?" We were flabbergasted.

But the matter was still not yet over. Some days later Little Jui told us when he brought the materials for our work that some of the other groups were going to hold a competition, and he wanted to know whether we would take part or not. We said we would. Little Jui then told us that Little Ku in their group had invented a way of pasting boxes that was at least twice as fast as the old method. We realized that we would have to raise our efficiency if we were to take part in the competition. Taking our cue from the reports of technical innovations that we had read about in the press, we started a production line in which each of us did one process. I liked this idea as it would make my work easier and might, I thought, cover up my incompetence. But before long there was a bottleneck at my stage in the line, and Old Hsien was the one who noticed it.

"One man's shortcomings are affecting the work of the group. What should we do about it?" He feigned an embarrassed expression.

I did not argue with him this time and stood there facing the pile of half-made boxes, just like the people who used to stand outside the Mind Nurture Palace in the old days waiting to be summoned to my presence. When the man who did the next process to mine pointed out that my work was not up to standard and was thus raising the rate of rejects for the whole team, I realized that nobody, however fair-minded, could refute Old Hsien's unkind criticism. I left the production line and went back to working by myself.

Once again I knew the misery of loneliness. Having been rejected by the group I felt that the contrast between me and them was as great as if I were standing there naked in front of them. I almost burst with rage when Old Hsien deliberately coughed as he walked past me, his pitted face revealing his delight in my misfortunes. I needed some sympathetic person to talk to, but the others were all far too busy. Then I caught flu and felt completely wretched.

That night I had a nightmare in which the face of Old Hsien was right on top of me saying evilly, "You are a reject. You're only capable of becoming a beggar." In my dream I saw myself squatting by a bridge like one of the "monkeys guarding the bridge" that the eunuchs had told me about when I was a boy. I felt a hand pressing on my head and woke up with a start. I saw an indistinct figure in white standing in front of me and feeling my chest. "You're running a high fever as your flu has got worse. There's nothing to worry about. Just let me take a look at you."

My head was aching and my temple throbbing violently as I took hold of myself and realized what was happening. The warder had heard me talking deliriously in my sleep, and when he could not wake me up he sent for a doctor. The doctor took my temperature, the nurse gave me an injection, and I drifted back to sleep.

I was ill for a fortnight, and I gradually got better under the daily attentions of the doctor and nurse. I spent most of my time in bed, doing no work or study. I thought a lot more in those two weeks than I had in the previous few years. My thoughts ranged from the cardboard boxes to the terrifying face of the Empress Dowager Tzu Hsi as I had seen it as a child.

Her dim memory had only seemed frightening to me in the past, but now I hated her. Why had she picked on me to be emperor? I was an ignorant and innocent child, in every respect at least as well endowed as Pu Chieh, but because I had been chosen to be emperor I had led a completely enclosed existence. I had not even been taught the most basic practical knowledge, with the result that I now knew nothing and was completely incapable. My knowledge and skills were less than those of a child, to say nothing of Pu Chieh. I was mocked and bullied by Old Hsien and his like, and if I were ever allowed to live by myself I would be incapable of surviving. Was not my present state the fault of Tzu Hsi, the princes and the Ching ministers?

Whenever I had been laughed at previously or been shown to be incompetent I had resented it bitterly, hating those who found fault with me and the People's Government that was incarcerating me. But now I saw that this was wrong of me. I really was laughable, incapable and ignorant. Previously I had resented the disrespect in which my nephews held me, but now I saw that there was no reason why they should respect me. I could not even recognize leek when I ate it, and I had acknowledged a foreign deity as my own ancestress.

What, after all, was so divine about me? The Mongol Old Cheng told me that when his father Babojab rebelled in the early years of the Republic the whole family had sworn to be prepared to die in support of my restoration; his mother had worshipped me as nothing less than a god. He observed that it was a great pity that she was now dead, as otherwise "I could have told her that Hsuan Tung is just a piece of rubbish". Could I blame people for saying things like this?

I only blamed the Empress Dowager and the rest of them, and hated the Forbidden City with a new intensity. I thought of it as an even bigger enemy than Old Hsien.

When I was nearly better the governor sent for me. After asking about my health he went on to inquire about the quarrel between me and Old Hsien. He asked if I had been shocked. After giving him a brief account of the affair I ended by saying, "I was very shocked at the time, but now I am not particularly angry. I only hate my own incompetence and all those people in the palace in Peking."

"It is good that you have recognized your own shortcomings; that shows progress. There is no need to be miserable about your inability, which can be overcome if you are willing to learn. It is even more important that you have recognized the source of your incompetence. You ought to ask yourself why those princes and court officials brought you up that way."

"They were only concerned about their own interests. They didn't care about me, only about themselves."

"I'm afraid you're not quite right there," the governor replied with a smile. "Can you really say that Chen Pao-shen and your father intentionally worked against you? Did they deliberately try to harm you?"

I could produce no answer.

"You should give this question careful thought. If you are able to find the answer, your illness will have been well worth while."

I continued to think about this after returning from the governor's office, and I went over my past life many times before the first criticism meeting I took part in after my illness. My failure to find an answer made me angrier and angrier.

At this criticism meeting someone criticized Old Hsien for his malevolence, saying that he was always deliberately attacking me. Most of the others expressed similar views, and some even put the blame for my illness on to Old Hsien and showed that he was having a bad effect on the remoulding of all of us. Old Hsien turned grey with panic and made a faltering self-criticism. I said nothing throughout the meeting although I was seething with hatred. When someone suggested that I speak Old Hsien turned paler than ever.

"I have nothing to say," I said in a low voice. "I only hate my own incompetence."

Everyone was astonished, and Old Hsien's jaw sagged. I started to shout, "I hate the place where I grew up. I hate that evil system. What is feudalism? Feudalism means ruining people from childhood."

There was a convulsion in my throat and I could not go on. The others were muttering something, but I could not hear what it was.

# The Investigators Arrive

From the end of 1953 onwards we studied *Imperialism* for three months, and after this we moved back to Fushun in March 1954. Before long the working party from the investigating organization arrived and began to question the prisoners.

We later found out that the government had made the most thorough preparations for investigating the crimes of the Japanese and "Manchukuo" war criminals, and had mustered strong forces for the job. A batch of Japanese war criminals was transferred to Fushun. The government had been collecting material for several years, and about two hundred investigators had been assembled and given special political and technical training.

The investigation of the "Manchukuo" war criminals began with a big meeting at the end of March. As far as we prisoners were concerned the investigations consisted of reporting others' crimes and admitting our own, and they were more or less finished by the end of the year.

The head of the group of investigators told us at the meeting that after our study and reflection over the past few years it was now time for us to acknowledge our guilt. The government had to examine our crimes, and we had to recognize the past for what it really was, confess our crimes, and report the crimes of the Japanese imperialists and the other Chinese traitors. Whether confessing our own crimes or reporting those of others we had to be honest, neither exaggerating nor minimizing. The decision that the government finally took on how to deal with us would depend on our crimes and our attitude, and its policy was one of leniency to those who confessed coupled with severity to those who resisted.

At the meeting the prison governor announced some new rules. We were forbidden to exchange information on our cases, to send notes to other cells, and so on. From that day on each group took its exercise in turn, so that it would be impossible to meet prisoners from other cells.

After this meeting each group returned to its cell for a discussion. Everyone said that they were going to make thorough confessions and reports, and intended to admit their guilt humbly in order to obtain leniency; but some of them, like Old Hsien, were visibly anxious about it.

I caught his alarm, and my belief in the policy of leniency gave way once more to doubts. If a former hospital director had grounds for fear, surely I, an ex-emperor, had far more. As I had already confessed my main crimes my principal worry was how to convince the investigators that I was being truthful. I therefore decided to rewrite my life history in greater detail, while bringing in all I knew about the crimes of the Japanese war criminals. I promised to do this at the meeting of our group.

Carrying out this promise was not easy. When writing about the end of the "Manchukuo" period I came to the declaration of war against Japan by the Soviet Union. I had been terrified that the Japanese might suspect me and kick me aside in that time of crisis, and had racked my brains for some way to ingratiate myself with them. On the night after hearing of the Soviet declaration of war on Japan I had sent for Chang Ching-hui and Takebe (the head of the "General Affairs Office of the State Council of Manchukuo") on my own initiative. I gave them an oral "edict" ordering them to mobilize speedily and do everything possible to support Japan against the attacks of the Soviet Red Army. What was I going to say about this now? I had to mention it as there was a chance that other people knew about this edict; but if I did mention it, then would not this one action I took without prompting from the Japanese make the investigators suspect that I had not, after all, been completely under the control of Yoshioka? If they did that, the whole of my autobiography would be invalidated.

379

I decided that I would not say too much about the matter. It could do me no harm to be a little reticent about some of the bad things that I had done. I put the blame for this edict on Yoshioka, then wrote the confession out again, going into greater detail about the things I dared to mention, and writing all I could about the crimes of others. I handed all this in and waited for the summons of the investigators.

I wondered what the questioning would be like. Would the interrogator look like an ordinary human being or like a monster? Would he use torture on me, as I had tortured offending servants and eunuchs in the Forbidden City and Changchun? I was sure that he would be cruel. I was more terrified of torture, or even a slap in the face, than I was of death. I had been in a Communist prison for three years and had seen that people were not beaten or cursed but were treated with the dignity due to them as human beings. This should have been enough to show me that my earlier fears of cruelty were groundless, but I was convinced that an interrogator was bound to be suspicious and use violence on his subject.

I spent ten uneasy days tormented by such thoughts. Then the dread moment came when a warder told me to go and see the investigators.

I was taken to a room that was about ten metres square. In the middle was a large desk, in front of which was a small table set with tea-bowls, a teapot and an ash-tray. Behind the desk sat two men, one middle-aged and one young. They indicated to me that I was to sit on a chair beside the table.

The older man asked me my name, age, place of origin and sex, and the younger man's pen scratched across a piece of paper as he wrote down my answers. "We have read your confession," the older man said, "and we would like to have a talk with you. You may smoke."

The older man asked me about a number of things from my childhood to the time of my capture. He nodded at my answers as if he were satisfied. "Very well, we'll leave it at that for the moment. Interrogator Chao may have some more questions to put to you later."

380

The atmosphere of the questioning, which had come as a complete surprise, ended my worries about torture.

I was a little disappointed at my next interrogation to find that only Chao was in the room. As I sat in front of this young interrogator I wondered if he would be any good. Would he be able to understand that I was telling the truth? Would he have a young man's hot temper? Whose word would he believe if others had written lying reports about me?

"There is a question I would like to ask you," he said, interrupting my train of thought. He wanted to know about the procedure for issuing imperial decrees and rescripts in "Manchukuo", and I replied truthfully. When he mentioned one decree, he asked me how long before its promulgation I had seen it. I was not sure and replied, "Probably one or two days beforehand, but it may have been three or even four."

"There is no need to give a reply at once. You can tell me when you remember. Let's go on to another question now." I could not think of the answer to that either, and got stuck. I wondered whether the interrogator would think that I was deliberately concealing something and lose his temper. Instead he said: "Let's put that one aside too. You can tell me when you remember."

I had to take my hat off to that young man in the end.

At one session — I can no longer remember which — he produced some of the materials I had written and laid them before me.

"You have written here that the Japanese invaders took sixteen million tons of grain from the Northeast in one year, following a plan made by Furumi Tadayuki, the war criminal who had been deputy chief of the 'General Affairs Office of the State Council of Manchukuo'. This is too vague. Which year was it? How do you know the figure of sixteen million tons? Please give me more details."

I had, in fact, overheard two former puppet ministers in my cell talking about it, but I could hardly admit this, so I said that the Japanese robbed the Northeast of all its wealth, and took all the grain that was grown. The interrogator interrupted me again at this point: "Do you know the annual grain production of the Northeast?"

I could say nothing.

"On what do you base the statement in the material you wrote?"

I saw that I could not bluff my way out of this situation, so I admitted that my only authority was gossip.

"So do you believe what you have written or not?"

"I. . . . I don't know."

"Hm. You don't even believe it yourself." The interrogator looked at me, his eyes wide open. "So why did you write it?"

I did **not** know what to say. He put the cap on his fountain pen and tidied up the thick *Manchukuo Yearbook* and *Government Report* on his desk. It was obvious that he did not want any more answers from me, and he closed the interrogation by saying, "Whether you are referring to yourself or to others you must always stick to the facts."

I looked at him silently, acknowledging to myself the truth of what he had just said. I was, after all, frightened that others might tell lies or exaggerate about me. I went out of the room wondering if all interrogators were as conscientious as this young fellow. What would happen if an incompetent one were to read some lies about me?

This question was soon answered when my cellmate Old Yuan told us about an experience of his. He had written down a figure he had worked out for the amount of iron and steel taken from the Northeast by the Japanese. The interrogator had not believed it and had given him a pencil, asking him to work out how much ore would be needed to produce so much iron and steel, and how much ore was actually mined in the Northeast each year. Old Yuan ended by telling us that the interrogator had files on the natural resources of the Northeast.

Now I understood why Interrogator Chao had all those reference books on his desk. To verify all the written evidence several hundred investigators had spent more than a year travelling all over the country and reading through files by the ton, as I found out when I signed the general conclusions on me written by the investigators.

The reason why I ran into trouble with that young investigator was because he was so conscientious in his search for the facts, and because I was stupidly worrying that he would think I was not being honest. I therefore hurriedly wrote out a self-criticism and sent it to him. With this done I felt that the situation was not too serious.

# The Sufferings and Hatred of the People of the Northeast

I never knew or cared much about the calamities that the Japanese had inflicted on the people of the Northeast, and I never thought they had anything to do with me. But when I attended a study meeting on the crimes of the Japanese war criminals in the Northeast I realized how serious they were. This meeting, in which the Japanese war criminals participated, made a very deep impression on me. The most striking testimonies were the confessions of Furumi Tadayuki, the former deputy head of the "General Affairs Office of the State Council of Manchukuo", and of a former "Manchukuo" gendarmerie commander.

Furumi had been a favourite of the Japanese military, and one of the real rulers of "Manchukuo". Acting on the orders of the Kwantung Army he and his superior Takebe Rokuzo had planned and carried out the rule and the looting of the Northeast. He spoke in great detail about the policy of forcibly seizing the land of the peasants in the Northeast for the resettlement of Japanese immigrants; about the "Five Year Plan for Developing Production" that was designed to plunder its natural resources; about the use of opium to poison the people; and about many other policies, including squeezing grain and other commodities out of the people as part of the preparations for the Pacific War. He told us about some of the results of these policies, and every example he cited was an atrocity. In 1944, for instance, over fifteen thousand labourers from all over the Northeast were conscripted for military construction at Wangyemiao in the Khingan Mountains. So bad were the conditions under which they were forced to work that more than six thousand of them died.

Furumi also had a lot to say about the Japanese opium policy. This was initiated in early 1933, when the Japanese Army was short of funds before its invasion of Jehol. As it did not then control the production of opium in the Northeast it imported over two million ounces of foreign opium and scattered leaflets by air all over Jehol encouraging the cultivation of the opium poppy. Around 1936 the Japanese Army greatly extended the area under opium cultivation in "Manchukuo", did all they could to expand production, and later gave themselves a legal monopoly of the sale of opium. The Japanese founded "Societies for the Prevention of Opium-Smoking" everywhere, set up opium dens with "hostesses", and made great efforts to spread the addiction among young people. In 1942 the Japanese "Asia Revival Council" held a "Conference on the Opium Needs and Production of China" which passed a resolution stating that "Manchukuo and the Mongolian border regions are to meet the opium requirements of the Greater East Asian Co-Prosperity Sphere"; after this the area under opium in the Northeast was increased to 3,000 hectares. According to Furumi's calculations, "Manchukuo" produced over 300 million ounces of opium before its collapse. The profit from it made up one-sixth of the revenue of the puppet government; in 1944 it reached a total of 300 million dollars, over a hundred times higher than it had been at the beginning of "Manchukuo", thus providing Japan with one of her most important sources of finance for her aggressive war. There were about 300,000 addicts in Jehol alone, and in the Northeast as a whole one person in twenty was an opium-smoker.

The gendarmerie officer testified that the gendarmerie often perpetrated mass slaughters, after which the local people would be assembled to see the corpses. Sometimes they would arrest a number of people they regarded as suspicious, line them up, select one of them at random, and then split him open with a sword in public. He had killed over thirty victims this way. Those the gendarmerie arrested had to undergo all kinds of tortures: they were beaten; they had cold water, peppery water and paraffin poured down their noses; they were burned with incense sticks or red-hot pokers; and were hung upside-down, to mention but a few of the torments.

Apart from what the people of the Northeast suffered directly from the Japanese invaders, it is not difficult to produce facts and figures about what they underwent at the hands of the puppet government and the Chinese traitors. Through various orders and grain policies, and through the system of supplying grain to Japan, the people of the Northeast were robbed of practically all the grain they produced every year, and at the end of the "Manchukuo" period they could only keep themselves alive by eating the "compound flour" they were supplied with that was made out of maize husks, bean-cake and acorn flour. The grain that was taken from them was either kept for military use or sent off to Japan. The amount sent to Japan annually steadily rose to 3,000,000 tons by 1944; and the total for the last six years of the "Manchukuo" period was over 11,100,000 tons.

As a result of the legislation controlling grain, cotton cloth, metals and other commodities the people found themselves being made into "economic criminals". Ordinary people were, for example, absolutely forbidden to eat rice, and they could be punished as "economic criminals" if the remains of rice were found in their vomit. In the year 1944-45 alone 317,100 people were punished for "economic crimes".

At the same time as their grain was being taken from them, the peasants of the Northeast were losing their land. In the last two years of "Manchukuo" 390,000 Japanese immigrants were moved into the Northeast, and the puppet government took 36,500,000 hectares of land from the people of the Northeast to give to them.

As they wanted to plunder the Northeast of its natural resources and turn it into their economic base, the Japanese used the puppet government to enslave the people of the Northeast through a variety of devices. After the "Labour Control Law" was issued in my name in 1938, 2,500,000 men (excluding those who were conscripted south of the Great Wall) had to do forced labour without payment every year. Most of them worked in mining and military construction, and they died in great numbers because of the terrible conditions under which they worked. Thus in 1944, during the "Flood-Prevention Project" in Liaoyang city 170 out of a force of 2,000 young labourers died of their sufferings.

Peasants, ordinary workers, clerks, students and young men who failed to pass the medical examination for the army all had to participate in this slave labour which was officially called "voluntary labour".

Those who suffered the worst were the inmates of the "reformatories". At the end of the "Manchukuo" era the savagery of Japanese rule neared the point of madness. The "Thought Rectification Law" and the "Security and Rectification Law" were proclaimed in 1943 in an attempt to solve the shortage of labour and curb the growing resistance of the people, and concentration camps were set up all over the Northeast under the name of "reformatories". People who had been reduced to destitution or who were dissatisfied were thrown into these institutions on charges of "vagabondage" or "bad thoughts" and forced to do hard labour. Sometimes the authorities stopped passers-by and labelled them as "vagabonds" without even bothering to question them, then threw them into a "reformatory" from which they would never emerge.

The inmates who had survived until the collapse of the "Manchukuo" regime were now telling the People's Government with bitterness and hatred about what the puppet rulers had done to them. A peasant of Hokang city was arrested in 1944 and taken to the police headquarters on a charge of anti-Manchukuo and anti-Japanese activities. There were seventeen others there with him, and after being viciously beaten they were moved to the Hokang Reformatory and forced to mine coal in the Tungshan mines. They had to work twelve hours a day, were only given a tiny ball of *kaoliang* at each meal, had no clothes or bedding, and were frequently and savagely beaten.

My mother heard that I was in the reformatory and she came to the place where I was working to see me through the barbed wire. When the police saw her they grabbed her by the hair and kicked her until she could not get up from the ground. Later they beat me with spades, so that I was covered with wounds and lay unconscious for seven days. Once, when we were not given any vegetables to eat with our meal, a fellow-prisoner called Sung Kai-tung bought some scallions from a passer-by with some money of mine. He was seen by the traitor Section Head Wang, who called the two of us over, took five dollars off me, and had me beaten up so badly that I bled from my mouth and nose. Then he forced me into a sack by hitting me on the head when I refused, and when I was in the sack they picked it up and dropped it three times, by the end of which I was unconscious. People died there daily, and every three or four days seven or eight corpses used to be carried out. Nine of the seventeen men who were arrested with me died there. I caught T.B. there, and I am still unable to work. My mother was driven mad, and my three sisters, of whom the oldest was only eleven, had to go out to beg for their food every day.

The oppression of the people of the Northeast by the army, police, law courts and prisons of "Manchukuo" was a story of bloody atrocities too numerous to enumerate. The sixty-one-year-old peasant Huang Yung-hung had been arrested for sending a letter to the Anti-Japanese Allied Army, and had witnessed a mass murder.

On the 26th day of the 2nd month by the lunar (Chinese) calendar the puppet police took over thirty of us prisoners to go and dig a pit outside the western gate of Chaoyuan. We returned to the prison after nightfall. On the 27th I and Wang Ya-min, Kao Shou-san, and Liu Cheng-fa were taken in one group and twenty others were taken in a second group to outside the west gate, where the group of twenty men were all shot. Then they brought along another batch of twenty-two men and shot them too. After shooting them the police poured petrol over their bodies and set them on fire. One of the men was not dead, and when he caught fire he tried to run away, but the police shot and killed him. When the bodies had all been burned they told us to bury the forty-two men. This grave is still there outside the west gate of Chaoyuan, and I could find the place again.

This hell on earth was the "paradise of the Kingly Way" that I had ruled as "Chief Executive" and "Emperor Kang Te". All these atrocities had been carried out in my name. No wonder that all of the testimonials of the victims of the "Manchukuo" regime ended with such expressions as:

"I demand that the People's Government avenge us. We want the Japanese and the Chinese traitors to repay their blood debt."

"Avenge our murdered families. Punish the Japanese and the traitors."

# "You Can Never Escape the Consequences of Your Sins"

The problem was even more serious than this.

The confessions and revelations of the Japanese war criminals and the accusations of the people of the Northeast stirred us "Manchukuo" war criminals. The reaction of the younger ones among us was particularly strong, and I was exposed by my nephews, my brothers-in-law and Big Li. I found myself surrounded by hatred, even within my own family. It was as if I were standing within a circle of mirrors, and wherever I looked I saw my own unpleasant image.

After attending the study meeting of the Japanese war criminals we were assembled and asked to talk about it. Some were still so moved that they swore to confess their own crimes and report those of others. The main target of accusations was Chang Huanhsiang, the former puppet minister of justice, who had gone to great lengths to ingratiate himself with the Japanese in the old days and was now very unpopular in the prison because he deliberately spoiled the food, broke prison rules, shouted at warders and so on. Some people warned him that if he did not behave properly in future the government would not be able to forgive him. As I was afraid of being treated this way myself, I was worried that the others might think I was not behaving properly. As we were not allowed at the time to tell each other anything about the confessions we had made and the information we had given, I was frightened that others might not know that I had already confessed, so I decided to speak at the meeting. When I had told the meeting about everything I had confessed and was just coming to my conclusion, Little Ku jumped to his feet and asked me, "You've said a lot, haven't you, but why didn't you mention that note?"

I was struck dumb for a moment.

"The note, Little Jui's note." Little Hsiu was standing up too. "You said just now that you handed over those jewels on your own initiative. Why didn't you say that Little Jui prompted you?"

"Yes, yes, I was just going to mention it. Little Jui was the one who enlightened me. . . ." I hastily filled in this gap in the story, but the glares I was getting from Little Hsiu and Little Ku made it clear that they were far from satisfied. Fortunately the meeting was then brought to a close.

Back in my cell I wrote out a self-criticism and handed it to the prison staff. I was sure that the governor would be angry with me, and was furious with Little Jui for having told the others about the note. Little Ku and Little Hsiu, members of my own family, were really heartless to do this to me. They were not even as loyal to me as Big Li. Not long afterwards I saw the reports on me that they had written, and then I realized that the change in my own family had been even more terrible than I had imagined.

There was a rule that every report had to be read by the person accused in it, and Interrogator Chao brought me the pile of ones about me. "When you've read them," he said, "sign the ones with which you agree. If you disagree, raise your objections."

The first ones I looked at were written by some former puppet ministers, and as they only referred to well-known facts about the "Manchukuo" regime I signed them all. But when I started reading the ones written by the members of my family my palm was soon sticky with sweat.

My brother-in-law Old Wan's report contained a passage that read:

On the evening of August 8, 1945 I went to the palace to see Pu Yi. He was writing something, and Chang Ching-hui and Takebe were waiting outside his room for an audience. Pu showed me what he had written and its general import was that all the "Manchukuo"

389

armed forces were to fight alongside the Imperial Japanese Army and smash the invading enemy (the Soviet Red Army). He said that he was going to give this order to Chang Ching-hui and Takebe, and he wanted to know if I had any suggestions to make. I said that there was no alternative.

This was a disaster, as I had put the blame for this on Yoshioka. Big Li's testimony was even more terrifying. He described my departure from Tientsin, and told how I had made an agreement with him about sticking to the old story before I wrote my auto-biography. This was not all. He exposed my daily conduct in great detail, showing how I had behaved with the Japanese and how I had treated the members of my household. If there had been only one or two cases of this sort mentioned in their reports that would not have mattered much, but as it was there was an enormous list of charges against me.

Old Wan, for example, had also written:

When films were shown in the palace we had to stand up if the Japanese emperor came on the screen, and clap any shots of Japanese soldiers making an attack. This was because the projectionists were Japanese.

There was a drive to economize on coal in 1944, so Pu Yi gave orders that there were to be no more fires in the Yi Hsi Lou (a building in the palace) in order to impress Yoshioka, but he used an electric fire in his bedroom without letting Yoshioka know.

When Pu Yi fled to Talitzukou he put the Japanese goddess and the picture of Hirohito's mother in his carriage on the train, and he made a ninety-degree bow whenever he walked past it. He ordered us to do likewise.

Little Jui's report included a passage about the orphans I employed as pages, and revealed how badly they had been treated and what cruel and unjust punishment I had so frequently inflicted on them. He also reported the death of the page who had tried to escape.

The wording of Big Li's accusations made no secret of his hatred.

This person Pu Yi was cruel, frightened of death, and extremely suspicious; he was also very cunning and thoroughly hypocritical. His treatment of his servants was inhuman. When he was in a bad temper he cursed them and had them beaten even if they had done nothing wrong. If he was feeling at all unwell or tired the servants suffered for it, and they were lucky if they got away with cuffs or kicks. But when he was with strangers he behaved as if he were the kindest man on earth.

In Tientsin he used to have people beaten with wooden rods or horsewhipped, and in the "Manchukuo" era many other new kinds of floggings and tortures were added. . . .

He made everyone act as his accomplice. When he wanted someone beaten, he suspected collusion if anyone refused to do the beating for him or did not hit hard enough. If that happened, the beater would be beaten himself, and several times harder. All of his nephews and attendants flogged people for him at some time or other. One page of twelve or thirteen called Chou Po-jen (an orphan) was once beaten so badly that he had wounds a foot long on his thighs which took two or three months to heal under the attention of Doctor Huang. While this boy was recovering Pu Yi told me to take milk and other things to him and say: "How kind His Majesty is to you! Did you get such good things to eat in the orphanage?"

By the time I had read this last accusation I began to have doubts about the self-justification I had resorted to in the past. Previously I had thought that everything I had done had been justified. I had only submitted to the pressure of the Japanese and done their bidding because I was forced to; and my treatment of the members of my household, even the torture, had always seemed to be my right. To cringe before the strong and bully the weak had seemed both natural and reasonable to me, and I had imagined that anyone else would have done the same in my position. Now I realized that not everyone was like me, and that my self-justification was completely void.

Nobody, after all, was weaker than prisoners stripped of all rights, but the Communists who held power did not beat or curse us, or regard us as less than human. As for power, the American troops with their first-rate equipment could be regarded as "powerful", but the Communist troops had not feared them despite the inferiority of their own equipment, and had dared to fight them for three years until they forced them to sign an armistice.

More recently I had seen new examples. From the accusations of the masses I had learnt that many ordinary people had not followed my creed in the face of violence and oppression. A peasant from Payen county called Li Tien-kuei had put his hopes in the Anti-Japanese Allied Army when he could stand the oppression of the Japanese and the traitors no longer. At the Chinese New Year in 1941 he had sent the anti-Japanese fighters ten catties of millet, 47 fried twists, 120 eggs, and two packets of cigarettes. This was later found out by the puppet police, and he was arrested. He had been hung up and flogged, and given electric shocks. Bloody corpses of men who had died under torture were put beside him to frighten him. All this was in an attempt to make him reveal some clue about the anti-Japanese forces. His tortures continued until he was freed after the Japanese surrender.

In 1943, when he was still a child, Li Ying-hua of Chinshan village had taken eggs to some passing anti-Japanese fighters, and when this was discovered by police spies he was taken to the police headquarters. First of all they had given him tea and cigarettes and invited him to eat *jiaozi*, saying: "You're only a kid and don't understand things, so if you talk we'll let you go." Li Ying-hua smoked the cigarettes, drank the tea, and ate the *jiaozi*. Finally he said: "I'm only a farmer and I don't know anything." The agents then suspended him upside-down and beat him, gave him electric shocks, burned him, stripped him naked and hit him with spiked rods, but they got nothing out of him.

I now knew that not all the people on this earth were weak. The only explanation for my past actions was that I bullied the weak and feared the strong, and that I feared death and was greedy for life. My basic justification had been that my life was the most valuable and that I was more worthy of preservation than anyone else. In the past few years I had learnt something of my true worth from my attempts at washing my clothes and making boxes, and now I had an even clearer idea of it from the accusations of the common people and the members of my household.

In the mirrors that surrounded me I saw that I was a guilty man, completely lacking in glory, and with no possible justification for my conduct.

I signed the last accusation against me and walked along the corridor, my mind full of remorse and sorrow.

"You can never escape the consequences of your sins."

# CHAPTER NINE

# I ACCEPT REMOULDING

# How Shall I Be a Man?

"A new year has begun. What do you think about it?" This was the question that the governor asked me on New Year's Day, 1955.

I said that I could only wait for my punishment. The governor shook his head and disagreed strongly.

"Why be so pessimistic? You should take a positive attitude to your remoulding and try hard to make a new man of yourself."

These words calmed me, but they did not eradicate my gloomy pessimism. I fell deep into a pit of self-contempt, which now played a bigger part in my thinking than the worries I had about my sentence.

While we were in the prison yard during a recreation period one day a reporter came with a camera to take pictures of us. As the period of accusations and recognition of our guilt was over we were allowed to take our recreation in the yard together, and an extra half-hour had been added to it. The yard was very lively, with some people playing volleyball and pingpong while others talked to each other, sang, and did all sorts of things. After putting all this on film the reporter finally got round to taking a picture of me. A former "Manchukuo" official who had been standing beside me watching a game noticed what the reporter was up to and hurried away with the words, "I'm not going to be photographed with him." Immediately afterwards all the others who were standing near me went away.

During March a group of Liberation Army generals came to inspect the prisons for war criminals that were under the control of the Shenyang military district, and the governor sent for me and Pu Chieh to go and see them. When I saw the room was full of gold epaulettes my first thought was that this must be a military tribunal, but then I discovered that the generals wanted to know how my studies were going. They were very friendly and showed a great interest in what I had to say, and they asked me about my childhood and my life in "Manchukuo" days. Finally one bearded general said, "Study well and remould yourself. In the future you will be able to see the building of socialism with your own eyes." As I went back to my cell I thought that he must be a marshal, and Pu Chieh told me that he was not the only marshal among them. I was greatly impressed. The Communists, whom I had not expected to show the least tolerance for me, actually treated me as a human being, whether they were marshals or warders. But my fellow-prisoners were not even prepared to stand beside me, as if I were something less than human.

Back in my cell I told my cellmates what the marshal had said. Old Yuan, a former "Manchukuo" ambassador to Japan and the quickest man in our cell, said: "Congratulations, Old Pu. If the marshal said that you will be able to see socialist construction, that means you're safe."

This cheered all the others up greatly. If the number one traitor was safe, they would certainly be all right.

After the end of the period of accusations and acknowledging guilt, many of us had been most concerned about the future. Old Hsien, for example, had not smiled once since the beginning of this period, but now his face broke into a broad grin and he patted me warmly on the shoulder. "Congratulations, Old Pu, congratulations."

The ban on talking during the rest period had now been lifted, and during the day our cells were no longer locked. Someone happened to come into our cell just at this moment, so the good news was immediately spread round the whole prison. It was still being discussed at rest time. I thought of my nephews and Big Li, who had been ignoring me since the period of accusations and acknowledging guilt; I was sure that this news would have cheered them up, so I took this as an excuse to go and talk to them. I saw Little Ku and Little Hsiu beside a tree in a corner of the yard. But before I got there they went away.

In April the prison authorities made us elect a study committee as the Japanese war criminals had done. This committee, which was under the supervision of the authorities, enabled us prisoners to organize our own study and daily life; it was responsible for passing on to the prison staff any problems that arose, and for reporting on discussions and criticism meetings. It could also make suggestions on its own initiative. It had five members, who were chosen by election and had to be approved by the prison authorities; there was a chairman, and four other members responsible for study, daily life, sport and recreation respectively. The study head and the daily life head of each cell had to report to the responsible committeeman every day. This innovation stirred the prisoners, and we regarded it as proof that the authorities were confident we would re-mould ourselves. Some of us realized more clearly than before that remoulding was up to ourselves. Facts later proved that this committee did a lot to help our remoulding. But at first my feelings about it were not the same as those of others. This was because two of the five members were the relations of mine who had made the most unflinching accusations against me. One was Old Wan, the chairman, and the other was Little Jui, the member responsible for our daily life.

Soon after its creation the study committee decided that we should build a sports ground. We had been using one that had been made by the Japanese war criminals, but now we were going to level a piece of land for ourselves. Little Jui was in charge of the job, and he gave me a dressing down in public when we were about to start work on the very first day. I was late for the roll-call because of some trifle, and as I ran to my place in the ranks hastily buttoning my clothes I heard my name being shouted.

"Coming, coming," I replied, hurrying to the end of the line.

"You're late every time we assemble," shouted Little Jui with a grim expression on his face. "You keep all the rest of us waiting just for you. You haven't the least consideration. Just look at yourself, you're a complete mess. You can't even button your jacket up properly."

I looked down and saw that my buttons were all in the wrong holes. Everyone turned round to look at me as I fumbled ineffectively.

I was worried that now they kept the records of the weekly criticism meetings, they would put a most unfavourable light on my actions. The weekly criticism meetings in our group were different from before, when we had either shouted at each other or else exchanged only polite remarks. Now we talked much more sensibly and seriously. This was partly because some of us had thrown off our ideological burdens or learnt something about remoulding, and thus took a more positive attitude. Another difference was that the irrelevant speeches we used to make would not get past the study committee. One reason why I felt that the weekly criticism meetings had changed was because when other people spoke about me they no longer did so with any reservations; and another more important one was that among the new members who had been moved into our group was Big Li, who knew me only too well and was in charge of our daily life. When others spoke about my shortcomings his introductions and analyses would enable them to go to the root of the trouble and hit me where it hurt. When the explanations of Little Jui and Old Wan on the study committee were added to all this, I would scarcely seem human.

When in the past some external shock reduced me to the depths of despair I would sometimes blame myself and take it as the retribution for my own actions, but at other times I would feel indignant with fate and with others for deliberately making things difficult for me. At the beginning I also used to be angry with the Communist Party, the People's Government and the prison authorities. Now I had no reason to complain about the last three, and felt more strongly that things were my own fault, but I still tended to blame my troubles on others. When I read the reports that had been written about me and realized that all the things I had wanted to keep secret had now been revealed, so that the government knew everything, I had thought that it would only be natural if they either took their revenge on me or at least abandoned their hopes of remoulding me. But the interrogators, the prison governor, and the marshal had all said that I should study, remould myself, and become a new man. All the prison staff shared that view, as they showed in many practical ways.

After we built the sports ground the study committee decided that we should make our prison yard more beautiful in preparation for May Day by planting flowers and trees, weeding, and levelling the ground.  We all set to work with enthusiasm.  At first I was helping to fill in a big pit, but Warder Chiang said that as my eyesight was so bad there was a danger that I might fall into it, so I was transferred to weeding a flower-bed.  After I had been working there for a while the Mongol Old Cheng came up to me, snatched the plant I had just uprooted from my hand and shouted, "What's this you've pulled up?  Eh?"

"I was told to weed, wasn't I?"

"Do you call this a weed?  Can't you see that all the things you've pulled up are flowers?"

I was the focus of attention once more as I squatted there, not daring to raise my head.  I wished that all the flowers and weeds would disappear.

"You really are a reject," Old Cheng went on shouting as he held the plant in his hand.  Warder Chiang came up, took the plant from Old Cheng, looked at it, and threw it on the ground. "What's the good of laying into him like that?  You should help him by teaching him to weed properly so that he won't do it wrong next time."

"I'd never imagined that there were still people who didn't know the difference between flowers and weeds," replied Old Cheng offensively.

"I'd never imagined it either, but now that we know differently, we must work out how to help him."

Previously the words "I'd never imagined" had always been connected in my mind with unpleasant remarks, such as "I'd never imagined that Pu Yi was so stupid — he isn't worth saving", or "I'd never imagined that Pu Yi was so hypocritical or so evil — you could never remould him", or "I'd never imagined that Pu Yi was hated by so many people — he can't be saved".  But now "I'd never imagined" was actually followed by "but now that we know we must work out how to help him".

One day my glasses broke again. After some hesitation I had to ask for Big Li's help once more. "Please help me," I asked in a weak voice. "I've tried to do them myself several times, but I just can't. Nobody else can do it, so please could you mend them for me?"

"You still want me to wait on you," he replied with a glare. "Haven't you been waited on long enough?" He went off angrily to another place at the table. I stood there helplessly, wishing that I could dash my head against the wall. Less than two minutes later Big Li came back and took the glasses from me, snorting angrily.

"Very well then, I'll mend them for you. But let me tell you this, I'm only doing it to help you reform. Otherwise I wouldn't have time."

When it was time for the break I went to the new reading-room to relax by myself, and there I met Pu Chieh. I told him what was on my mind, and mentioned that I had sometimes spent sleepless nights because of the hostility of the members of my household. He asked me why I didn't talk it over with the prison authorities. "Why?" I asked. "I made them suffer in the old days, so it's only natural that they should hate me." Pu Chieh replied that he had heard the prison staff telling them to forget old grudges and help me. Only then did I understand why Big Li had swallowed his temper and come back from the other side of the table.

I divided the help that I received into two categories. One was practical, such as Big Li repairing my glasses and the others helping me to stitch up my quilt and mattress after washing them; without this assistance I would have wasted a whole day on the job and thus hindered collective activities. The other kind of help was verbal, and this was the category into which I put the criticisms of me that others made. The prison staff often said that we should help each other through criticism, self-criticism and the exchange of opinions. I gave very little of this kind of help to others, and I was not at all willing to accept it from them either. So although Big Li had told me that his aim in mending my spectacles was to help me remould myself, and although the governor had told me that criticism was one of the ways of helping each other reform our thought, I was still unable to see any connection between any of these forms of help and my thought reform and remoulding. I thought that the practical help that others gave me only proved my own incompetence and showed their contempt for me; and I regarded criticism as being no more than a way of re-opening my wounds and causing me pain. I would have preferred no help at all.

Whenever government officials talked about becoming a new man they always linked it with reforming one's thought and changing one's outlook. But what worried me was the question of face. I wondered how I would be treated by society and my family, and whether I would be rejected or not. Even if the Communist Party and the People's Government were to allow me to survive, society might not tolerate me, and even if I was not beaten I was afraid that people would abuse me and spit on me.

Whenever the prison authorities talked about thought reform they pointed out that a man's actions were always supported by a particular ideology, so that it was necessary to analyse the ideological roots of a man's crimes in order to prevent him from committing them again. I, on the other hand, was convinced that I could never repeat what I had done in the past. If the people of New China were prepared to tolerate me I could guarantee this. What need was there to go into my thinking?

I thought that the key to becoming a new man lay not in myself but in the way others treated me. The governor said that if we reformed properly the people would treat us leniently, but they would not tolerate any refusal to remould ourselves. It was, in fact, up to myself. I only began to understand this because of a little thing that happened to me after many days of distress.

## It Is Up to Me

One Sunday I was washing my clothes as usual. When I had finished it was time for recreation, and what I felt like doing was going to read by myself in the reading-room. I had just sat down when I heard voices outside.

403

"Can't any of you play tennis?"

"I can't, but Pu Yi can. You should ask him."

"Even if he can he'll never have time for it. Goodness knows when he'll finish washing his clothes."

"He's much quicker now."

"I don't believe you."

This infuriated me. I had undoubtedly finished washing them, and I'd done just as many as the others, but there were still people who would not believe it, as if I were fundamentally incapable of making any progress. I fetched my racket and went out into the yard, not so much because I wanted to play as to show the others that I had finished my washing. When I reached the court the people I had heard talking a moment ago were no longer there, so I played with some others who wanted a game. Some spectators gathered to watch. I played with spirit, sweating heavily.

When I went to wash my hands at a tap afterwards I met the governor, who often spent his Sundays in the prison.

"You've made progress today, Pu Yi."

I was pleased to hear this. "I haven't played for a long time."

"I was talking about that," he said, pointing at my washing drying on the line. "As you can now do your washing as quickly as the rest you can enjoy the same amount of rest and recreation as they do."

I nodded and walked round the yard with him.

"In the old days you were too busy to enjoy rest and recreation like everyone else, so you were not equal with them and resented it. But now that you are equal, you are much happier when it comes to washing clothes. So you see, you hold the key to the problem yourself. There is no point in worrying about how other people treat you."

A moment later he went on: "The Second World War turned you from an emperor into a prisoner. At present there is a great battle going on in your mind, a battle to turn an emperor into an ordinary worker. You've already learnt something about what an emperor really is, but this battle is not yet over, and you still don't think of yourself as the equal of others. You must get a better understanding of yourself."

I thought about what he had said for a long time. While I agreed that I held the key to the question, I could not see that I was still giving myself an emperor's airs. But as time went on life gradually taught me that this was true.

When our group had returned to the cell after removing the rubbish one day the member of the study committee who was responsible for daily life criticized us. "You didn't turn the tap off after washing your hands, and the water is still running. This was irresponsible, and I must ask you not to do it again."

Big Li immediately asked me if I had been the last to wash, and when I admitted that I had probably forgotten to turn the tap off, he said that this was an example of the way I still behaved as I had done when I was an emperor. "In those days you never even touched a door handle as you always had others to open and close doors for you. Even now you only open doors and never close them behind you. You haven't stopped behaving like an emperor yet."

"Now I think of it," said Old Yuan, "you often cover the door-handle with newspaper when you open the door. Why do you do that?"

"It's because you're afraid it's dirty, isn't it?" interrupted Big Li.

"Everyone touches it, so of course it's dirty," I replied.

This brought an avalanche of attacks down on me. "Why are you the only one to mind dirt?" "Is it a dirty door you're worried about, or dirty people?" "Doesn't this show that you think you're a cut above everyone else? You think we're all lower than you, don't you?"

I protested vigorously that I entertained no such feelings, but I could not dispel my own doubts. Did I really do this? Did I really have such thoughts? Later someone pointed out to me that when we bathed I was always the first to get into the bath and always got out when the others followed me in; and another fellow-prisoner reminded me that I had always taken the first bowl of *jiaozi* in the

405

Soviet Union. I had to admit to myself that Big Li was right when he said that I had still not got rid of all my emperor's airs.

When I look back today I see that Big Li was a teacher to me, albeit a stern one. Whatever his motives may have been, he was always making me see things that I had never thought of for myself, and I finally came to understand that I had only myself to blame for most of my troubles.

Once I lost our group a number of points in a hygiene inspection because I had made a splash on the floor when cleaning my teeth and only rubbed it with my feet instead of cleaning it up properly. Big Li came up to me with a rag and asked me why I had not used a cloth.

"I didn't think of it."

He laid into me for this reply, accusing me of only thinking of myself. "You can only think about your rights, never about your duties." He was on the point of doing it himself, but he flung the cloth on the floor and told me to wipe up the mess myself. I obediently did so.

From the time of the discovery that the Americans were using germ bombs in Korea and the Northeast and the consequent nation-wide patriotic hygiene movement there were several campaigns in the prison at fixed times each year to eliminate pests. Among my many memories of these campaigns is the fly-swatting affair.

Big Li brought in some new fly-swatters one day. There were not enough to go round, and the others were all asking for them. I made no effort to get one, but Big Li handed the first one to me. This was the first time I had ever handled a fly-swatter, and I felt rather awkward as I had, to tell the truth, never killed a single fly in my life.

There were not many flies in the prison, and by the standards of the "New Capital" of "Manchukuo" they were virtually extinct. I hunted for a fly and when at last I found one on the sill of an open window I waved my swatter to drive it out.

"What do you think you're doing?" shouted Big Li from behind me. "Are you killing pests or saving life?"

406

This may have sounded like a joke to the others, but I knew what he was getting at. I blushed and said in a forced voice, "Of course I'm not saving life." At the same time I wondered why I had let the fly go.

"You won't kill because you're afraid of retribution. Isn't that it?" As he glared at me I felt guilty but put on a bold front.

"What are you talking about? The fly got away, that's all."

"Think it over."

At the criticism meeting that evening nobody mentioned the affair at first, but then Big Li told everyone how I had forbidden the killing of flies in Changchun and even directed people to rescue a mouse from the jaws of a cat. Everyone roared with laughter, then they criticized me for my superstition. While I had to admit to myself that they were right, I heard myself saying: "I'm certainly not superstitious. Didn't I kill flies last year?"

Old Yuan could not restrain his guffaws. "I remember — thanks for reminding me. You gave your swatter to someone else and fanned all the flies away with a newspaper to let them escape."

Amid the peals of mocking laughter that followed only Big Li kept a straight face. "I don't know what it means when other people save life, but in your case I'm sure that it's complete self-ishness. You do it to get the blessing of the Buddha. It doesn't matter if everyone else is killed provided that you stay alive. You think that you're the most valuable person on earth."

"That's an exaggeration," I protested.

"Pu Yi does sometimes humble himself," put in Old Yuan.

"Yes," I added, "I don't regard myself as at all superior to anyone."

"Perhaps you do humble yourself sometimes," said Big Li, "but sometimes you still think of yourself as higher and more important than everyone else. I've no idea how you got that way."

Later I gradually came to understand. After forty years of living as a very superior being I had been suddenly brought down to earth. This explained why sometimes I disagreed with the others, lost my temper, and nursed grievances. On the other hand, I was constantly seeing that I was inferior to others, and this made me dispirited, full of hatred, self-abasing and miserable. In short, I had lost my emperor's airs but I still kept my old standards. I realized this later when I discovered that it was impossible to judge some people by these standards. While I was in the same cell as Big Li before I came to understand this, I could only see what the governor had been talking about. I realized that I did not treat others as my equals in my relations with them, which aroused their resentment and prevented them from treating me as an equal or respecting me. It was only when I encountered the generosity of people who could not be measured by my yardstick that I found out what sort of person I really was.

## Why So Magnanimous?

One day soon after the Chinese New Year of 1956 the governor made an announcement at the end of a talk on the growth of the national economy:

"You have already studied documents on the First Five-Year Plan, agricultural co-operation, and the socialist transformation of handicrafts and privately-owned industry and commerce. You have also read in the papers about the appearance of joint state-private enterprises in some of the big cities. But all you know about socialist construction is what you have learnt from books. You need to see the present state of the country with your own eyes to be able to link your studies with reality. For this reason the government will arrange for you to make visits outside in the near future. You will see Fushun first, and later you will go to other cities."

That day the atmosphere in the prison was much more cheerful than it had ever been before, and some of the prisoners even saw this as a sign that we would soon be released. I did not share their hopes, convinced that I would certainly not be released even if they were. I was even alarmed about the prospect of showing my face in public on a visit. That afternoon I heard some of the others talking about the problem that was on my mind.

"What do you think the people will do when they see us?"

"Nothing will happen as we'll be taken by government personnel. Otherwise they wouldn't let us go."

"I'm not so sure. What happens if they get excited?" asked Old Fu, minister of agriculture of "Manchukuo". "My goodness, I used to be a petty official, and I've seen the masses when they get worked up. If they turn nasty, surely the government will do what the people demand."

"Don't worry, the government wouldn't let us go if it wasn't quite sure of what it was doing."

The new head of our cell's study group, a former official in the Wang Ching-wei puppet government, came over and said, "I don't think that the government will reveal who we are."

"Whether they reveal it or not, people will know," said Old Yuan with a laugh. "Do you think it will be all right just because the Northeasterners won't recognize you? Once they spot one of us, which they're bound to do, they'll know what sort of people we are."

I thought of the pictures of me that the people of the Northeast had been forced to bow to in the past, and was sure that they would have no difficulty in identifying me. How could the government prevent them from getting worked up and demanding my public trial? As Old Fu had suggested, wouldn't the government do what the people demanded?

In those days I still thought of the common people as completely ignorant and barbarous. Surely they would deal with me, their hated enemy, with ferocious cruelty, ignoring the government and Party policy of leniency and remoulding. I doubted whether the government would be able to prevent this, and suspected that it might be prepared to "sacrifice" me to win popular support. But I was quite wrong.

I shall describe many amazing things I saw on the visit in the next section, but first I want to describe the astonishing people I met.

The first was an ordinary young woman. She had survived the Pingtingshan massacre, and was now the head of the kindergarten

409

of the Fushun Open-cast Mine. Some of the mine staff told us about the history of the mine and the massacre.

In the eastern part of the mining area was a village of about a thousand households called Pingtingshan. Most of the inhabitants were destitute miners. After the Japanese occupation of the Northeast, anti-Japanese fighters appeared in this district as they did elsewhere. One night in the autumn of 1933 the South Manchurian Anti-Japanese Volunteers clashed with the Japanese at Pingtingshan, killing a Japanese official and about a dozen Japanese guards, and burning a Japanese store.

The next day, when the resistance fighters had gone, about 190 Japanese guards and some Chinese quislings surrounded Pingtingshan and drove the whole population — men, women and children — at bayonet point to the hill outside the village. Here all three thousand of them were machine-gunned, and then the soldiers bayoneted all the bodies to make sure they were dead. After this they soaked the corpses in petrol, burnt them, and bombarded the hill with heavy artillery to cover the remains. Finally they surrounded the village with a fourfold barbed-wire fence and allowed no strangers in. A warning was issued that anyone who harboured fugitives from Pingtingshan would be killed with his whole family. Thus it was that Pingtingshan was turned into a desolate hillside covered with bones. A popular lament was sung in the Fushun area that went like this:

> Pingtingshan used to be full of life,
> But now it's covered with blood and weeds.
> Gather some bricks,
> Pick up a bone,
> The Japanese have slaughtered our parents and cousins,
> The sea of blood is deep; our hatred will never die.

But the Japanese were unable to slaughter all of the villagers or to cow the workers of Fushun. A little girl of five called Fang Sujung had escaped from the pile of bloody corpses and had been looked after secretly by a disabled old miner. Thus a witness of the atrocity had survived.

After we prisoners had seen the mine it was time for us to look over the welfare facilities, and so we went to Fang Su-jung's kindergarten. As she was in Shenyang at the time the kindergarten staff told us about her meeting with the Japanese war criminals the previous day.

The kindergarten staff had at first refused to let her meet them as it might be too much of a shock for her. The Japanese criminals discussed the matter and then begged to be allowed to see her as they wanted to apologize to her. After the hesitation of the kindergarten staff had been overcome she finally came in to see them. The war criminals bowed low to her as an expression of their guilt and asked her to tell them about the massacre.

She told them how her father had led her out while her mother carried her baby brother. "The Japanese soldiers and the traitors were shouting that we were to go for a photograph. I asked granddad what a photograph was and he gave me a windmill he had just made and told me not to ask any questions." Thus she had gone with all the other villagers to the execution ground. When the machine-guns started firing her grandfather had covered her with his own body, and she had passed out without even crying. When she came round she found herself surrounded by blood and gore; smoke blotted out the sky.

She was in terrible pain from the eight bullet and bayonet wounds in her body, and was suffering even greater agonies of terror. Her grandfather was silent and she could not see her mother or brother. She climbed out of the pile of corpses and went back to the village, only to find that it had been reduced to smoking rubble. She climbed through the barbed wire and crawled across a field of *kaoliang* stubble, covering her face with her hands. An old man found her and wrapped her in his jacket, after which she had passed out again.

This man was an old miner, crippled after a life of hardship and suffering, who was now reduced to selling cigarettes to keep himself alive. He kept her in a sack, only opening it at night to feed her. Realizing that he could not go on like this for long he had smuggled her in his sack past the Japanese and taken her to the house of an uncle of hers. This uncle had kept her outside in a straw rick, tended her wounds, and fed her at night. When winter approached he took her to some other relations in a more distant village, and she lived with them under a different name.

Wounded in mind and body, Fang Su-jung had grown up nursing the deepest hatred. But when at last the Japanese surrendered they were only replaced by corrupt and venal Kuomintang officials, and to her hatred of the murderers of her family was added loathing for the Chiang Kai-shek troops, who killed, burnt and looted just as the Japanese had done. Finally her village was liberated, and light came into her life. The Party and the government supported and educated her. Later she found a job, married and had children. Now she was a well-known Fushun model worker.

What did this woman say to the criminals who had committed such appalling crimes against China when she met them face to face?

"Even if I were to bite you to death my hatred of you would not be sated. But I am a member of the Communist Party, and the great cause of socialism and changing the world means even more to me than my private feelings. Our Party had made all kinds of policies to achieve these ends, and I believe in them and will carry them out. For the sake of this cause I have put my private hatred to one side."

This amazing forgiveness struck the hundreds of Japanese war criminals dumb for a while, and then they began to weep for shame and kneel before her, asking the Chinese Government to punish them.

Fang Su-jung's magnanimity was astounding enough, but then as a Party member and a cadre she was obliged to take such an attitude. What was even more unimaginable was the magnanimity shown me by an ordinary peasant of Taishanpao.

Taishanpao is a village on the outskirts of Fushun that then formed an agricultural co-operative. We went there on the day after we visited the kindergarten, and my heart was pounding with fear on the way. I remembered the accusations written by peasants that I had read and wondered how I would be treated, convinced that the "crude" and "ignorant" peasants would be incapable of behaving as Fang Su-jung had done. In fact we had met a number of workers and members of their families the previous day, but I had attributed their behaviour to an ignorance of who we were. The previous evening we had visited the home for retired miners. Old men who had worked in the mines all their lives or who had been kicked out by the Japanese after suffering some incapacitating injury had been saved from destitution immediately after the formation of the People's Government, and a former Japanese luxury hotel had been turned into a home where they could end their lives in peace. They spent their time playing chess, growing flowers, reading the papers, and in any other way that suited them. When I visited one of them with a few other prisoners he told us about the wretched life of miners in "Manchukuo" days. I felt ashamed and frightened, hiding in the corner and saying nothing for fear of being recognized. I noticed that instead of the family snapshots that we had seen on the walls of the workers' quarters he only had a picture of Chairman Mao, who was clearly dearer to him than his relations — that is, if he had any relations left alive. I wondered if he understood Chairman Mao's policy of remoulding criminals.

During the first day of our visit we had all tried to make ourselves inconspicuous. Big Mouth, who had once been in charge of building a Japanese Shinto shrine in Fushun, was ashen-faced, and tried all the time to hide in the middle of our group. When we reached Taishanpao not one of us dared to raise his head. In this uneasy state we listened as the chairman of the co-op told us about the co-op's past and present. We went round and saw new tools, poultry, hothouses full of vegetables, livestock, granaries and other things. Everyone we met was kind to us, and some people stopped the work they were doing to stand up and greet us. I congratulated myself on going unrecognized for so long. But when I was in the house of a co-op member at the very end of the visit I was unable to conceal my identity any longer.

The house that I and a few others visited was that of a family named Liu. The parents both worked in the fields, the eldest son was a book-keeper for the storage pits, the second son was at middle school, and the daughter worked at a hydro-electric plant. Only Mrs. Liu was at home when we arrived. She was cooking, and when she saw the commune cadre leading us in she took off her apron and asked us to sit in the north room, which was newly built of concrete. She treated us as real guests, asking us to come right inside and sit on the *kang* in the Northeastern manner. There was a chest of drawers by the wall, and on it stood a large clock, a gleaming tea-service, a number of vases, and a tea-caddy.

The cadre who had brought us did not tell Mrs. Liu who we were, just saying that we were visitors who had come to see the co-op. Then he asked her to talk to us. Although she was not a good talker she told us that they had originally been a family of seven tilling seven *mou* of land (a little over an acre), and that during "Manchukuo" they had lived almost like beggars. "We grew rice, but we had to eat acorn flour. We had to hand over all the rice we grew, and if they found a single grain of it in the house we were 'economic criminals'. Once a man was arrested when he was sick in the road and the police found rice grains in his mess. We all dressed in rags. Some families were even worse off than we, and grown-up girls only had sacking to wear. . . . One New Year the kiddies had nothing to eat, and I can't tell you how cold it was, so my old man said we should secretly have a meal of rice. The police came to the village in the middle of the night, and that really gave us a fright. In fact they had come to seize men for forced labour, and they sent them out to fell trees and build defences. They said it was for protection against bandits, but really it was because they were scared of our Anti-Japanese Allied Armies. My old man was dragged off. Hardly any of the men who were taken off from our village for forced labour came back alive. . . ."

Her son came in while she was speaking. He was very short, and on closer examination we could see that he had been born a cripple with stunted legs. In answer to our questions he told us that in the old days his deformity had forced him to lead a dog's life, whereas he now worked as the book-keeper for the storage pits with as much dignity as everyone else. His eyes were full of hatred for the past, but when he talked of the present his voice and manner became cheerful and confident, just like his mother. He told us about all the vegetables that had never been grown in the village before, and his mother showed us the large crock of rice in the corner. "Who wants to look at rice?" her son asked with a laugh. "There's nothing to it these days," she riposted, "but how often did you see it in the time of Kang Te?"[1]

This last remark stung me to the quick.

I had been frightened when we first came into this house that they would ask me my name, and now I felt that it would be unforgivable dishonesty if I did not tell them who I was before I went. I stood up and said with my head bowed, "The Kang Te of whom you speak is Pu Yi, the traitorous puppet emperor of 'Manchukuo'. I am he. I owe you my apologies."

Before I had finished speaking the former puppet ministers and generals who were with me rose to their feet and told her who they were. One had been the minister responsible for forced labour, one had been in charge of sending grain to Japan, and one had been a military commander who forced men into the puppet army to fight for the Japanese.

The old lady was dumbfounded. Although she had guessed we were "Manchukuo" war criminals she had clearly not known who we were, nor had she imagined that we would ask her to deal with us.

How in fact did she deal with us? She did not curse or weep, nor did she call in the neighbours or the widows and orphans of men killed in the old days to vent their wrath on us. Instead she said with a sigh that wrung my heart, "It's all over now. Don't let's say any more about it." She wiped away her tears. "As long as you're willing to study, do what Chairman Mao says, and become decent people, you'll be all right."

We had been weeping silently before, but with these words we broke into sobs.

"We know what sort of people you are," said her son in a low voice. "Chairman Mao says that the great majority of criminals can be remoulded, and what he says can't be wrong. If you reform and acknowledge your guilt the common people will forgive you."

---

[1] The reign title used when I was "Emperor of Manchukuo".

Such was the magnanimity of the peasants whom I had thought crude, ignorant and liable to take their revenge without caring about the policy of leniency and remoulding.

They were now their own masters, and behind them they had a powerful government and army led by the Communist Party. Yet when faced with prisoners who had committed the most appalling crimes against them they were able to show such generosity. It was on this visit that I learnt the answer why.

## The Changes Explain Everything

Our mood at the end of our three-day visit was in sharp contrast to that in which we had set out, lively conversation replacing grim silence. For our first two days back in prison we talked all the time, and the topic was always our trip. The recurrent theme was, "Things have changed, society has changed, all Chinese have changed." Of course, the theme of change was one we had often read about in the papers and in family letters or heard about from the prison authorities during the past few years, but some of the more worldly-wise among us had wanted to check on this at first hand. One of these was Old Yuan in our cell, and this time he too was convinced.

One evening we were talking about the cakes we had tasted ourselves in the workers' canteen. One of us said that while we had seen the food provided at work it was a pity that we had not seen any meals being cooked on the gas rings in the workers' flats. Then Old Yuan told us what he had discovered. While the rest of us had been looking at the workers' rooms he had gone behind the building to look in the dustbins, where he had found fishbones, eggshells and other food remains.

Old Fu, who had been a supply officer with the old Northeastern army before becoming the "Manchukuo" minister of agriculture, was normally a taciturn fellow, but today he was rather animated. "In the days of 'Manchukuo' you wouldn't find fish or meat in workers' houses, and even before that they were a rare sight. I ought to know — I started out in life as a petty official."

Old Cheng, who had been brought up by the Japanese, said frankly: "When I read the papers and studied political documents in the past I was sometimes convinced and sometimes suspicious, and I used to think that this Northeastern industrial base was something left by the Japanese. But at the factory attached to the Industrial School I saw that the old Japanese belt-driven lathes there had been replaced with brand-new Chinese-made equipment; now I believe that the Chinese have indeed stood up. They really have changed."

I certainly agreed that they had changed, and I had other feelings about the visit as well.

The astonishing magnanimity that the people had shown me during the three days of our visit had made me wonder whether this could be real. Were they prepared to ignore the crimes that traitors had committed against them? Did they really have such faith in the policy of remoulding criminals? How could this be?

The changes explained everything. From the late nineteenth century onwards Fushun had been famous for its mineral wealth, but those who had benefited from it had not been the wretchedly poor miners. In 1905 the open-cast mines had come under Japanese control after the defeat of tsarist Russia, and in the four succeeding decades it is estimated that between 250,000 and 300,000 miners died of their sufferings in the mines.

The miners, who were mostly destitute peasants from Shantung, Hopei and the Northeast, came in droves every year. They worked over twelve hours a day. Most of them lived in "big houses" with one or two hundred men to a room, and wore rags all the year round. Some of them could not afford clothes for their new-born babies, and when the children died of starvation, they were forced to bury them naked. Low as their wages were, they had to pay a proportion of them to the managers and the gangers. What was left was not enough for adequate food and clothing. Few of them could afford to marry, and before liberation 70 per cent of the men in the Lungfeng Mine were bachelors.

There was no question of safety precautions in the mines, and explosions and cave-ins were common events. As the workers used to put it, "If you want to be a miner, you have to risk your life." After a gas explosion in 1917 the Japanese owners sealed off a mine to prevent losses of coal, leaving 917 men inside to be burnt alive. A flood in the same mine killed 482 miners in 1928. According to "Manchukuo" official statistics, 251,999 men were killed and injured in these mines between 1916 and 1944. A mountain valley was filled with the bodies of those who were not buried inside the pit, and was called the "Ten Thousand Men's Grave".

The Japanese opened a place they called the "Pleasure Garden" where there were over a thousand whores, gambling houses, and opium and morphine dens.

In old Fushun there were luxury homes for Japanese and the towering head-gear for the mines, but there were also beggars and dead cats and babies beside the Yangpai River and floating in the sewers. In winter new corpses were found every day by the Yangpai bridge. Fushun also had a "reformatory" during the "Manchukuo" period, a concentration camp for the workers who opposed "Manchukuo" and Japan.

There had been enormous changes since then. On the remains of the shacks with 3,500 square metres' floor-space that the Japanese had built for the workers in thirty-one years, new workers' quarters of 170,000 square metres had been erected in the seven years since liberation. We visited one worker's home here, probably belonging to one of the 80 per cent of the miners who had married since liberation.

In these rooms I saw the blue flames of a gas ring.

The head of the mine office told us something about gas as we walked along one of the underground roadways of the Lungfeng Mine. The Lungfeng, Shengli and Laohu collieries had been exceptionally bad for gas, the great enemy of miners all over the world. The three mines were in a terrible state immediately after liberation, particularly the Lungfeng, whose roadways had been obstructed by falls as a result of sabotage first by the Japanese and then by the Kuomintang. It was also so full of gas that blasting and electrical equipment could not be used in it.

In the autumn of 1949 one of the mine's engineers proposed to the Party committee that the gas should be piped to the surface and put to good use above ground, which would also end the gas danger in the mine. The committee gave the engineer their full support, and the workers, particularly the older men and their dependants, said that they were willing to do anything to make this plan succeed. An experimental project was organized. The workers who were members of the Party were in the forefront of the struggle that was waged day and night in the gas-filled underground roadways. At first they met with difficulties. They were often surrounded by dense gas and attacked by cowards and conservatives; but on July 1, 1950 the experimental project was completed, and a blue flame shot from the nozzle of the pipe bringing the gas up from underground. The old workers wept, and the youngsters shouted, "We've won again."

This story made me think of a song I had heard some chubby youngsters singing in a kindergarten that morning:

> Without the Communist Party
> There would be no New China.

As we walked along the underground roadway we came across a brightly-lit shop selling fruit, sweets, towels, handkerchiefs and so on. We stopped here, and our guide explained that a filthy and rat-infested stream flowed here in "Manchukuo" days. "No one dared to touch the rats as supersitition was widespread and people said that they were the horses of the Taoist god Laotzu. The miners used to worship him in the hope of getting some security in their lives. Nowadays they have all thrown the pictures of Laotzu out of their houses." Pointing at the clean concrete floor he told us that the miners used to walk barefoot in the filthy water here in the old days, and that at some faces they used to work stark naked.

We walked on past electrically-drawn wagons that were carrying the coal away.

"In the old days there were roadways where trains went but people couldn't. Men were often run over, but of course the number killed that way was nothing compared with those who died in explosions. The miners used to say that they were 'lumps of flesh stuck in the coal-face'. They would return each night from their long labour underground thankful that they had survived another day. There was always a crowd of women and children waiting at the pithead when the miners came off, and if a man was missing they knew he was dead. Often the bodies weren't even recovered." He pointed to the wall. "I saw four men buried alive there. I first came down the pit when I was fourteen, and I wouldn't like to say how many times I've brushed with death since then."

He told us how terrified the workers used to be of sickness. Their resistance was low as their shacks were unheated, they had rags for clothes and sacks for bedding, and their food ration was only eight tiny corn buns a day. If the Japanese found that a man was sick they would put him into a heavily guarded isolation centre and give him only a bowl of rice porridge at each meal. Some of the inmates were incinerated before they were dead, or buried alive in "Ten Thousand Men's Grave". Our guide told us that the father of the man we had just seen driving the train had been buried alive.

After a moment's silence he went on to tell us that once he had almost suffocated in the foul atmosphere there used to be down the mine. He had been ill when he went up, but the ganger had threatened to flog him if he did not go down the pit again. As he was the youngest miner in the shack in which he lived the others came and chased the ganger away. He said that the workers most feared by the Japanese and the overseers were the Eighth Route Army prisoners, who were prepared to kill their oppressors if they caught them underground. This meant that the Japanese were forced to treat them better. Although these prisoners were rigidly segregated from the other miners, their resistance showed the rest of the miners that the gangers and the Japanese were no more formidable than the mine rats, and that their days were numbered.

I was conscious of the contrast between this self-confident miner and myself as I was in those days, sick of eating meat, taking my daily injections and medicine, overcome with feelings that my end was near, and with all my human dignity lost. In those days he would have thought of me and my kind as no more than rats. What was his view of us now?

I thought of the tears shed by the older workers when the gas was first successfully piped off and the confident victory cries of the younger men. In their eyes all secrets had been revealed and everything and everybody could be remoulded. What did they care about an emperor when the future was theirs? This was another reason why they were able to be so forgiving towards me. Everything had changed, and the most basic change was the one that had taken place in people. Without the Communist Party all these changes and the magnanimity extended to us would have been impossible.

## Meeting Relations

I learnt from this visit that if the people were to forgive me I would have to become a real human being. I had learnt other things too. On the first day of the visit I had looked at the new government through old-fashioned spectacles, refusing to believe that any regime could be on terms of mutual confidence with the masses, as I had read in books. I thought that the reason why the Communist Party had such powerful armed forces and so strong a government was because of its great cunning and its demagogic skill. This was why I had feared that they might sacrifice me to the wrath of the masses. Now I knew that the reason why the people supported and trusted the Party was because of the unprecedented benefits it had brought them, benefits that I had seen with my own eyes during our visit. No previous regime had even wanted, let alone been able, to bring about such progress.

I had also thought that even if the poor did well in the new society, those who had been rich or important in the old days, people closely connected with myself, and members of the minority national groups would not be at all satisfied. Soon after our trip I was visited by some of my own relations, and I learnt that this view was as absurd as the other. In fact an unprecedentedly large proportion of all social strata was pleased with the new state of affairs.

We prisoners had started to exchange letters with our relations in the summer of 1955. We found out from them that they were not being discriminated against because we were criminals. Some of the children were at school and some at work; some had become specialists and some had joined the Communist Youth League or the Party. Many of us were greatly encouraged by our family letters, and realized a little more clearly what the changes in society meant to ourselves. Some of the more suspicious of us were only half convinced, and a few were so biased as to put the most fantastic interpretations on them. When Old Chang, a former puppet general, received the first letter from his son he found that it began "Mr. Chang, I am sorry, but I cannot address you in any other way. . . ." Old Chang went almost mad with grief, and many other prisoners sympathized with him. "So this is how the new society brings up the young," some people muttered. "Because the father's in jail the son wants no more of him." I could not help remembering how Chen Pao-shen had said that the Communists were heartless and unjust. Old Liu, another former general who was in the same cell as Pu Chieh, was very fond of his daughter and was deeply worried that she might be the victim of discrimination. Previously he had been thoroughly sceptical about New China, but now he read in a letter from her that she was well provided for and had been admitted to the Youth League. Her organization was taking good care of her, she had plenty of friends, and had been sent by the state to an art school, which was the fulfilment of her old ambition. Old Liu shook his hoary head over the letter, saying, "Even if every word in it is true I won't believe it until I can see her with my own eyes." From 1956 onwards all our questions were answered, and I learnt that the problems that had been solved were not just those of single families but those of a whole nationality and a whole younger generation.

On March 10, three days after our trip, the warder told me, Pu Chieh, my two brothers-in-law and my three nephews to go to the governor's office. We went into his reception room, and to our astonishment we saw my uncle Tsai Tao and my third and fifth sisters. We had been separated for over ten years.

When I saw my uncle looking as fit as ever and my sisters in their cotton-padded clothes I felt as if I were dreaming.

Tsai Tao was the only surviving close relation of mine from the previous generation. In 1954 he had been elected to the National People's Congress as the representative of China's two million Manchus. He was also a member of the National Committee of the Chinese People's Political Consultative Conference. He told me that he had met Chairman Mao a few days back at the second meeting of the Congress. Premier Chou En-lai had introduced him to the Chairman as Mr. Tsai Tao, the uncle of Pu Yi. Chairman Mao had shaken him by the hand and said, "I have heard that Pu Yi's studies are going quite well; why don't you go and visit him?"

As my uncle told us this his voice shook so much with emotion that it was almost inaudible, and I was unable to hold back my tears. We all wept, and my nephew Jui finally sobbed out loud.

In this meeting with my relations I learnt that not only had I myself been saved but that the entire Aisin-Gioro clan and Manchu nationality had been rescued.

My uncle told me that while there had been only 80,000 registered Manchus before liberation the present figure was thirty times as high. I understood the significance of this change. I knew what a wretched state the bannermen had fallen into under Peiyang warlord rule and the Kuomintang government, when they had found great difficulty in getting jobs unless they pretended to be of the Han nationality. Many of the members of the Aisin-Gioro clan had changed their surnames to Chin, Chao or Lo; my father's family in Tientsin, for example, had taken the name Chin. After liberation more and more Manchus acknowledged their nationality, and when all of them registered after the proclamation of the Constitution the total of 2,400,000 surprised even the Manchus themselves.

I remembered my anger at the time of the robbery of the Eastern Mausolea and the vow I had sworn before the tablets of my ancestors that I would avenge them. In fact all I had done had been to speed the destruction of my own people and clan; and it was only after the collapse of my clique and the Japanese who claimed to support me that the Manchus and the Aisin-Gioro clan had found a secure future. The proof of this was the change from 80,000 to 2,400,000.

This historic change affected not only the younger Aisin-Gioros but also the *beileh*[1] Tsai Tao and my own sisters. My uncle was now 69, but such was his mental and physical vigour that I could see little of the old man about him. I noticed that his customary way of talking to me was unchanged. He explained that after liberation he had worked for a department of the People's Liberation Army that was in charge of horses, and he was very pleased to tell me that he had spent some time in the steppes of the Northwest. At the moment he was planning to make a trip to inspect the work of the national minorities as a part of his duties as a member of the National People's Congress.

Immediately after the entry of the People's Liberation Army into Peking many of the old Manchus had been worried, particularly those of the Aisin-Gioro clan, and they did not lose their doubts even after reading the Proclamation of the People's Liberation Army.[2] Most of these old Peking Manchus had not been members of the "new nobility" of the "Manchukuo" or Wang Ching-wei puppet regimes, but some of them had not yet lost their superstitious respect for my person and were more alarmed than ever when they heard that I had been imprisoned. The combination of this, the ever diminishing number of Manchus, and their destitution meant that they had no "illusions" about the People's Liberation Army. Their first surprise came when they learnt that the Northeastern People's Government had opened a special school for Manchu children. Later on they saw representatives of the Manchu nationality take part with representatives of all other circles in the meetings of the Chinese People's Political Consultative Conference that discussed the Common Programme.[3] Then cadres from the People's Government visited the homes of quite a few of them to invite them to be representatives in

---

[1] A Manchu noble title.

[2] This was made public in April 1949. It contained an eight-point covenant, promising, among other things, to protect the lives and property of all the people except counter-revolutionaries and saboteurs.

[3] The Common Programme served as a provisional constitution before the adoption of the Constitution by the National People's Congress in September 1954.

local political consultative conferences. The cadres asked them to make suggestions on behalf of themselves and the Manchu people and to contribute their efforts to the building of a new society. In Peking all the descendants in my generation of my great-grandfather the emperor Tao Kuang and of Prince Tun, Prince Kung and Prince Chun were over sixty except for a few cousins of mine who were a little younger. My second cousin Pu Chin (also known as Pu Hsueh-chai), an outstanding painter, calligrapher, and player of the *ku chin* (an ancient Chinese stringed instrument), was now over sixty, and to his surprise he was able to take his *ku chin* down from the wall again and go once a week to the banks of Peihai Lake in Peking to indulge his passion for this ancient art with his old and new friends. He saw a bright future for Chinese classical music in the youngsters who were his students. In addition to this he had been elected vice-president of the *Ku Chin* Research Association and president of the Calligraphy Research Association; he had been invited to attend a district political consultative conference; and he had become a teacher at the Academy of Chinese Painting. His brother Pu Chien was also teaching Chinese painting. His cousin Pu Hsiu had been a "Companion of the Chien Ching Gate" in the Forbidden City and looked after my Tientsin property while I was in Changchun, but had since lost his eyesight and been unable to earn his living. After liberation his experiences and the historical materials that he carried in his brain were valued highly by the new society, and he was asked to become a member of the Institute for Classical and Historical Studies. These institutes have been founded all over the country, and their members include scholars who passed the imperial examinations of the Ching Dynasty, witnesses of the events of the warlord and Chiang Kai-shek periods, participants in the Revolution of 1911, members of the early revolutionary organization, the Tung Meng Hui, and even people who had seen behind the scenes at the last feudal court. Pu Hsiu was full of confidence in life, and he recounted what he remembered about Ching history for others to write down on his behalf.

These phenomena, that already seemed normal to the new society, were fresh to me and made a deep impression. But what made the deepest impression was the change I could see in my sisters.

Some six months previously I had exchanged letters with my brothers and sisters in Peking. I had realized from what they wrote that big changes were taking place in my family, but I had never given the matter much serious thought. During the "Manchukuo" days all of my brothers and sisters except Fourth Brother and Sixth and Seventh Sisters had lived in Changchun and accompanied me in my flight to Tunghua. After my capture I had been worried that they might be discriminated against as traitors. Second Sister's husband was the grandson of the "Manchukuo" premier Cheng Hsiao-hsu, while Third Sister was married to the younger brother of my first wife; and Fifth Sister had married the son of the chief of staff to Chang Hsun, the monarchist general who had put me back on the throne in 1917. These two husbands had both been "Manchukuo" lieutenant-colonels. The father-in-law of my fourth sister had been the Manchu official who was notorious for having killed the outstanding woman revolutionary Chiu Chin in 1907. All of my sisters' husbands had been either military officers or civil functionaries of the "Manchukuo" regime. Sixth and Seventh Sisters alone had been regular students, but I was still worried that they might have suffered because their eldest brother was a leading traitor. Such anxieties were shared by all of us prisoners, but mine were worse than those of the others. Later my family correspondence showed me that my fears were groundless. My brothers and sisters enjoyed the same right to work as other people and their children could go to school and receive scholarships in the normal way. Fourth Brother and Seventh Sister were still primary school teachers, Sixth Sister was a freelance painter, Fifth Sister was a seamstress, and Third Sister was a social activist who had been chosen by her neighbours as a member of the street committee responsible for security. Although they were doing their own cooking and looking after their own children, their letters showed that they were satisfied and happy. I stopped worrying. Now that I had seen these two sisters again and heard what they said to their own husbands, I started to think about them even more.

I can still remember how Old Wan, the husband of Fifth Sister, stared wide-eyed as he asked her, "Can you really ride a bicycle?

Can you sew too?" These were things that had astonished him in her letters, and he wanted to ask her about them in person. He had good reason to be surprised. As a child she had not even dared to run, and when she grew up she had been surrounded by maids and waiting women. She had never even entered a kitchen or touched a pair of scissors; could she now ride a bicycle to work and use scissors to make clothes? Was she really a self-supporting seamstress?

What was even more amazing to him was the way she answered quite naturally, "What's so strange about that? There's nothing to it."

Third Sister had been through rather more than Fifth Sister. As her son was ill she had not gone straight back to Peking after the Japanese surrender but had stayed at Tunghua with two nurses. She had no property, and as she was afraid of attracting attention because of her origin and her fine clothes she set up a cigarette stall in Tunghua. She was nearly forced to leave by Kuomintang agents and was swindled by a merchant who sold her some matches that would not strike. After a few years of this insecure life she returned to Peking in 1949. Since liberation she had regularly taken part in meetings of the street committee. She had known something about the policies of the government as she had been in contact with the People's Liberation Army and the People's Government in the Northeast; and as she enjoyed the confidence of her neighbours she had been elected to work for the street committee. The part of her job that she spoke about with the greatest enthusiasm was explaining the new Marriage Law.

This would not have been particularly fascinating to other people, but it gave me rather a surprise. She had been even more the "refined young lady" than Fifth Sister in the old days, and was always asking me about the presents I gave to other people. Who would have expected that this spoilt, lazy girl, capable only of asking me for things, was now a social activist? It sounded incredible at first, but this change made sense. I came to understand why she was an enthusiastic propagator of the new Marriage Law and why she sometimes burst into tears when reading the papers. I knew she meant it when she said, "In the old days I was nothing but an ornament."

Although she was quite well educated and a noblewoman, her life in the old days was futile and jejune. When she and her husband were staying in Japan I once wrote and asked her to tell me about everyday life in that country. Her reply read like this: "I am sitting in a room with my maid ironing my clothes beside me. Outside the window an old servant is watering flowers, and a puppy is sitting on the floor gazing at a box of sweets. . . . That's all there is to it." Now her life had much more meaning because her neighbours were so eager to hear her read the papers to them.

Later she told me about an experience of hers when she was in Tunghua after the Japanese surrender. "One day the people's militia came for me and said that the common people were holding a meeting at which they wanted me to tell them about my past. I was scared stiff of struggle meetings against traitors and said that I would do anything they liked if they let me off. Then I saw some cadres who told me not to be frightened as the masses were very reasonable. I had no choice and had to go on the platform, shivering with terror as I was, and tell the meeting about my life. There were huge crowds of people there including some who had come just to see the princess. When I had finished speaking a whispered discussion started. Finally someone got up and said, 'She hasn't done anything wicked herself, so we don't have anything against her.' Everyone agreed with this and the meeting ended. Then I realized that the common people are very reasonable."

This last point was something that I had just come to understand myself.

On the second day of meeting the family I happened to receive a letter from Second Sister in which she said that her eldest daughter was in the second year at a physical training college and had become an outstanding spare-time driving instructor. She had recently ridden a motor-bicycle all the way from Tientsin to Hankow. My sister wrote happily that her daughter, an aristocratic young lady 12 years ago, had become an athlete, and her other children were also doing well at school. When I mentioned this to Fifth and Third Sisters they wiped the tears from their eyes and told me about their own children. This convinced me that the fate of the Aisin-Gioro clan had really changed.

I once made a calculation on the basis of the "Jade Register" of the imperial family compiled in 1937 and the information provided by my brothers and sisters about the rate of infantile mortality in my branch of the Aisin-Gioro clan. Thirty-four per cent of the children had died in the Ching Dynasty, 10 per cent during the Republic, and none in the ten years since liberation. The figures for the whole Aisin-Gioro clan would be even more staggering, with something like 45 per cent of the boys and girls of my and my father's generation dying in childhood, mostly under the age of two.

I had not made these calculations when I met my uncle and sisters, but the early death of so many of the children of my family in the old days occurred to me then. And those who grew up were capable of nothing except carrying a bird-cage around; there were no other possibilities open to them. Apart from strolling in the Hou Men district with their bird-cages in their hands, the older generation would drink tea every day from dawn until lunch, when about ten dishes of cheap food would be laid out for show, and after that they would throw their weight around at home. That was all the older generation was capable of, while the youngsters were rarely aware of the need to learn anything but how to serve and imitate their seniors. Even if they were driven by penury to look for work or tried to find some job in which to use their talents they never found anything. I had known so many cases of this during the Republic.

But things had changed completely. The fate of my juniors was something that I could never even have hoped for in the old days. My brother and six sisters in Peking had twenty-seven children between them, and all of them who were of the right age were in school or university. My uncle Tsai Tao had sixteen grandchildren and great-grandchildren, of whom one was a technician at a hydro-electric station, one had distinguished himself with the People's Volunteers in Korea, one was an army cultural worker, and the others (except for those who were below school age) were all studying or working. In the eyes of this generation the idle life of their elders was just a joke.

One member of the younger generation had met with a different fate. Pu Chieh's wife had written to him from Japan telling him that their elder daughter, a girl of eighteen, had killed herself in a suicide pact with a young man because of a love affair. I have since heard many different versions of this story, and I am convinced that the boy was as unfortunate as my niece. Such are the contrasts in the fate of young people in different periods and societies.

From that year onwards there were continual family visits to the prison. It is worth mentioning the meeting between Old Liu, the most resolute sceptic of us all, and his daughter who was studying to be an artist. She brought her future husband along with her.

"Don't you believe it yet, Dad?" she asked him. "I'm at art school, and this is my fiancé."

"I believe it now," her father replied.

"Do you understand that I would have been unable to go to art school if it were not for the leadership of Mao Tse-tung?"

"I understand."

"If you understand that, you should study properly and reform."

Previously Old Chang had almost gone out of his mind when he received a letter in which his son addressed him as "Mr.". But now his daughter came to visit him with a letter from her brother. Old Chang showed this letter to almost everyone in the prison.

Dear Father,

I now see that I was too "leftist". The teaching that I have been given by the Youth League and the criticisms of my comrades are right: I should not have taken such an attitude to you. . . . What difficulties are you having with your studies? I thought that you were bound to be using a pen in your studies, so I have bought one and asked Sister to bring it to you. . . .

# The Japanese War Criminals

In June and July I went with some other prisoners to appear as a witness at the military tribunal hearing the cases of the Japanese war criminals at Shenyang.

I had read in the press that over a thousand Japanese war criminals had been in captivity in China, some in Fushun and some in Taiyuan. They had all committed crimes during the Japanese invasion of China. In June and July of 1956 forty-five of them were sentenced at Shenyang and Taiyuan, while the rest were not put on trial but were repatriated with the help of the Chinese Red Cross. Thirty-six prisoners from the Fushun group were tried at Shenyang in two groups. I had known about some of them during my "Manchukuo" days, and had heard others of them speaking at a meeting in the prison at Fushun. One of these was Furumi Tadayuki, the former vice-head of the "General Affairs Office of the Manchukuo State Council". It was against him and his superior Takebe Rokuzo that I and four former puppet ministers were to give evidence. Furumi was the first to be tried by the court, and he was later sentenced to eighteen years' imprisonment.[1]

As I went into the courtroom I thought of the victory in the Korean War, the successful signing of the Geneva Agreement, and China's position in the world since the founding of the People's Republic. The trial of Japanese war criminals on Chinese soil was unprecedented.

When the Chinese People's Volunteers and the Korean People's Army won in Korea I had thought that there was no hope for me except to acknowledge my guilt and throw myself on the mercy of the Chinese people. Now that the Japanese war criminals were being tried I was not worried about my own future and was instead filled with national pride. In addition I thought about many other problems.

---

[1] He was released in February 1963 before serving his full sentence.

In the last part of the speech he made before his judgement Furumi said something like this:

There is not a square inch of land in the whole of the Northeast that bears no trace of the barbarity of Japanese imperialism, and the crimes of imperialism were my crimes. I most deeply acknowledge that I am a war criminal who has openly violated international law and humanitarian principles by committing the gravest crimes against the Chinese people, and I sincerely apologize to them for this. Over the past six years the Chinese people have treated me with kindness although I am so horrible a criminal, and they have given me the chance to reflect coolly on my crimes. Thanks to this I have recovered my conscience and my reason, and I have learnt which road men should take. I do not know how I can possibly repay this gift of the Chinese people.

I remember that after I had given my evidence the judges asked him what comments he had to make. He bowed deeply and said that every word of my testimony was true.

My thoughts went back to the International Military Tribunal in Tokyo. There the Japanese war criminals had used lawyers to make trouble and attack the witnesses. In the hope of lightening their sentences they had used every conceivable method to cover up their crimes. But at this court all the war criminals admitted their guilt and submitted to punishment.

My brother and brothers-in-law told me a great deal about the Japanese prisoners. They had helped in translating the confessions of the Japanese prisoners and the letters that some of them had sent from Japan after they were repatriated. When my brothers-in-law were released this work was done by Pu Chieh, Old Pang, and others. From 1956 onwards I heard quite a few stories about the Japanese war criminals.

One of them had been an army general, and when the investigating body began its work in 1954 he told them almost nothing. But at this military tribunal he admitted that he had directed his men to perpetrate six different massacres of civilians in Hopei and Honan. In October 1942, for example, a unit under his command had butchered over 1,280 residents of Panchiatai Village and burnt down some thousand houses. After being sentenced to twenty years' imprisonment he said to a journalist that he deserved to have been sentenced to death and told him how fairly he had been interrogated and tried. He had even been provided with a lawyer. "When I remember how many Chinese people I have killed and how difficult I made life for their dependants, my heart is cut to shreds at the thought that it is those very relations who are now looking after me."

A former Japanese colonel was interviewed by journalists on the Japanese boat in which he was being repatriated without having been tried. As he had been very angry when his former subordinates had questioned him in prison about his crimes they were hoping that he would have something uncomplimentary to say about China. When he failed to give them what they wanted, one of the journalists asked, "Why do you go on talking that way? Are you still frightened of China?" "I'm on board a Japanese boat," the colonel replied, "so why should I be afraid of China? I'm telling you the truth, that's all."

Third Sister's husband had been head patient in one of the sick-rooms. There was one Japanese war criminal who always made trouble for the nurses and warders and disregarded the prison regulations; but at a farewell party after his release was announced he burst into tears and made a speech about his mistakes. There was another invalid who, although not as troublesome as the previous one, refused to see his guilt. He was sent to hospital for two emergency operations on a malignant rectal cancer, and the doctor gave some of his own blood to save his life. After leaving the hospital he told a large meeting how he had butchered and tortured the Chinese people in the past, and he compared this with the way the Chinese people had saved his life when he lay dying. Both he and his audience were in tears throughout his speech.

Once when we were levelling the ground to make flowerbeds we dug up a bone with a bullet hole in it. Old Yuan and Old Hsien, who had studied some Western medicine, said that it had belonged to a young girl. Later on my brother-in-law Old Wan translated an article by a Japanese war criminal, who had been the governor of this prison in the old days, describing the hellish life of the patriots who had been incarcerated there. The place rang with the screams of the tortured and echoed with the clanking of chains. It was

433

stinking and filthy; in winter the walls were covered with ice and in summer it was swarming with flies and mosquitoes. The prisoners were only given one small bowl of *kaoliang* a day and had to do heavy labour from dawn to dusk. Many were beaten or worked to death. This article went on to describe the changes in the prison since then and the sharp contrast between the conditions in the old days and those he had experienced as a prisoner himself.

Many of the war criminals wrote in letters and articles that they had felt fear and hatred when they were sent back to China by the Soviet Union. Some of them, like myself, had tried to understand things in terms of their old ideology, and had failed to see why the Chinese people were treating them as they did. When they saw the boiler-room being built they imagined that it was going to be a death house and when they saw medical facilities being provided they assumed that they were going to be used in experiments as prisoners had been in the time of Japanese rule. Others saw in their lenient and humane treatment a sign of weakness, but the victories of the Chinese People's Volunteers in Korea showed them that the people who were reasonable to them were certainly not weak, whereas the true sign of weakness was cruelty.

Even before these stories came out nearly everyone except me knew about the changes that had taken place in the Japanese war criminals; I was too preoccupied with my own problems to think about them. In fact the changes had become more and more obvious ever since 1954 or thereabouts. In his diary for 1955 Pu Chieh described plays and performances of music and dancing put on by the Japanese prisoners. One play was about the horrible effects of the atom bomb explosion at Nagasaki. He also mentioned sports meetings the Japanese prisoners held on the ground they had levelled themselves.

Now I look back on it the changes that took place in them are very clear. Why did these prisoners become so happy and high-spirited? Why was it that after their release they took with them the musical instruments they had been given by the prison authorities and played with tears in their eyes as they looked back towards China from the Japanese boat that was taking them home? Why

434

were they so fond of singing "Tokyo-Peking"? Why was it that even those who had served sentences said, "We are grateful to the Chinese people and are ashamed of. . . ."

Letters sent back from repatriated Japanese war criminals often contained such sentences as: "I learnt in China how one should live"; "Now I know what life is"; and "As I take the first steps along the course of a human life I wish to say, Mr. Governor, that I shall never forget the warmth of your handshake as you wished me good health".

Some prisoners read in the Japanese press about girls who went around with the American troops like the "jeep girls" of pre-liberation China, and they roundly condemned these women. One prisoner wrote a letter to his wife asking her if she was doing this. When the letter was checked by the prison authorities they took it back to the writer and asked him with great patience to reconsider it. "Is it proper to write a letter like this to your wife? Even if you had any grounds for asking such a question — and you don't — whose fault would it be? Not hers, surely." The prisoner said nothing, crumpled the letter into a ball, and threw it on the floor. Then he put his head into his hands and burst into tears.

They were grateful to the Chinese people for teaching them to recognize the truth as well as for treating them leniently. Just as I had learnt what in fact emperors were, they had come to see what militarism and Japan were really like. In letters written from Japan they described the startling increase in juvenile delinquency.

In the U.S. bases American tanks were rolling over their land; U.S. military aircraft were soiling their skies; and G.I.s were debauching their women. One letter from a man who had returned to his village was full of the changes that had taken place among the youth there. "Some have become gangsters, others kill because of women, and some have joined the Self-Defence Force and are living a depraved life, besotted with liquor and girls." The young people did not obey their parents, and culture was decadent and full of violence.

The released prisoners spoke about the new China and Japanese militarism, opposing the restoration of the latter and pleading for independence, peace, and democracy. They did this in spite of sur-

435

veillance and restrictions that they avoided with great ingenuity.
When reactionaries did not allow them to perform Chinese dance
themselves, they taught them to professional dancers, so that they
spread throughout the whole of Japan. They were asked to speak
about their life in prison and about New China. They spoke about
the friendship of the Chinese people for the people of Japan, of their
attitude to war now that they were strong, and of their hopes and
ideals. Some people doubted, some had their reservations, and
others were convinced. The pro-American government disliked them
more and more, while the people's belief in what they said grew.

They published a book called *The Three-All Policy*[1] in which men
who had themselves participated in the savageries committed by the
Japanese army in China described how they had exterminated the
populations of whole regions, used the Chinese people as the subject
of experiments in bacteriological warfare, dissected people alive, and
so on. The first printing of 50,000 sold out in a week.

When a number of retired generals heard a former fellow-soldier
of theirs describe his experiences in China they were silent for a
long time before one of them said, "Our instincts and what we know
of you are enough to convince us of the truth of every word you
have told us. But we can only say so behind closed doors."

When one ex-soldier went back to his village the local people
came to greet him with a banner reading "Eternal Victory". But
when he got off the train the returning soldier made a very painful
speech, after which the local people understood the causes of the
Hiroshima disaster and wept. The banner was dropped to the
ground.

Many of the dependants of the war criminals were simple working people and men of goodwill. Quite a few of them had written
to the Chinese government in the past asking for the release of
their "innocent" husbands and sons. Later some of them were
allowed to come to China to visit their imprisoned relations. When
they heard what their menfolk had to say and listened to recordings

---

[1] The policy of "burn all, loot all, and kill all" carried out by the Japanese
invaders in China.

436

of the accusations made by the Chinese people before the court they wept with the prisoners. They understood now that the men were guilty and had been deceived by militarism.

The changes among the Japanese war criminals, like those that took place in my family, shook me to the core. One fact stood out clearly in my mind: the Communist Party used reason to win people over.

# "The World's Glory"

From the second half of 1956 onwards I was often interviewed by foreign journalists and visitors, and other foreigners wrote to me asking for my picture. In February 1957 I received a letter from a Frenchman in which he asked me to autograph a picture of myself. In addition to some photos of my past there was an article, though what the point of it was I do not know. It read as follows:

### THE IMPRISONED EMPEROR OF CHINA

The world's glory is meaningless: this sums up the life of a political prisoner now awaiting sentence in Red China's Fushun Prison. As a child he wore precious silks, but now he is dressed in tattered clothes of padded cotton as he walks alone in the prison yard. This man's name is Henry Pu Yi. Fifty years ago his birth was marked with a lavish display of fireworks; now he lives in jail. When he was two, Henry became the emperor of China, but six years of civil war threw him off his imperial throne. 1932 was an important year for this "Son of Heaven": with Japanese support he became Emperor of Manchukuo. After the Second World War he was not heard of again until the present, when this striking photograph revealed his tragic fate. . . .

Had he sent me this two years earlier I might have shed a few tears over it, but it was too late now. In my reply I wrote: "I am sorry, but I am unable to agree with your interpretation. I cannot sign the photograph."

Not long before that I had been asked a number of similar "sympathetic" questions in interviews with some foreign journalists: "Don't you feel sad at having been the last emperor of the Ching Dynasty?" "Don't you feel that it is unfair that you have not been tried after so long a time? Don't you find this surprising?" I replied that what was sad was my past life as Ching emperor and puppet emperor, and that when it came to surprises, I was astonished by the leniency with which I was being treated. The journalists did not seem to understand me, and I imagined that the French gentleman who had written to me would doubtless share their incomprehension when he read my reply.

In my view what was truly glorious was the magnanimity of Fang Su-jung, the girl who survived the massacre, the simple words of the Taishanpao peasants, the great changes that had taken place among the younger members of the Aisin-Gioro clan, the gas jets in the kitchens of the Fushun miners, the Chinese lathes that had replaced Japanese ones in the industrial school I visited, and the peaceful life of the retired workers in the old people's home. Was all this "meaningless" to me? Was it meaningless that others had put their hopes and trust in my becoming a real man? Was this not the most valuable judgement that could have been passed on me?

I am convinced that my feelings were shared by many of the other criminals, and that some of them had come to this conclusion before me. Indeed, so many of us were now determined to remould ourselves through our own efforts that the New Year of 1957 was quite different from previous ones.

At New Year and other festivals we had parties at which the talented ones among us would perform. The corridor where the parties were usually held would be hung with lanterns and decorations, and this combined with the good food we were given for the occasion to give us a sense of well-being. But some time before the New Year of 1957 we felt that this was not enough, and we wanted to hold a big party in the hall as the Japanese war criminals did. The prison authorities told our study committee that if we thought we could manage it we could go ahead, and could have the newly-arrived Chiang Kai-shek war criminals to fill the hall as our audience. When the study committee passed this news on to the cells we all set to with great enthusiasm.

We prisoners were all pleased because we reckoned that we would have a happy New Year, and the prison authorities gave us their backing because this method of enabling prisoners to educate themselves had been very successful with the Japanese war criminals. The Japanese prisoners wrote plays themselves on the basis of what they read in the Japanese press. One of them was on the horrors of the nuclear explosions in Japan and the crimes that Japanese militarism had committed against the people of Japan and the rest of the world. They had a great educational effect on writers, performers, and audience alike. Our study committee therefore decided to include plays of this sort in our show. This proposal was generally supported, and two plays were soon outlined. One was a "living newspaper" called "The Defeat of the Aggressors" about the repulse of the British invasion of Egypt; and the other was to be about the transformation of a "Manchukuo" traitor. They were written by Pu Chieh and a former official of Wang Ching-wei's puppet government.

As the work on the plays went ahead all kinds of other performances were in preparation. Our conjurer Old Lung, for example, announced that he was going to do some bigger trick than producing eggs from a hat or swallowing ping-pong balls. The busiest man was Old Wan, the head of the study committee, who was in charge of all the arrangements. Little Jui was responsible for the decorations, and Big Li, now an accomplished electrician, looked after the lighting.

In previous years, I had not performed in the corridor parties and had been thought too clumsy to be of much use in the preparations. This time too I expected that the others would not want me to get in their way, but then to my great surprise our cell-chief, Old Chu, discovered that I could sing passably well and signed me up for the choir. I was deeply moved, and I sang with gusto. Just when I had learnt my songs Old Wan, the chairman of the study committee, sent for me.

439

"Pu Yi, there's a part for you in the first play. It's not too difficult and there aren't many lines to learn. Anyhow you can improvise if you feel like it. This is a worthwhile job and a part of our mutual education. . . ."

"You don't have to persuade me. As long as you think I'm up to it, I'm game."

"Of course you can do it," grinned Old Wan. "You're certainly up to it. You have a strong, clear voice. You. . . ."

"Take it easy. What do you want me to play in?"

"We've called it 'The Defeat of the Aggressors', and it's about the British invasion of Egypt and the uproar it caused. It's based on press reports. Old Jun is playing the main role — the Foreign Secretary Selwyn Lloyd. You will be a left-wing Labour M.P."

I went to see Pu Chieh to read the script, hear his explanation of it, and copy down my lines. Then I had to choose my costume. As I was playing a foreigner I would naturally have to wear Western clothes, of which there was no shortage in the prison as the suits of many of the prisoners were kept there. I went back to my cell with the blue suit I had worn at the International Military Tribunal in Tokyo, a shirt, a tie and other clothes. As nobody else was in the cell I dressed up by myself. Just when I had put on a white shirt Old Yuan came in and asked me with astonishment what I was doing.

As I was excited and my shirt collar was too tight I could not answer at first. Finally I panted, "I'm going to be in a play. Come and loosen the belt at the back of my waistcoat."

He did this for me, but the waistcoat was still too tight. I realized that I must have put on weight. My leather shoes from England pinched my feet, so I asked Old Yuan in irritation whether I would need to wear leather shoes to play a British Labour M.P.

"You certainly will. Some British Labour M.P.s even use scent, so of course you can't wear padded cloth boots. Don't worry, your leather shoes won't pinch after you've worn them for a while, and the waistcoat can be altered. Go and learn your lines. It's great news that you will be acting." He ended with a laugh that still rang in my ears as I went out into the corridor. I was in very high spirits: Old Wan had said that this would be self-education and a kind of mutual help. This was the first time I had been in the position of helping other people instead of just being helped. After all, I had my abilities just like everyone else, and was on equal terms with the rest when it came to helping each other.

From then on I recited my lines incessantly. As Old Wan had said, they were very short, and my part was probably the smallest in the play. At the very end of the play Selwyn Lloyd made a speech in the House of Commons trying to justify the failure of the invasion, and some opposition members started to question him and then joined in an attack on him. At this point I was to stand up in their midst and say to Selwyn Lloyd, "There is no need for you to continue to defend your actions. They are disgraceful, disgraceful, and, I say it again, disgraceful." The chamber was then supposed to be filled with angry insults and demands for Lloyd's resignation, during which I was to shout "Get out! Get out!" This play had a very simple plot, in which the most important element was this parliamentary debate which only lasted some fifteen minutes. I spent many dozens of fifteen minutes preparing my part for fear I would forget my lines or say them wrong and thus disappoint the hopes that had been placed in me. In the past I had suffered from insomnia or talked in my sleep because I was worried or frightened. This was the first time that excitement and nerves had kept me awake.

When New Year came and I went into the hall for the party the festive atmosphere and the magnificent stage made me forget my nerves. Our show compared well with the parties of the Japanese war criminals: choral and solo singing, Mongol songs and dances, crosstalk, ballads sung to the clappers, conjuring, the living newspaper "The Defeat of the Aggressors", and the play "From Darkness to Light". When we saw how impressed the Chiang Kai-shek war criminals were we winked at each other in our excitement.

The other acts went off successfully, drawing plenty of applause, and the first item after the interval was the living newspaper. The debate began. Old Jun had dressed himself up to look just like

Selwyn Lloyd. As he had a naturally big nose he was the only "M.P." who looked like an Englishman, and his acting was outstanding: in his anger, fear, desperation and arrogance he was the living image of a defeated Foreign Secretary. After about ten minutes Old Yuan whispered to me (an action that was in the script), "Don't be too wooden. Put some movement into it." I peered forward and looked at the audience. I had the feeling that the attention of all of them was focused on me, the left-wing M.P., and it made me very nervous. Nobody had noticed me when I was singing in the choir, but now all their eyes were on me. Before I could recover my calm Old Yuan nudged me: "Say something; say something to refute him." I stood up in a panic, turned towards Old Jun, who was still spouting away, and realized that I had forgotten my words. Inspiration came to me in my despair, and I shouted "NO! No! No!" in English. My outburst cut Old Jun short, and then I remembered my lines. When I had said them I heard a burst of applause from the audience and cries of "Get out! Get out!" from the stage. The Foreign Secretary scuttled off stage in confusion.

Old Yuan was the first to congratulate me after the show: "You didn't do at all badly. Although you were a bit nervy, you weren't at all bad." Then others expressed their satisfaction and roared with laughter at the words I had improvised.

The hall gradually calmed down and the play "From Darkness to Light" began. This took us into a different world. The first scene showed how two down-and-out Northeastern officials became leading traitors. In the second scene they tried to get in with the Kuomintang after the Japanese surrender but were captured by the Soviet Red Army. In the third they attempted to deceive the authorities after being sent back to China but without success, and they finally responded to the education they received from the government and its policy of leniency: they acknowledged their guilt and accepted remoulding. Although the play was nothing wonderful in itself, all of us war criminals could see ourselves in it. It reminded us of our own pasts, held our attention, and made us feel more and more ashamed of ourselves. In one part of the play some traitors forced the people to work on the building of the Emperor Jimmu Shrine. Big Mouth saw that this was his story, and he was heard to mumble, "What's the point in showing that disgraceful business?" In another scene a group of traitors were sitting round in a room fawning on the Japanese and making suggestions about how to steal grain from the people of the Northeast. I heard someone next to me sighing and saying "How filthy!" I felt that the filthiest thing was not any of the characters in the play but the curtained niche in the corner of the room in which hung the "True Imperial Image" of the traitor emperor. When the characters in the play bowed to it every time they came on stage I realized that it was the dirtiest thing in the world.

The climax of the evening came in the last scene, when government personnel explained the policy of remoulding criminals. The applause and shouting of slogans was louder than anything I had ever heard before. This was due not so much to the play itself as to the combined effects of family letters and visits, our trips outside, the confessions of the Japanese war criminals at the military tribunal, and other factors. Amid the ear-splitting shouts and applause could be heard muffled sobs. Old Liu, who had not believed that his daughter was being looked after until he saw her with his own eyes, was shaking with sobs; and Old Chang, who was on good terms with his son again, was crying out loud as his fountain pen shone from his breast pocket.

The emotions stirred up at this meeting showed us what kind of "glory" was still possible for us in the present world, a "glory" that was shining ever clearer. Soon after the New Year thirteen prisoners were released without trial, and they included my three nephews and Big Li. After seeing them off we had an even better party to celebrate the Spring Festival with a play about a Northeastern village in "Manchukuo" days and after liberation. Then four more prisoners were released, including my two brothers-in-law. This was the time when I received the letter from the Frenchman about "the world's glory".

# Another Visit

In the second half of 1957 we went on another trip, this time to Shenyang, Anshan, Changchun and Harbin. We saw the Tahuofang reservoir project near Shenyang, eighteen factories, six technical organizations and schools, three hospitals, two exhibitions, and a sports palace. In Harbin we visited the area that had suffered disaster from the Japanese 731 Bacteriological Unit and the Hall of the Northeastern Martyrs. This trip made an even deeper impression on us than the previous one.

The great majority of the enterprises we visited were newly built, the exceptions being a few that were left from the time of the Japanese. These Japanese factories had been almost completely wrecked when they were taken over. The Anshan Iron and Steel Works and the Shenyang Machine-Tool Plant, for example, had been sabotaged both by the Japanese and the Kuomintang. After they were taken over by the People's Government they were rebuilt, and expanded to their present gigantic size. Many of the former "Manchukuo" ministers who had seen these plants in the old days were astonished by their growth. What surprised me most was the amount of equipment with trade marks and specifications in Chinese on it. Even I, inexperienced as I was, thought of "Made in USA", "Made in Germany" when machinery was mentioned, but now I saw whole sets of equipment made by China herself. Some of the products of these plants were even going for export, and all of them bore the proud words: "Made in the People's Republic of China".

At the Anshan Iron and Steel Works I stood in front of the enormous iron and steel structures and tried unsuccessfully to think how all this could have grown out of a heap of scrap. But that was what had really happened. When the Japanese left Anshan they said: "Give Anshan to the Chinese to grow *kaoliang* on. Even if they want to start it up again they'll need twenty years at a calm estimate." But the Chinese people had taken not twenty years but three to start it up and reach an annual output of 1,350,000 tons, far above the highest figure ever obtained in the "Manchukuo" period. Five years later annual production was up to 5,350,000 tons, more than the total output for the whole thirty-one years from the foundation of the Showa Steel Works by the Japanese in 1917 to the final withdrawal of the Kuomintang in 1947.

I saw many other things like this on the trip, and they all told me that the Chinese people had stood up. Not only could they win military victories, but they could triumph on the economic front as well. If I had not seen this with my own eyes, or if someone had predicted it ten years earlier, I would have been as sceptical as the Japanese who advised the Chinese to plant *kaoliang*.

During the previous forty years I had forgotten that I too was Chinese. I had joined the Japanese in praising their nation as the most splendid one on earth; I had shared Cheng Hsiao-hsu's illusions about using "foreign officials" and "foreign strength" to develop China's resources; and I had often sighed with Pu Chieh over the stupidity of the Chinese as compared with the intelligence of the white races. Even after going into prison I had still refused to believe that the new China would be able to keep its place in the world. So far from being elated when the Chinese and Korean people's forces won battles in Korea I had been terrified that the Americans would drop atom bombs. I had not been able to understand why the Chinese Communist Party dared to expose U.S. imperialism at the rostrum of the United Nations or why the delegates of the Sino-Korean side dared to warn the Americans at the Panmunjom talks that they would not be able to gain at the conference table what they had failed to win on the battlefield. In short, I had suffered from a very bad case of "soft bone disease".

After the Korean armistice was signed and China played a new role in world affairs at the Geneva Conference I had thought about China's international relations since the Opium Wars: from the time of my great-grandfather Tao Kuang to the Kuomintang and Chiang Kai-shek they had been a continuous record of "soft bone disease". During those 109 years the bringers of cannons and opium, the pseudo-missionaries — the foreigners who thought themselves so civilized and superior — had come to China and burned, killed, plundered and cheated. The foreign invaders had stationed their troops in China's capital, ports, big cities and forts, and had all regarded the Chinese as slaves, savages and targets. They had caused China so many days of national disgrace, and made China sign so many treaties turning her own people into slaves. So many humiliating terms had appeared in the diplomatic history of the period: equality of opportunity, the open door, most favoured nation treatment, leased territories, mortgaged tariffs, consular jurisdiction, garrison rights, railway-building rights, mining rights, river transport rights, air transport rights, and so on. The foreigners had even once enjoyed the special privileges of paying one hundred U.S. dollars as compensation for killing a donkey, eighty dollars for killing a man. They had not been liable for trial by Chinese courts if they raped Chinese women.

But this shameful period was now gone for ever. The Chinese people had stood up and were now confidently building their own country, making the foreigners who had laughed so insultingly shut their mouths.

I heard an anecdote in the Changchun Number One Motor Works. When the factory had just started production some children from a primary school wanted to visit it. The factory planned to send an imported bus to fetch them, but the children insisted on a Chinese-made lorry.

Their country must have meant a lot to those children, but for forty years it had been nothing to me.

Whether in one's own society or on the world stage one could now be very proud of being Chinese.

I had always been curious in the past about how other people lived — with the exception, that is, of the late "Manchukuo" period. The first time I had gone out to satisfy this curiosity was to visit my father's mansion, and the second time was when I used the excuse of Chen Pao-shen's sickness to go and see him. I had been most impressed by the freedom of their lives. When I moved to Tientsin I felt that the "top Chinese" I saw in Western restaurants and foreign amusement parks were more free than I was but not so well born; for this reason I did not admire them much, but I was still curious about them. In "Manchukuo" I was too worried about my own position to be very curious. After my repatriation I took no interest in such matters at first, feeling that other people's lives were no concern of mine, but as I took a rosier view of my future these things meant more to me. On this trip I paid a great deal of attention to the way people lived, and what I found out brought back memories and caused me great pain.

Harbin made the deepest impression. The children's railway in the Children's Park there reminded me of how I had played with ants in my own childhood. The survival rate of new babies at the children's hospital and the general level of health would have been beyond the imagination of the Ching imperial family. Sitting on a bench on Harbin's Sun Island as I looked at the pleasure boats on the river and listened to the youngsters singing and playing accordions made me think back to the first part of my life. I had never sung for joy nor had I ever known the pleasure of sunning myself on the grass, to say nothing of being able to walk about as I pleased. In those days I had been worrying whether the kitchen was cheating me and frightened that the Japanese were going to kill me. But here people seemed to be carefree. On an island a few yards in front of me a young artist was painting from life. He was sitting with his back to me, and he did not turn round once although his bag and canvas were leaning against a chair with nobody looking after them. He seemed to be quite confident that nobody would take them. This would have been inconceivable in the old society, but now it was a fact.

Here was another fact: there was a wooden box inside a telephone booth in the park with a piece of paper stuck on it: "Please put four cents in the box for each call made."

One of my fellow-prisoners told me that there used to be a club on Sun Island in the old days in which you had to give a tip every time you visited the lavatory. But now letters from home told us that the staff in any restaurant, hotel, bath-house or other such place would be insulted if you tried to tip them. This was another fact.

Two visits we made in our last days in Harbin showed me the difference between two kinds of people in the world. The first place was where the Japanese 731 Bacteriological Unit had committed its atrocities and the second was the Hall of the Northeastern Martyrs.

A book called 731 *Bacteriological Unit* was published in Japan after the Second World War by a man called Akiyama Hiroshi who had been a member of the unit. According to this book there was a group of buildings about four kilometers in circumference, and the main one was four times the size of the Marunouchi Building in Japan. There were about 3,000 personnel, and they raised tens of thousands of rats. In addition they had 4,500 Ishii style incubators in which they reared astronomical numbers of fleas and produced 300 kilograms of bubonic plague germs a month. There was a prison there where up to four or five hundred prisoners of war or anti-Japanese patriots were kept to be used in experiments. Some were Chinese and others were citizens of the Soviet Union or the Mongolian People's Republic. They were referred to not as men but as "logs". At least six hundred of them would be tortured to death there every year, and the experiments performed on them were of indescribable cruelty. Some men were skinned alive; some were put into refrigerators for experiments and the bones of their hands would go on shaking after the flesh had been frozen off; others were laid on operating tables like frogs while white-coated personnel dissected them; some were tied to stakes in nothing but their underpants while germ bombs were exploded in front of them; and others were fed well and then infected with germs, and if this did not kill them the experiment was repeated until they died.

When he was in this 731 Unit the author heard that the germs bred there were more powerful than any other weapon and could kill 100,000,000 people, a claim on which the Japanese Army prided itself.

When the Soviet Red Army was approaching Harbin this Unit tried to cover up all trace of its crimes. The Japanese poisoned all the surviving prisoners, planning to burn them to ashes and then bury them in a large pit. As the executioners were in a panic they did not burn the corpses thoroughly and could not get them all into the pit. They pulled out the half-burned corpses and divided the flesh from the bone. The flesh was then burned to ashes and the bones were put through a pulverizing machine. Finally the main buildings were destroyed with explosives.

Not long after someone from a nearby village was walking past the ruins when he saw some fleas jumping around in a broken pottery jar. One of these fleas bit him. Little did he realize that it had infected him with the bubonic plague that the murderers had left behind them. Plague broke out in the village, and the local people's government at once sent an army of medical workers to deal with it, but for all their efforts 142 lives were lost in this village of only a hundred or so families.

This shocking event had been witnessed by Chiang Shu-ching, a co-operative member and model worker we visited. After telling us about the crimes that had been committed against this village during the "Manchukuo" days she said, "The Japanese surrendered and laid down their arms and the people's government let us live happily. We had our own land and kept the crops we harvested for ourselves. We were all so pleased and saying that everything was just fine because life was going to be good with the people's government leading us. We didn't know that we hadn't seen the end of the evil caused by the Japanese, or that they had left this behind after they went. The bastards."

I noticed one thing that was the same both in Chiang Shu-ching's spick-and-span little house and in the spacious offices of the agricultural co-operative: whenever the members of the Gold Star Co-operative talked about the past they said little and spoke slowly, but the moment the subject turned to the present or the future the atmosphere change completely. When they talked about the harvests they were now getting, particularly the vegetable crop, they spoke with animation and went into great detail. To back up what they had said they took us to see their hothouses and the new things they had bought: drainage and irrigation equipment, heavy lorries and various kinds of chemical fertilizer. We saw a newly-built school and clinic as well as new electric power cables. When they talked about the targets for the next year they became even more excited. The co-op head pointed to some rows of new tiled houses and chose his words with great caution: "After next autumn I think we might be able to build a few more." None of us believed that "a few" meant only ten or a dozen.

As we were leaving this village the co-op members brought baskets of cucumbers and radishes to give to us. "Take them with you. We've just harvested them, and although they're not worth anything they're very fresh." The co-op head ignored our protests and thrust them into our coach.

I gazed through the windows at the rapidly receding tiled roofs of the Gold Star Co-op and thought of the extraordinary impression that the co-op head's very ordinary words "After next autumn I think . . ." had made on me. Ordinary men like him, whom I had despised in the past as being thoroughly uncivilized, toiled diligently with their own two hands, doing a job that was both ordinary and great. They turned thatched cottages into brick houses to give the people a better life. The Japanese imperialists, on the other hand, whom I used to regard with fear and trembling as the representatives of an outstanding nation, had used modern science and technology to create plague and death. They too had had their ideal: the enslavement and elimination of an oppressed nation.

The rubble of the germ factory at Pingfangchu showed the meaning of evil, while each relic of the martyrs in the Hall of the Northeastern Martyrs showed what was meant by good. Each exhibit told how its former owners had shed their last drops of blood for the sake of the finest human ideals, thus covering themselves with glory. Both the ruins of the germ factory and the bloodstained clothes and last messages of the martyrs were mirrors in which we visitors could see our own ugly past.

The Hall of the Northeastern Martyrs is a majestic building in the Roman style that was used as the Harbin police headquarters during the fourteen years of "Manchukuo". Countless numbers of the bravest Chinese were interrogated, tortured or sent to the execution ground from here in that bloody era. The martyrs whose photographs and relics are exhibited here are only a tiny proportion of the total. All the exhibits and the details about times and places brought back shameful memories. On September 21, 1931, three days after the outbreak of fighting in Shenyang, the Manchurian Committee of the Chinese Communist Party held an emergency meeting which called upon all Party members and all patriotic soldiers to take up arms and fight against the enemy. Pictures of this resolution and the house that was the committee's headquarters reminded me by contrast of my days in the Quiet Garden over twenty years previously. To save the nation in its hour of danger the people of the Northeast had risen under the leadership of the Party and fought, not heeding the obstruction put in their way by Chiang Kai-shek. I, however, had intensified my treachery. I remembered Doihara, Itagaki, Cheng Hsiao-hsu and his son, and Lo Chen-yu; I also recalled my stay in Tangkangtzu and Lushun.

When the guide told us about the life of Yang Ching-yu I thought of my various "imperial progresses" to Tungpientao — the region where the First Allied Anti-Japanese Army under Yang Ching-yu, Li Hung-kuang and other generals operated. I had seen the peaks of the Changpai Mountains as the sun rose above the morning mist. But I had not been moved by the beauty of my motherland as my attention had been on the Japanese gendarmes and the puppet troops and gendarmes on both sides of the railway tracks. The Japanese-run papers always said that the "bandits" in this district had been cleared up, but when I went there the Japanese were worried and gave the appearance of being faced with a mighty foe. When I fled to Tunghua and Talitzukou right at the end of "Manchukuo" I was told that this area was "unsafe". The Allied Anti-Japanese Armies fought there right down to the Japanese surrender, when it was not they who were destroyed but the Imperial Japanese Army that had so often pronounced itself victorious. The anti-Japanese forces had been faced by the powerful Kwantung Army and the "Manchukuo" troops who were better equipped than themselves, and the difficulties that surrounded them were almost unimaginable; but by looking at the cooking pots, water bottles, home-made knives and well-worn sewing machines that the resistance fighters had used I seemed to see the smiling faces of their owners — faces like that of the young director of the Lungfeng Mine, lit up with the smiles that come only from confidence and determination. As I looked at a pair of shoes made from birchbark a song echoed through my brain:

> Birchbark shoes,
> Chinese goods,
> We make them ourselves from our own materials,
> The straps are from the wild hemp,
> The soles from the birch trees.

> With birchbark shoes,
> Top-rate shoes,
> Soldiers can climb to mountain peaks.
> Fashionable girls can't buy them.
> Rich old ladies aren't lucky enough to wear them.

> Birchbark shoes
> Are really good.
> Soldiers in them run across the hills,
> Scaring the devils out of their wits,
> Chasing lorries honking in terror.

The Japanese had made me approve batch after batch of laws. With these in their hands they had herded families and villages together, instituted grain controls, blockaded mountain areas, and used every conceivable means to cut the economic links between the resistance fighters and the outside world. In this way they succeeded in surrounding General Yang Ching-yu and some of the anti-Japanese troops, but despite their desperate shortage of food they fought on — so long in fact that the Japanese began to doubt their own intelligence reports and common sense. How could these men go on fighting without grain? What were they eating? After General Yang Ching-yu laid down his life the Japanese cut open his stomach to solve this riddle, and all they found was grass and leaves.

I remembered the sighs of Yoshioka, the "Imperial Attaché": "The Communists are terrifying." In the eyes of the Imperial Japanese Army, equipped as it was with aircraft and tanks, even grass was frightening.

When General Yang Ching-yu and his comrades-in-arms were singing that song about birchbark shoes I had been terrified that the Japanese would leave me, and scared by my nightmares; and while they were eating grass I had been sick of eating meat and spent all my days practising divination and reciting sutras.

The maps, seals, bloodstained clothes and childhood compositions of Yang Ching-yu swam before my eyes. From behind me came the sound of my Chinese and Japanese fellow-prisoners weeping, a sound that grew louder and louder. As we looked at the photograph of one martyr called Chao Yi-man someone pushed his way forward and knelt before the picture sobbing bitterly as he kotowed to it.

"I was the puppet police chief. . . ."

He was Yu Ching-tao, who had been Harbin police chief before becoming "Manchukuo" minister of labour. When the martyr Chao Yi-man was held in this police headquarters and questioned in this very room Yu Ching-tao had been one of her interrogators. But now the interrogator had been judged by history and imprisoned. Needless to say, Yu Ching-tao was not the only man who should have cried.


## Labour and Optimism


After this visit I was firmly convinced that the gates to the new society stood wide open to me and that the only remaining problems lay within myself.

I began 1958 full of hope. This optimistic attitude had first revealed itself when we were carrying coal in the autumn of 1957. Every autumn the prison authorities moved in large quantities of coal, some for keeping us warm and some for making briquettes for the hothouses in which we grew our winter greens.

This was the first year we had taken part in the work of moving the coal in and making briquettes. I was by now far more capable than I had been in the past. In my cell there were four of us who did most of the heavy work: Old Wang, the Mongol Old Cheng, myself and a fairly young former "Manchukuo" general. The exercise was very good for me. I got much stronger and my old ailments all disappeared. When we were making briquettes I took the fairly heavy job of carrying the coal. As the prison governor and some other cadres were helping the work went with a swing. Just before we finished the job Old Hsien and I brought in three more basketfuls.

As we were handing in our tools I heard Warder Wang saying to one of his colleagues, "I see Pu Yi's working seriously. He doesn't try to show off."

Old Hsien and I put down the basket of coal that we had been carrying with a pole over our shoulders and took our clothes from the tree on which they had been hanging. The governor asked me with a smile how my shoulder was. I looked at it and replied, "It doesn't hurt and it isn't swollen. It's a bit red, that's all."

"How's your appetite these days?"

"Three large bowls of rice or thirty big *jiaozi*."

"Insomnia?"

"I go to sleep as soon as my head hits the pillow. There's nothing wrong with me at all now."

All the others laughed, but no longer with the mocking laugh of the old days. I would not be hearing that laugh any more.

I had also made progress in other fields. I did not find it nearly as much of an effort to study *Political Economy* and *Historical Materialism* as I had before, and my clothes were now very nearly as clean as everyone else's. But what I had most confidence in was labour. As long as I was not asked to do such delicate jobs as making paper flowers I was always first-rate, and even those who were better at theoretical study than me had to take their hats off to me in this respect.

The admiration of my companions and the growth of my own confidence were due not so much to the implanting of a proper attitude to labour as to the new enthusiasm for labour that existed throughout society. From late 1957 onwards we noticed this from the press, family letters, and the prison staff themselves. It seemed that everyone was striving to participate in physical labour, which they saw as something glorious. Tens of thousands of government personnel went to the countryside, schools added periods of labour, and all kinds of voluntary short-term labour units appeared. In the prison itself the staff helped to make briquettes, prepared vegetables in the kitchen, looked after fires, and even brought the food to our cells. Before we were out of our beds in the morning we heard the sounds of wheelbarrows loaded with picks and shovels. This meant that the governor and staff had already set off to clear waste land outside the prison. All this showed us that in the new society labour was the standard by which men were measured. Those who were being remoulded could clearly be no exception. I forget who it was who told me that many people were under the delusion that labour was a punishment that God had inflicted on the human race, and that only the Communists saw it correctly as one of the human rights. I had by then lost all interest in gods or Buddhas and failed to see any connection between God and labour. We could all see that from the Communist point of view labour was something natural. I remember that once when we were clearing out a pile of rubbish the intellectual Section Head Li happened to come past. He picked up a shovel and set to, working more quickly and efficiently than we did and not thinking that there was anything odd in what he was doing.

The importance attached to labour and the enthusiasm for it in 1958 made a still deeper impression on us. I learnt many amazing new things from the letters I received from Peking. Second Sister, who had always stayed at home and taken no interest in anything else, now took part in the activities of her street committee by helping to set up a nursery for the children of working mothers. Fourth Sister, who worked in the former imperial palace, joined in a voluntary lake reconstruction project outside the Te Sheng Gate of Peking and was named as a "five good" activist. Third Sister and her husband participated in political studies organized by the committee of a district people's political consultative conference. Old Jun worked on the Ming Tombs Reservoir together with some other old men of the district people's political consultative conference and they were praised for a technical innovation they made. Fifth Sister and her husband Old Wan told me with pride that their eldest son, who had studied geology at university, was doing research on the uses of snow and ice and was now with an expedition exploring the mountains of the Northwest. Some of my nephews and Big Li were working as team leaders on a state farm on the outskirts of the capital. Everywhere was work and enthusiasm, and the war drums were pulsing for the attack on nature. In this historic campaign to lift the country out of backwardness everyone was doing his bit. My fellow-prisoners all got the same impression from their family letters. When we heard that Chairman Mao, Premier Chou and government ministers all took part in the building of the Ming Tombs Reservoir we could no longer be held back. We asked the study committee and the prison authorities to organize us for productive labour.

The prison authorities met our request. First they set up a workshop to manufacture electric motors, but as we were too few for the job it was given to the Chiang Kai-shek war criminals from other sections of the prison. We were then given other work that would train us in productive skills. We were put into five groups according to our abilities: animal raising, food processing, horticulture, market gardening, and medicine. I and four others formed the medical group. We combined labour with study. We had to clean up the clinic every day, do all the odd jobs, and help with auxiliary medical work; we also spent two hours a day reading up medicine and held discussions under the direction of Dr. Wen of the prison staff. My four colleagues had all been doctors before, and three of them revised their Western medicine while the other studied Chinese medicine with me. In addition we all did a course on acupuncture and moxibustion. This period of working in a small group gave me new confidence.

I was not as good as the others at helping with the medical work at first. The surgical cotton-wool swabs I made looked like lumps of worn cotton padding; when I took blood pressures I would concentrate on looking at my watch and forget to listen to the stethoscope, or else listen and forget to look; when I was learning to use the electrical equipment for treating blood pressure I was always in a muddle and could not do things right. I was only better than the others when it came to odd jobs and manual labour. I made up my mind to master my medical work. When the doctor or nurse had taught me something I would ask my fellow-students to go over it again with me and then practise it endlessly myself. Thus I gradually learnt to master my job as a medical assistant. One of the Japanese war criminals used to come in every day for electrical treatment, and he would always bow low to me afterwards and say "Thank you, doctor" to my great delight. As I wore a white coat and spectacles it was not surprising that he made this mistake; it also showed that my technique was good enough to win the patient's confidence. At the end of the first course Dr. Wen examined us, and I got full marks as well as the others.

When we were trial-producing electric motors I had been frustrated in my attempts to get any but the simplest jobs given me and I had regarded this as prejudice against me. But now I had learnt to be a medical assistant, had been mistaken for a full-fledged doctor, and had got full marks in my first exam. I was confident that I was not a complete idiot and would be able to master this skill; I would no longer need my 468 pieces of jewellery to support myself.

One day I asked to see the governor. As the old governor had been transferred to another post in which he had other responsibilities apart from our prison he did not come regularly, so I saw a deputy governor by the name of Chin who was now running the prison.

"The government ought to accept that jewellery formally," I said. "Anyhow, I lost the receipt for it ages ago."

I thought that I would have to explain about the jewellery to the deputy governor, but to my surprise he replied at once with a smile:

"I know all about it. Well then, are you confident that you will be able to support yourself through your own work?"

I spent the rest of that day giving information about each of the 468 pieces of jewellery while a secretary wrote it all down. When this was over I went into the courtyard with a feeling of relief, thinking that the words of the deputy governor were proof that I had made good progress. Was the day in sight when I would be a real man?

# The Test

I had rated myself too highly, as I found out when I was faced with a test.

At the time when the Great Leap Forward was taking place throughout the country, the prison governor put it to us that we needed to review our thoughts in order to clear away the ideological obstructions to our progress. The method used was for each of us to discuss in our study meetings the changes that had taken place in our thinking and the questions that we still did not understand.

When my turn came I had trouble. After I had spoken about my old ideology and the changes in many of my attitudes someone asked me: "A person with your background must have had very close ties with Japanese imperialism, and you may still hanker after it in your private thoughts and feelings. Your connections with it were no looser than ours, so why are you the only one not to mention this? Don't tell me that you have no such feelings."

"I have no feelings for the Japanese besides hatred. I differ from you on this."

This provoked a storm of protest. "Why aren't you more humble? You still think you're a cut above the rest of us, don't you?" "What sort of feelings for them do you have now? Are you more advanced than the rest of us?" Someone cited many examples from my past, such as the poems I had written when I went to Japan and the way I had helped the Japanese empress dowager up some steps, to show that in those days I had been more grateful to the Japanese than anyone else; he found my complete denial hard to accept. I replied that in the past I and the Japanese had made use of each other, so that there was no question of gratitude. I was not trying to cast aspersions on the others when I made this denial that was completely true, but nobody was prepared to accept my explanation. When I described my terror during my flight to Talitzukou I was asked:

"When the Japanese were going to send you to Tokyo they sent you three hundred million yen for your preparatory expenses. Didn't that make you grateful to Japanese imperialism?"

"Three hundred million yen?" I was astounded. "I don't know about any three hundred million yen."

This was not in fact a great mystery. When the Kwantung Army took the last gold reserves from the "Manchukuo" treasury it had announced to the world that they were being transported to Japan for the "Emperor of Manchukuo". I had never seen a cent of this money, and everyone knew this, which was why it had not been held against me. The only reason it had been brought up now was because they wanted to know about my state of mind at that time. Had I thought back calmly or humbly listened to what others had to say I would have been able to remember about it; but instead I asserted with confidence that I knew nothing whatever about it.

"You don't know about it?" Many of those who did know about it started shouting. "This business was handled by Chang Ching-hui and Takebe Rokuzo. Are you trying to repudiate your responsibility because Chang Ching-hui has died recently?" Someone else asked, "Didn't you write about this in your confession?" When I said that I had not they were even more incredulous: "But everyone knows about it." "This isn't a matter of three hundred or three thousand but of three hundred million."

That evening I cast my mind back and recalled that Hsi Hsia had told me in Talitzukou that the Japanese had taken all the gold of the "Bank of Manchukuo" with them on the pretext that it was to be used to support me in Japan. This must have been the three hundred million yen the others were talking about. But at the time I had been too worried about the immediate threat to my life to pay any attention to the matter. The next day I asked whether this was the money in question and was told that it was. I therefore told my study group about it.

"Why did you conceal this before?" asked several of the others in chorus.

"I didn't conceal it. I forgot about it."

"Do you still maintain that you forgot about it?"

"I've remembered about it now."

"Why didn't you remember about it before?"

"I've told you: I forgot. It's only natural to forget things sometimes, isn't it?"

This stimulated another storm of objections. "The further back you go the better your memory is, and the nearer things are the more you forget them. Most peculiar." "It's quite obvious that you were too scared to admit to it before." "If you haven't got the guts to admit your mistakes you'll never be remoulded." "None of us believe you. I can guarantee that the government will not fall for your stories again." "You're a word-twister and a liar." "How can as dishonest a man as yourself ever be remoulded?"

The more I tried to defend myself the less the others believed me. I was worried: obviously they all thought that I was lying. If they were unanimous would the governor take my word against theirs? These thoughts rushed through my brain, possessing me like devils, and I went silly. I had never been worried about this before, but I was now. At the thought that my word was not likely to be taken against all of theirs my courage melted away and I fell back into my bad old ways; I was prepared to forget about my principles so long as I could weather this storm. Wouldn't I be able to muddle my way through this crisis if I made a confession? Very well then. I said that I had not dared to mention this before as I was frightened that the government would punish me, but now they had all persuaded me to overcome my fears.

Although I had really forgotten about the three hundred million yen it seemed as if something that had been hidden in the bottom of my soul had now been exposed.

The members of my group showed no more interest in my problem after that, but I could not put it out of my mind. The more

I thought about it the uneasier I became, convinced that I had made a mess of the whole business. Although there was no shadow of doubt but that I had forgotten about the money, I had said that I had concealed the fact. For fear that the government would think me dishonest, I had told a lie. This affair had given me a sick conscience, and I was now suffering for what I had done.

In the past when I had suspected that every act of the prison staff implied their hostility towards me, I had been tortured by the fear of execution. Now I knew that the government did not want to kill me and was even helping me to become a new man. But just when I was full of hope I had encountered this new tribulation, and the more encouragement I received from the prison staff the worse I felt.

One day a warder told me that the governor wanted to see me. I assumed at once that it would be about the three hundred million yen, and I reckoned that he would probably be angry with me for continuing to try and conceal my crimes despite the way I had been treated. The other possibility I thought of was that he might be pleased with me for owning up to my crimes and writing a confession; he might even praise me for it, and that would be even worse. I went to the governor's reception room in fear and trepidation, only to find that he wanted to talk to me about something completely different.

This interview with the governor plunged me into still deeper gloom. The old governor had not been in the prison for a long time, and today there was another senior official with him. After inquiring about my studies and manual labour they asked what I was doing in the campaign to eliminate pests. The governor said he had been told that I had made some progress in killing flies and done my duty, but he did not know how successful I had been in the current campaign against rats and mice. I replied that I had not yet made a plan, but I thought that everyone in our cell would destroy at least one.

"What about you?" asked the senior official sitting next to the governor. I then recognized him to my horror as the man who had asked me in Harbin why I had not protested at the massacres committed by the Japanese. Without waiting for me to answer he asked another question: "Are you still against killing?" He roared with laughter and his guffaws calmed me down. I replied that I had long given up such ideas and was planning to destroy at least one mouse during this campaign.

The governor shook his head. "Your plan is too conservative. Even the children in primary schools plan to destroy more than one each."

"I'll do my best to kill at least two."

The governor interrupted to say that he would not set a limit for me and would let me kill as many as I could. With this he sent me back to my cell.

I returned to my cell with a heavy heart. This was not because I was alarmed at the prospect of catching mice, a thing I had never done in my life, but because of the thoughts that this conversation had aroused. I remembered how the governor had specially inspected my plan during the anti-fly campaign and how he had encouraged me when I had learnt to wash my clothes. The prison authorities had devoted so much effort to teaching me how to become a man; but now I felt that even if I caught a hundred mice I would not be able to atone for my wrongdoing.

When Warder Chiang, who had just come off duty, saw me sitting in the club by myself he asked me if I had thought of any way of catching mice and offered to help me make a trap. In my total ignorance of how to catch them I did not even know where mice lived. I gladly accepted his offer, and as I was learning to make mouse-traps my worries came back to me.

We talked as we made the traps, and Warder Chiang told me about his childhood. Thus it was that I chanced to hear about the sufferings he had endured. I had never imagined that this calm and kind young man had suffered so much injustice in the days of "Manchukuo". He had been a typical victim of the policy of combining households and villages. After his family had been compulsorily moved several times they spent the winter in a shack and all caught typhoid fever. His seven brothers all died, leaving him as the only survivor. The dead brothers had to be buried naked.

His story ended when we finished making the mouse-traps. He took me to find some mouse holes, and I followed silently, wondering how a young man whose brothers had all been killed by the "Manchukuo" regime could today be helping me. Had all the other warders, who were so kind to us prisoners, suffered like him in the past? I asked him, "Did Warder Wang and Warder Liu suffer such injustice under 'Manchukuo'?"

"Everyone was ground down in those days. Warder Wang was taken for forced labour three times, and Warder Liu was left with no choice but to join the anti-Japanese army."

I realized without having to ask again that all the members of the prison staff who were of Northeastern origin had suffered in the days of "Manchukuo".

The guidance of Warder Chiang enabled me to kill six mice. When Warders Wang and Liu heard that I had caught some mice they came in to see my "captives" as if this were a marvellous achievement, and they praised me for my progress. Their congratulations made me feel most uneasy: while these former victims of the "Manchukuo" regime were attaching such importance to my progress I was still deceiving them.

I went to work in the clinic every day as usual, sweeping the room, taking blood pressures, giving electric therapy and studying Chinese medicine; and the short Japanese war criminal continued to bow to me. But now I did not hear what he was saying, the *Outlines of Chinese Medicine* became hard to understand, and I often had to take people's blood pressure several times over. My sisters and brothers-in-law wrote about their new triumphs in their letters and expressed the hope that I would soon be remoulded and able to share their happy life. I now read such words as a rebuke.

When autumn came round we did a crash job of making coal briquettes, and the deputy governor and cadres all lent a hand in preparing the fuel to be used in the hothouses in the winter. I put all my energies into carrying coal while avoiding drawing the attention of the governor. If he had praised me then it would have been worse than a dressing down.

One day I had been busy with something else and by the time I came round to giving electric therapy there were two people waiting. One was the Japanese who always bowed to me, and as he was a regular patient I decided to treat him first. To my surprise he gestured to the other man and said in Chinese, "Please be first. I'm in no hurry."

"You came first, so you should be treated first," said the other man, a Chiang Kai-shek war criminal.

"Thank you very much, but I'm in no hurry. I can sit here and wait. I'm going to be released shortly," he added as an explanation.

I had not known before that he spoke such good Chinese, and as I arranged the equipment for the Chiang Kai-shek war criminal I cast several glances in his direction. He was looking gravely at the wall opposite. A moment later his gaze turned to the ceiling.

"This room was a torture chamber in the 'Manchukuo' days," he said in a low voice. I did not know whether he was talking to himself or to us. "Who knows how many patriotic Chinese were tortured here?"

After a pause he pointed to the ceiling. "In those days chains used to hang from there and the walls were covered in blood." His eyes swept the walls and settled on the glass-fronted cabinet. After another period of silence he spoke again. "When the Chinese gentlemen were repairing this building we thought that it was being restored as a torture chamber where revenge would be meted out to us. Later on, when we saw white-coated doctors we thought that we were going to be dissected in experiments. We never imagined that a clinic was being built to cure our illnesses." His voice was choked with sobs.

The Chiang Kai-shek war criminal had gone now, so I asked the Japanese to come over for his treatment. He stood up and said respectfully, "No, thank you. I came to look at this room. As I have missed Dr. Wen, would you please tell him that while I have no right to thank him, I would like to thank him on behalf of my mother. Thank you too, doctor."

"I'm not a doctor; I'm Pu Yi."

I do not know whether he replied or not. He bowed, turned, and went out of the room.

I could not hold out any longer. No matter how hard it might be for the governor to understand, I had to put an end to my lie.

It happened that the old governor was in the prison at the time, and he asked me to come for a talk. I opened the door of his reception room and saw the familiar grey-haired figure behind the desk looking at a pile of papers. He asked me to sit down, and a moment later he put the papers away and looked up.

"I've been looking at the record of your cell. How are things? Have you been having any ideological problems recently?"

Now that the vital moment had come I hesitated. I looked at the minutes of our cell's meetings and thought of the unanimity with which the others had attacked me. I could not help wondering whether there was any point in telling the truth as it was my word against all of theirs. But I could not keep the deception up any longer.

"Tell me what the meetings of your group are like."

"They're good. They have summarized our thinking correctly."

"Hm?" The governor raised his eyebrows. "Give me more details."

I realized that I was breathing unnaturally. "I spoke the truth when I said that," I replied. "The conclusion that I had been too worried to mention things was quite true. But there were one or two cases. . . ."

"Go on. You know how much I want to understand your thinking."

I knew that I had to speak out now, and with my heart pounding I poured out a breathless account of the whole business. The governor listened with close attention. When I had finished he asked:

"Why was it so difficult to say that? What were you frightened of?"

"I was scared because it was my word against all of theirs."

"If you speak the truth you have nothing to fear," said the governor with the utmost gravity. "Do you think that the government can't investigate the matter for itself and reach its own verdict? You still don't really understand that to be a real man you need courage. You must have the courage to speak the truth."

I wept. I had not imagined that he would be able to see everything so clearly. What else was there for me to say?

# Special Pardon

### PROPOSAL OF THE CENTRAL COMMITTEE OF THE COMMUNIST PARTY OF CHINA TO THE STANDING COMMITTEE OF THE NATIONAL PEOPLE'S CONGRESS

The Central Committee of the Communist Party of China proposes to the Standing Committee of the National People's Congress that in celebration of the tenth anniversary of the foundation of the great People's Republic of China a number of reformed war criminals, counter-revolutionaries and common criminals should be granted special pardons.

We have won a great victory in the socialist revolution and the socialist construction of our country. Our motherland is flourishing, production and construction are forging ahead, and the living standards of the people are being steadily raised. The government of the people's democratic dictatorship is unprecedentedly consolidated and strong. The people of the whole country are more politically conscious and better organized than ever before. The political and economic state of the nation is excellent. The policy of the Party and the People's Government of combining punishment with leniency in dealing with counter-revolutionaries and other criminals, and the policy of combining reform through labour with ideological education have achieved great successes. The majority of the prisoners now under detention have been remoulded to a greater or lesser extent, and a considerable number of them have genuinely reformed.

In these circumstances the Central Committee of the Communist Party of China believes that at this time, when we are celebrating the tenth anniversary of the founding of the People's Republic of China, it would be fitting to announce and put into effect a special pardon for a number of war criminals, counter-revolutionaries and common criminals who have really reformed. The adoption of this measure will help to change negative factors into positive ones and be of great assistance to their further remoulding, as well as to that of the other criminals still in captivity. It will enable them to realize that under our great socialist system their future lies in reform.

The Central Committee of the Communist Party of China requests that the Standing Committee of the National People's Congress will consider this proposal and reach an appropriate decision.

Mao Tse-tung
*Chairman of the Central Committee*
*of the Communist Party of China*

September 14, 1959

A resolution on these lines was passed by the Standing Committee of the National People's Congress, and on September 17 Chairman Liu Shao-chi proclaimed the special pardon.

The delight with which Chairman Mao's proposal and Chairman Liu's order were greeted in the prison was unforgettable. After the announcer had read the last sentence there was a moment of silence around the radio followed by an explosion of cheers, slogans and applause. It was as if ten thousand strings of firecrackers had been let off at once, and it went on for a long time.

From that moment on the morning of September 18 onwards the whole prison was excited. All sorts of views were expressed: the Party and Government were always as good as their word; we now had a future and it would not be long before we were out; we would be pardoned in batches; we would all be let out at once. Who would be in the first group to be released? Most of us realized that pardon would depend on whether one had reformed or not, and some regretted their tendency to slack off recently. There were those who said modestly that they were not yet up to the standard while they discreetly packed their clothes, burnt their discarded notebooks and threw away their worn-out socks.

The yard was a hubbub of voices during the break. I heard Old Yuan asking Old Hsien, "Who's going to be in the first lot?"

"It's bound to be those who have done best in their studies recently. You've got a good chance."

"No, I'm not good enough; but I'm sure you are."

"Me? If they let me out I'd go to Peking and send you some Peking specialities. I'd fancy some Peking dates."

I heard Big Mouth's voice from another part of the yard. "They should either let all of us out or none."

"You've got no confidence in yourself," someone said to him. "You're scared of being left behind."

"Leave me behind? Unless they keep Pu Yi here they won't keep me."

Even I was quite sure that he must be right. On the following day, I think, the deputy governor asked me what I thought of the special pardon.

"I think that I am bound to be the very last — that is, if I can ever remould myself. All the same, I shall try my hardest."

For most of the prisoners pardon and release meant reunion with their families, but this did not affect me. My mother had died long ago, my father had been dead since 1951, and my last wife had divorced me in 1956. Even if they had still been alive none of them would have understood me as well as the people here. Nobody I had known before could teach me how to be a real man as the staff here did. One might say that release meant regaining freedom and light, but it was in prison that I had found truth and light, and won the freedom of knowing about the world. From my point of view pardon would mean that I was qualified as a human being and could begin a new life that would have real significance.

I had received a letter from Old Wan recently. He told me that the son of his who was studying to become a geologist had led a team of mountaineers in the conquest of the Chilien Mountains. After this he had gone on to Tibet just at the time when the serf-owners rebelled, where he and his fellow-students had fought on the side of the serfs. After the crushing of the rebellion they had gone on to assault new peaks. In his letter that was so full of pride and happiness Old Wan often mentioned how glad he was that his son had been brought up in the present and not in the accursed past.

Today his son had a brilliant future. Were it not for today he would not have had such a son, nor would he himself have been working alongside all other true Chinese citizens as a translator and a builder of socialism. He hoped that I would soon be sharing this happiness that we had never known before. He believed that I was heading that way.

A month after the proclamation of the special pardon we went on another visit, this time to the Tahuofang Reservoir near Shenyang. When we had last come here in 1957 we had seen an endless mass of people working in the valley, and I had learnt from a table-top model that it was going to have a capacity of 2,110 million cubic metres — enough to hold a flood that might only occur once in a thousand years — and would irrigate 80,000 hectares of land. When we made our second visit this mighty project had been completed for a year, and a vast man-made sea stretched before our eyes, bounded by a dam that was 48 metres high, 8 metres wide at the top, 330 metres wide at the base and 1,367 metres long. When Furumi Tadayuki, the Japanese war criminal who had been deputy head of the General Affairs Office of the "Manchukuo State Council", came back from this visit he told all of us about his impressions in the club. Part of his talk went something like this:

"As I stood on the dam at the Tahuofang Reservoir I was struck with its grandeur, beauty and peace. I felt that this was a victory that had been won over nature and a source of pride and joy to the Chinese people as they continue the conquest of nature. . . . The sight of this reservoir reminded me of when I stood on the dam of the Shuifeng Reservoir in the old days as head of the planning department of the General Affairs Office, deputy minister of economics, and deputy head of the General Affairs Office of 'Manchukuo'. In those days I thought with pride that the only people in Asia who could wage such struggles against nature and build so big a project were the Japanese; I despised the Chinese and thought them completely incapable of such a thing. The Chinese workers were dressed in rags, and I thought of myself as an entirely different kind of being from them: I looked down upon them with arrogance as if I were great, brilliant and exalted.

"But the men who worked on the Tahuofang Reservoir now had tremendous energy because they were full of confidence. They toiled selflessly. They were full of life, their faces shining with pride and happiness. I, standing on a corner of the dam and surveying the scene, was a war criminal who had committed the most serious crimes against the Chinese people. Who was right?"

On one side were the Chinese people, "their faces shining with pride and happiness", and on the other was a war criminal. In my mind I was leaving one side and crossing over to the other, the right side. This was the only solution I had found after ten years of thinking it out.

The past ten years had taught me the rudiments of the difference between right and wrong. The victory in the Korean War; the confessions of the Japanese war criminals; China's diplomatic successes and unprecedented standing in world public opinion; the changes in the country, society, my nationality, my own clan and myself — all this had happened under the leadership of that very Communist Party that I had viewed with hatred, prejudice and fear ten years ago. The events of these ten years and the history of the past century or so had taught me that the decisive force in history was the common people whom I had so despised. It was inevitable that the first part of my life should have ended in disaster, and that imperialism and the reactionary Peiyang power on which I had relied should have collapsed. I now understood that Chen Pao-shen, Cheng Hsiao-hsu, Yoshioka, the gods and the Bodhisattvas had been unable to tell me what my destiny was. I now knew that my fate was to be a man who supported himself through his own labour and brought benefits to humanity. The best fate was one that was linked with that of the people.

"One must take the side that is right."

This needed courage, and the proclamation of the special pardon gave me courage, as it did to all the others.

We put more effort into our work and study, and many of us were awaiting eagerly the next assessment of our studies. The food-processing team now made bean-curd that was both soft and white, the stock-breeding team had fattened up their pigs so that they were even finer than ever, and in the medical team we had stopped making mistakes. Even Big Mouth had started to behave himself and was not quarrelling any more.

More than a month passed. One evening the deputy governor came to talk to me about the special pardon. "What have you been thinking about for the past couple of months?" he asked me.

I told him what I have mentioned above and also said that some people seemed to me to have been remoulded quite well. I mentioned the food-processing and pig-breeding teams and some individuals who had been praised for their studies recently.

"You find it quite easy now to think of the good points of others," said the deputy governor with a smile. "What would you think if you were included in the special pardon?"

"It's out of the question," I replied, laughing.

Out of the question. That was what I thought as I went back to my cell. "But . . . if?" The very thought of this made me tense. Later I concluded that I might be pardoned in the future, but it would be bound to be a long time. My prospects were not so dim. I imagined myself, Old Wan, Little Jui and the others taking our place among ordinary people and doing ordinary things. In these daydreams I was given a job as a medical assistant in a hospital, the sort of job I had read about in the papers. But I was sure that it would be a long time before the people gave their approval and accepted me as one of them. At the thought of my future happiness I was almost unable to sleep.

The next day we were ordered to assemble in the club. Facing us was a broad strip of crimson cloth stretched across the stage that took my breath away. On it was written "Fushun War Criminals Prison Special Pardon Meeting".

A representative of the Supreme People's Court, the two governors and some other people were sitting on the platform. Below the platform all was silent except for the pounding of my heart.

After a few words from the prison governor the representative of the Supreme People's Court went to the middle of the stage and read from a sheet of paper. "Aisin-Gioro Pu Yi".

471

My heart leapt. I went and stood in front of the stage and heard someone reading out:

NOTICE OF A SPECIAL PARDON
FROM THE SUPREME PEOPLE'S COURT OF
THE PEOPLE'S REPUBLIC OF CHINA

In accordance with the Special Pardon Order issued by the Chairman of the People's Republic of China on September 17, 1959 this Court has investigated the case of the "Manchukuo" war criminal Aisin-Gioro Pu Yi.

The war criminal Aisin-Gioro Pu Yi, male, 54 years old, of the Manchu nationality, and from Peking, has now served ten years' detention. As a result of remoulding through labour and ideological education during his captivity he has shown that he has genuinely reformed. In accordance with the stipulations of Clause I of the Special Pardon Order he is therefore to be released.

Supreme People's Court of
the People's Republic of China

December 4, 1959

Before I had heard this to the end I burst into tears. My motherland had made me into a man.

# A New Chapter

I was on the train. Outside was a snow-covered plain, bright and vast, unfolding before me like my own future. Inside the train I was surrounded by ordinary workers. This was the first time in my life that I had sat with them or shared a train with them. I was going to live with them and build with them; I was going to — no, I had already — become one of them.

Soon after boarding the train at Fushun something happened that showed me at once the quality of the society that I was coming into and of the people I was among. A train attendant and a woman passenger came into our carriage looking for a place for a little girl they were carrying. There was an empty seat behind me, and the man sitting next to it vacated his seat as well for them. The woman laid the girl down on the seats while she stood over her, clearly most anxious. Another passenger asked her if the child was ill, and, if so, why she was out of doors. The woman's reply astonished us. She was a teacher in a primary school near the station, and the girl was a pupil of hers who had suddenly felt a bad pain in her abdomen during class. The school health worker had suspected appendicitis and said that she should be sent to hospital immediately. As the girl's parents both worked in a distant mine there was not time to ask them to come and take the child to hospital, and it would also have taken too long to send her to the mine hospital to be operated on. The teacher decided to put the girl straight on the Shenyang train. The platform staff had allowed her to pay for the tickets on the train itself and told her that they would tell Shenyang by phone to look after them. This incident made me think of the words of Tao Yuan-ming:[1] "From the time of our birth we are brothers, needing no kinship of flesh." This thought is shared by many people today. Then it occurred to me that what Mencius[2] had said about looking after the aged and young of other families as well as one's own had actually come about in the present day. Judging by such conduct, the society into which I was moving was even finer than I had imagined.

On December 9 I arrived in Peking, the home town that I had left thirty-five years earlier. On the platform of the magnificent railway station I saw Fifth Sister and Fourth Brother whom I had not met for over ten and more than twenty years respectively. As we took each other's hands I heard them call me "elder brother", a familiar form of address that my brothers and sisters had never used with me in the old days. I felt that a new life was beginning in my family.

I said goodbye to Section Head Li who had come with us and to Old Meng. Old Meng was one of the eight Chiang Kai-shek war

---

[1] A poet of the Eastern Tsin Dynasty who lived in the late fourth and early fifth centuries A.D.

[2] Thinker and educationalist (372-289 B.C.).

criminals in our prison who had received a pardon, along with Kuo Wen-lin, a former "Manchukuo" general, and myself. He went off with his wife who had come to meet him. Fourth Brother carried my black leather case as I walked off the platform with Fifth Sister and her husband Old Wan on either side of me. When we were off the platform I looked at the station clock and pulled out my pocket watch. Before leaving Fushun the governor had chosen this watch from the pile of things I had presented to the government in jail and told me to keep it. I protested that as it had been bought with money derived through exploitation I did not want it. The governor replied that the people were giving it to me now, so I should keep it. This watch was the French gold watch I had bought in the shop on the edge of the Legation Quarter in Peking when I was trying to shake off my father's chief steward on my way to the foreign legations in 1924. On that day my record of disgrace had started. Now this same watch was marking the beginning of my new life as I set it by Peking time.

On the day he gave me that watch the governor had said to the ten of us who were being released that when we went back home to our families and our neighbours we should apologize to them for the wrongs we had done them in the past. "I believe," he said, "that your neighbours and relations will forgive you, provided that you behave well and serve the people conscientiously." These words were fully borne out when I went to the home of Fifth Sister and Old Wan. Everyone in their compound was kind to me. The next morning I wanted to do something for the neighbours, and when I saw that some people were sweeping the lane I took a broom and joined them. When we had swept as far as the entrance to the lane I could not find my way back home and went into a stranger's home. They guessed what had happened and took me home. They said there was no need for me to thank them as we were all from the same street, and even if we had not been there was nothing odd about people helping each other in the new society.

I went to see my uncle Tsai Tao and his family. I learnt that our clan was flourishing. He had addressed the National People's Congress on his findings during his tour of the minority areas. I heard my cousin Pu Chin play his *ku chin* and watched while he did some calligraphy for me that was better than ever. I also saw a picture of flowers and birds that Pu Chien had recently painted. I went to visit Second Sister and found that she was now running a nursery. Her husband, a postal engineer, told me that she was so busy that the headaches she used to suffer from had disappeared. I also visited Fourth Sister, and Third, Sixth and Seventh Sisters and their husbands. Fourth Sister was working in the archives of the former palace, Sixth Sister and her husband were both painters, and Seventh Sister and her husband were teaching.

I was even more struck by the second generation. On the day of the Spring Festival countless youngsters with red scarves round their necks swarmed all over my uncle's house. Of the older members of that generation I met the former member of the People's Volunteers who had distinguished himself in action, the Peking woman motor-bicycle champion, the leader of the mountaineering team, the doctor, the nurse, the teacher, and the car driver. Most of the youngsters were doing specialized vocational training or studying in middle school. Some of them had joined the Communist Party and the Youth League, and all the rest of them were doing their best to attain these honours.

I also met many friends from the old days. Shang Yen-ying was now a member of the Institute of History and Literature. When I saw him he was lying on a couch; he was so old he could no longer speak clearly. When he saw me his expression became constrained and grave, and he tried to get up. I took his hand and said, "You are old and ill, so you should lie down and rest. We are members of the new society now, and we can enjoy a normal relationship. When you are better we will serve the people together." The formal expression vanished from his face and he nodded to me with a slight smile. "I'll go along with you," he said. "I'm going along with the Communist Party," I replied. "I will too," was his answer. I met some of my old friends who had been palace eunuchs and found out how they were doing. The local authorities ran a special home for them where they could spend their declining years in peace.

Practically everyone I met on the first day said: "Now that you're back you must have a good look around — you've never been able to wander round Peking before." I told them that the first thing I wanted to see was Tien An Men, the Gate of Heavenly Peace.

I already knew Tien An Men Square well from films, papers and letters. On the screen I had seen the parades being reviewed by Chairman Mao, and I had watched festival celebrations. I had seen pictures in the papers of traffic policemen taking kindergarten children across the road, and of Chinese-made Red Flag and East Wind cars parked there. I knew that the Great Hall of the People had been built in ten months, and I had heard about the reactions to the square of foreign guests from all over the world. At last I was here in the place I had dreamed about for so long.

The majestic Tien An Men Gate that stood in front of me was a witness of the motherland's change from misery to happiness, and of the change from the old Pu Yi to the new Pu Yi. On my left was the imposing Great Hall of the People in which the affairs of the nation were decided, including the special pardon under which I had been allowed to start a new life. On my right was the Revolutionary Museum and behind me was the Monument to the Revolutionary Heroes. They told me what a bitter struggle so many heroes and martyrs had waged for over a century to achieve the fruition of today, of which I too was a beneficiary.

It was in Tien An Men Square that I took my first walk feeling free, safe, happy and proud. I, Fifth Sister and my cousin Pu Chien strolled slowly to the west. When we reached the Cultural Palace of the Nationalities with its white walls and blue roof my sister asked me with concern: "Elder brother, are you tired? Is this the first time you've walked so far?" "I'm not tired," I replied, "for the very reason that this is the first time."

"The first time" were three words that constantly cropped up as I began my new life. "The first time" was always difficult, but I was too excited to feel uneasy about it.

I went to the barber's for the first time, or, strictly speaking, for the second time, as I had once been out to the Chung Yuan Company for a haircut thirty years ago in Tientsin. At any rate, what happened now happened to me for the first time. I sat in the chair and saw a mysterious object I had noticed in a Harbin department store. I asked the barber what it was that was making a humming noise at the next chair and he told me it was a hair-drier. "Do you dry or cut the hair first?" I asked. This question astonished him. "Haven't you ever had your hair cut before?" He thought I was trying to pull his leg. When I realized this I burst out laughing, and when I heard the hair-drier humming over my own head I felt more pleased than ever.

The first time I rode on a bus I gave my cousin Pu Chien a fright. As I was waiting in the bus queue I saw other people standing aside for old people and children to get on first, so I let a woman who was standing next to me get on before me. I did not realize that she was the conductress. Seeing that I was not getting on, she jumped aboard; then the door closed behind her and the bus moved off. A few moments later my cousin came rushing back from the next stop, and we started to laugh out loud at each other when he was still some way off. "Don't worry," I said with full confidence, "nothing can possibly happen." With so many people looking after me what had I to worry about? That very morning I had collected a leather wallet from a shop near Third Sister's place where I had left it by mistake. It was impossible for me to get lost.

The Peking municipal authorities organized a series of visits for a number of us who had come here after special pardon, including the former Kuomintang generals Tu Yu-ming, Wang Yao-wu, Sung Hsi-lien and others. This was to help us to know Peking better and get used to everyday life. We saw some new factories, all kinds of public utilities that had been expanded since liberation, some urban people's communes, and other places; these visits went on for about two months. Finally the others insisted that we go to the former palace with me as temporary guide.

What I found most surprising was that the air of decay and collapse I had known there when I left had disappeared. There was fresh paint everywhere. The curtains for the doors, windows and beds, the cushions, the tablecloths and everything else were all new. I heard later these were all made in the Palace Museum's own factory after the original patterns. Very little of the palace collection of jade, porcelain, calligraphy, paintings, and other *objets d'art* had been left after the depredations of the Peiyang warlord government, the Kuomintang government, and its various guardians, myself included. I did find, however, that quite a few things had been bought back by the museum or presented by collectors. The picture "River-side Scene at the Ching Ming Festival" by the Sung artist Chang Tse-tuan, for example, which had been stolen by Pu Chieh and myself, had now been bought back.

In the imperial garden I saw children playing in the sun and old men sipping tea. I sniffed the spring fragrance of the ancient cypresses and felt that the sun was shining brighter here than it had ever done before. I was sure that the former palace had taken on a new lease of life.

In March 1960 I was sent to the Peking Botanical Gardens of the Institute of Botany of the Chinese Academy of Sciences. Here I spent half my time working and half studying. This was a preparatory stage before I took up the post in which I was to serve the people. Under the guidance of the technical personnel I learnt how to plant seeds, look after seedlings, and transplant them in the hot-houses. I spent the other part of the day either studying or writing this book.

In the first part of my life I did not know what the world "family" meant, and I only began to have some family feeling in my last years in Fushun. Before I had been in the Botanical Gardens for long I felt that I had a second home, living as I was in a friendly and co-operative atmosphere. Once I realized when I came back from a walk that I had lost my watch; I was sadly convinced that I had gone too far to be able to find it again and I gave it up for lost. When Old Liu, my room-mate, heard that I had lost it he asked me in detail about the route I had taken, and set off at once although he was off duty. To my great embarrassment many of the others also found out what had happened, and all of them who were off duty went out to look for the watch. In the end Old Liu found it in front of the dining-hall of a brigade of the Evergreen People's

Commune and brought it back in the highest of spirits. I felt that I was being given back much more than just a watch.

That summer a militia unit was formed in the Botanical Gardens, and it drilled every day. I applied to join, but the others all said that I was over the age limit. "I am a member of the big family of the motherland," I protested, "so I too should be allowed to defend her." I made my point and was allowed to join in the training as an over-age militiaman. Soon I was able to achieve another ambition and demonstrate in Tien An Men Square. The occasion was the march in support of the Japanese people's struggle against the Japan-U.S. Security Treaty.

This was the time when I began to undertake social activities, which made me feel that I was on the same side as the people of the whole of China and the rest of the world who were fighting for peace, democracy, national independence and socialism.

On November 26, 1960 I received a voter's card with my name on it. It seemed the most valuable thing I had ever had in my life, and when I put the ballot-paper into the red box I felt that I was the happiest man on earth. I, along with my 650 million compatriots, was now the owner of our 9,600,000 square kilometres of land. The help that was being extended from this land to the oppressed peoples and nations of the world was great and reliable.

In March 1961 I completed my preparatory stage and took up the post in which I was to serve the people: I became a literary and historical worker for the Historical Materials Commission of the National Committee of the Chinese People's Political Consultative Conference.

In this job I worked on literary and historical material of the late Ching and Peiyang warlord periods. I often came across familiar names and historical events with which I was connected. Most of the authors of these materials were participants in or eyewitnesses of the events they described, and they and I were all witnesses of the history of this period. I gained a clearer view of the developments in the period from these rich source-materials. The lady Yehonala (Empress Dowager Tzu Hsi), Yuan Shih-kai, Tuan Chi-jui, Chang Tso-lin, and all those other figures who were cast aside by history had seemed in their day to wield overwhelming power; while the people, whom they butchered and oppressed, had seemed helpless. Writers of the type of Hu Shih had cheered such figures on; the old-timers had put their hopes of restoration on them; and they had inflated themselves to ever greater proportions in the belief that the powers who backed them would support them for ever. But they turned out to be only paper tigers when they perished in the flames of history, and history was the people. "In appearance, the reactionaries are terrifying, but in reality they are not so powerful. From a long-term point of view, it is not the reactionaries but the people who are really powerful." My own experiences had made me accept the truth of this, and I was going to proclaim it to the people through my work and in my capacity as a witness.

I also continued to write this book.

My office helped me in many ways and provided me with much valuable material, and with the enthusiastic help of many other friends I was able to use many books and documents from archives as well as information that had been specially hunted out. Some of this was hand-copied for me by friends I had never even met, some of it was checked by comrades in my publishing house who went on long journeys to do so, and some was recorded by old gentlemen who had witnessed the events with their own eyes. Much of the inaccessible material was provided by archives and libraries; I should like to mention in particular the National Archives, the History Museum, Peking Library, and the Capital Library, where the comrades made special searches and compilations for me. I was embarrassed by the amount of concern and support I received, but there is in fact nothing unusual about it in our country, where anyone who is doing something that will be useful to the people or is proclaiming the truth will find interest and help everywhere; apart from what he gets from the Party and government.

My book drew the interest of many foreign friends. I was visited by foreign journalists and visitors who asked me about my experiences, particularly my reform over the past ten years. One Latin American said that it showed him once again how great Mao Tsetung's thought was, and urged me to finish my book soon. An

Asian friend said: "I hope you will send me a copy of the English edition of your book as soon as it comes out so that I can translate it into my own language and let the people of my country read your amazing story."

In 1962 our bitter struggle against the difficulties originating at home and abroad was brilliantly successful, and that year brought me further happiness. I was invited to sit on the National Committee of the Chinese People's Political Consultative Conference and to hear the reports at the National People's Congress on the construction of the motherland. On May 1, I and my bride Li Shu-hsien started our own little home, and this ordinary home was, to me, something extraordinary.

This is the new chapter. This is how my new life began. When I think of my home, my voter's card, and the boundless prospects that stretch out before me I will never forget how I gained this new life.

There is another story I should tell about the policy of remoulding criminals, the policy that gave me a new life. As my nephew Little Jui said, I have to include it in this book.

In the summer of 1960 I went to Fragrance Hill Park with Little Jui, and we talked about the very first changes in each of our minds and what it was that first shook us.

Little Jui talked about Little Hsiu first. Little Ku had been shaken when he saw a Chinese train at Suifenho Station where only foreign trains had been seen before, and Little Hsiu had been made to feel that his past life had been futile by the welcome given to the girl worker who had lost a hand. Then Jui talked about himself. "There were many things I shall never forget. The first was when I broke a window-pane while cleaning it soon after I started work. The moment the pane hit the floor a warder came running in. I was terrified, but to my surprise he asked me if I had hurt myself. I said that I was all right, though I had smashed a pane of glass. He said that a piece of glass did not matter, but I had better be careful not to cause anyone injury."

"Things like that have happened to me," I replied. "At first I was most concerned about whether I would be killed or not and doubted whether the policy of leniency would apply to me. What made me see that I had some chance and thus gradually brought me round to a more optimistic view was the unexpected way I was let off scot-free after handing over the stuff I had been hiding in the bottom of my suitcase. Talking of that, I must thank you for the help you gave me then."

"My help?" asked Little Jui, his eyes wide open. "Didn't the prison governor tell you what really happened?"

"Yes, he did. During the time of accusations and acknowledging guilt I wrote a self-criticism about it to the governor after I owned up under Little Ku's questioning at the big meeting. After the New Year I told the governor that I had not mentioned the note you sent me for fear of getting you into trouble. He told me that he knew all about the business and had asked you to write the note in order to help me hand the stuff over on my own initiative. The governor was very conscientious, but you helped me too."

"So you still don't know the details. I didn't want to write that note and was in favour of searching you and confiscating the things to punish you. This is something I have to tell you, and you must include it in your book."

Only now did I learn the full story. Little Jui had divulged my secret to the governor some time previously and asked him to confiscate the stuff. The governor had refused: "It would be very easy to find it but it wouldn't help him in his remoulding. Be patient. It will be much better for him to take the initiative in handing the things over when he's more politically aware." A long time later Little Jui had asked the governor to make a search. The governor's reply had been that different people's thinking developed at different speeds and that it was no use being impatient. The Communist Party was sure that the great majority of criminals could be remoulded when they were in the power of the people, though the process varied. What mattered was not the jewels or the prison rules but how best I could be helped to remould myself. "You must understand," the governor had said about me, "that because of his unique background he finds it hard to believe immediately in the People's Government's policy of leniency to those who confess. If we were to make a search he would lose this chance of understanding the policy. Leave the initiative to him. Rather than make a hurried search you should think out some way of hastening his awakening." Little Jui then thought of writing me a note. When nothing happened for several days after he had passed it to me he grew impatient again and said to the governor, "Pu Yi will never wake up and he hasn't got a scrap of awareness. Why don't we search him?" "It is more important than ever not to be impatient at this point," was the governor's reply. In the end, of course, I had handed the jewels over in desperation; and from that moment on I began to see that there was a new way out for me.

"From then on I understood that the government really believed that the majority of criminals could be reformed," said Little Jui with emotion. "You know yourself that you were still trying to resist and deceive the government then, and the prison authorities knew all about it. Even before the investigators came we had told the government about everything. But from that time on the prison authorities believed that you could be remoulded and were anxious for you to study and reform."

We were standing on the slopes of Fragrance Hill looking towards Peking, which was bathed in sunlight. I thought of one thing after another that had happened in the past ten years. I recalled the grey hair of the old prison governor and the lively speech of the younger deputy governor. I thought of all the warders, doctors, nurses, and other members of the prison staff. When I tried to deceive them; when I used all kinds of shameful methods to resist them; when my ignorance, incompetence and stupidity were thoroughly revealed; when I was in total despair about myself and felt that I could not bear to live a moment longer — at those times these Communist Party members had held firmly to their belief that I could be remoulded and led patiently to becoming a new man.

"Man" was the very first word I learnt to read in my first reader, the *Three Character Classic*, but I had never understood its meaning before. Only today, with the Communist Party and the policy of remoulding criminals, have I learnt the significance of this magnificent word and become a real man.

# INDEX

## A

Academy of Chinese Painting, 425
"Administrative Committee for the Northeast", 240
Aisin-Gioro clan, 3, 17-18, 129, 196, 228, 275-276, 423-424, 429, 438
Akiyama Hiroshi, 448
Aldrovani, Count, 268
"All-Manchurian Assembly", 253
Alston, Beilby (British minister), 107
Ama-terasu-o-mi-Kami, see Heaven Shining Bright Deity
Amakasu Masahiko, 234-235, 237-239, 254
America, 13, 83, 157, 187, 189, 190-191, 210, 242, 267, 269, 293, 324, 435
Amur River (Black Dragon River), 205
An Te-hai (eunuch), 5
Anhwei, 88, 98, 184
Anhwei clique, 105
Anshan, 444
Anshan Iron and Steel Works, 444
"Anti-Communist Autonomous Government of Eastern Hopei", 283
Anti-Japanese Allied Armies, 288, 320, 387, 392, 414, 451
Anti-Japanese National Salvation Society, 288
Antung, 309
Arita Hachiro, 206
"Army of Pacification", 176, 183
Articles for Favourable Treatment, 36, 37-38, 79, 85, 96, 123, 157, 165, 175, 228
Ashikaga Takauji, 219
"Asia Revival Council", 384
Asnis (Captain), 333-334
"Autonomous Military Government of Inner Mongolia", 283
Awaji Maru, 233

## B

Babojab, Prince, 86-87, 97, 376
"Bank of Manchukuo", 459
"Big Mouth", see Chang Huan-hsiang
Black Dragon Society (Black Ocean Association), 197, 203-206, 225, 275
"Boxers", see Yi Ho Tuan
Britain, 4, 13, 108, 115, 189-190, 197, 210, 221-222, 268, 293, 302, 324, 439-440
Buddhism, 110, 266
Bungei Shunju, 232
Burnell-Nugent, F. H., Brigadier, 222

## C

Calligraphy Research Association, 425
Capital Library, 480
Central Committee of the Communist Party of China, 466-467
Chang Chieh-ho, 63-67, 69, 77, 79, 84
Chang Chih-tung, 59
Chang Ching-hui, 105-107, 240, 254-256, 283, 286-287, 292, 317, 319-320, 324, 338, 374, 379, 389-390, 459
Chang Hai-peng, 224, 255-256
Chang Hsueh-liang, 139, 184, 186-188, 194, 218, 226, 229, 268
Chang Hsun, 87-92, 94-100, 105-107, 120, 142, 145, 162, 180, 192, 426
Chang Huan-hsiang ("Big Mouth"), 360, 388, 413, 443, 468, 471
Chang, Little, 338
Chang, Old (former puppet general), 422, 430, 443
Chang Pi, 146
Chang Tso-hsiang, 220
Chang Tso-lin, 105-108, 120, 123, 145, 153-154, 156, 158, 163, 175-177, 179-188, 190, 192, 194, 197, 225, 246, 284, 479

485

Chang Tsung-chang, 105, 175, 183-186, 189, 194, 255
Chang Yen-ching, 256
Chang Yu-ching, 276
Chang Yuan-fu, 69
Changchiakou (Kalgan), 86
Changchun, 72, 245, 254-255, 257, 265, 276, 278-279, 282-283, 289, 293, 300, 305, 307, 319-320, 334, 337, 349, 362, 380, 407, 425-426, 444
Changchun Number One Motor Works, 446
Chao (Interrogator), 336-337, 380-382, 389
Chao Erh-sun, 81
Chao Hsin-po, 256
Chao Kuei-lan, 363
Chao Ping-chun, 80
Chao Yi-man, 453
Chaoyang, battle of, 144
Chaoyuan, 387
Chekiang Province, 174
Chen Pao-shen, 51, 58-61, 70, 78-79, 81-82, 84-85, 88-94, 101, 109, 113-114, 116, 138-140, 143, 145, 147, 152-153, 157, 158-161, 173, 175-180, 182, 186, 189, 191, 193-194, 200-201, 203-204, 206, 208, 212-213, 221-222, 224, 227, 230, 238-239, 257, 264, 377, 422, 446, 470
Chen Tseng-shou, 208, 221, 238-239, 241, 255
Cheng, Old (Mongol), 376, 401, 417, 454
Cheng Chih-yuan, 256
Cheng Chui, 223-224, 230-236, 239, 247, 256, 265, 267-269, 271-272
Cheng Hsiao-hsu, 108, 131, 138, 140-142, 151-154, 157-162, 168, 174-175, 189-191, 194, 196, 200-201, 203-208, 213, 217-219, 221-225, 227, 229-231, 233-235, 237-241, 243, 246-247, 253-256, 259, 261-265, 267-269, 271-272, 274-276, 282-284, 300, 426, 445, 451, 470
Cheng Yu, 256
Chi Chi-chung, 204, 228-229, 231, 235
Chi Hsiang, 4
Chi Ling, 140, 150
Chia (section head), 355
Chiang (warder), 359, 401, 462

Chiang Kai-shek, 177, 183-185, 188, 194-197, 217, 222, 228, 267-268, 273, 319, 334, 412, 425, 438, 445, 451, 456, 464
Chiang Shu-ching, 449
Chiao (family name of Pu Yi's nurse), 72-73
Chichibu, Prince (Chichibu-no-Miya Yasuhito), 276, 280-281
Chien Lung (emperor), 46, 58, 60, 65, 105, 133, 181, 194-196, 357
Chihli (now Hopei Province), 12, 72-73, 98, 184
Chihli army, 107, 144
Chihli clique, 102, 105, 107-108
Chihli-Fengtien war, 118, 144
Chilien Mountains, 468
Chin (a deputy governor), 457, 471
Chin-Doihara Agreement, 283
Chin Liang, 139, 155, 223, 227
Chin Pi-hui (Kawashima Yoshiko), 372
Chin Pi-tung, 256
Chinese Academy of Sciences, 478
Chinese People's Liberation Army, see People's Liberation Army
Chinese People's Political Consultative Conference, 424
Chinese People's Volunteers, 349-352, 357, 363, 430-431, 434, 445, 475
Chinese Red Cross, 431
Ching Dynasty, 3, 19, 32, 36, 40, 54, 56, 60, 72, 77-84, 90, 98, 100-101, 104, 111, 120, 132, 140, 146, 174, 176, 195, 239, 241, 243, 246, 270, 275, 284, 294, 425, 429, 438
Ching house, 34-37, 54, 80-82, 85, 88, 95-96, 110-111, 119, 125, 134-135, 146-147, 155, 163, 166, 186, 189, 196, 208-209, 214, 270, 447
Ching Fang-chang, 208
Ching, Prince (Yi Kuang), 17-18, 20-21, 34, 36-37, 61
Ching Yi, 65, 117-118
Chita, 323
Chiu Chin, 426
Chou An Hui, 83
Chou En-lai, 334, 423, 456
Chou Po-jen, 391
Chu, Old (cell chief), 439
Chu Chi-chien, 79

Chu Yi-fan, 58-60, 90, 109, 147, 152
Chuang Ho, 116
Chukeh Liang, Second, *see* Liu Feng-
    chih
Chun, 1st Prince (Pu Yi's grandfather),
    3, 7, 10-11, 15, 23-26, 53, 73
Chun, 2nd Prince (Pu Yi's father), 3,
    7, 10-11, 15-16, 105-106, 126, 136, 148-149,
    150-152
Chung Lun, 69
Chung Yuan Company, 212, 476
Chungking, 319
*Chuokoron*, (Japanese magazine), 269
Claudel, Henri, 268
Columbia University, 83
Common Programme, 424
Communist Party of China, 176, 201, 314,
    320, 333, 335, 352, 365, 369, 387, 392,
    400, 403, 409, 412, 414, 416, 419, 421,
    437, 445, 451, 475, 480, 482-483
Communist Youth League, 422, 475
"Concordia Association", 261-262, 278-
    279, 288
"Concordia Party", 261-262
Confucianism, 110, 266
Confucianists, 241
Confucius, 81, 100-111, 242, 261
Constitution of the People's Republic
    of China, 423-424
*Coup* of 1898, 13, 15
Cultural Palace of the Nationalities, 476

D

"Declaration of Independence of the
    Manchu and Mongol People", 245
*Defeat of the Aggressors, The,* 439-441
Demchukdongrub, *see* Te, Prince
*Diamond Sutra,* 327
Dipper, Dr., 160
Doihara, 205, 225-230, 233, 236, 240, 268,
    371, 451

E

East Asia, 182, 241-243
East Wind Car, 476
Eastern Dowager, *see* Tzu An

Eastern Mausolea, 194-195, 198, 228, 254,
    299, 423
Egypt, British invasion of, 439-440
Eighth Route Army, 314, 420
Elizabeth, *see* Wan Jung
England, 111, 113, 116, 128, 157, 211, *see
    also* Britain
Europe, 116, 157, 191-192, 242
Evergreen People's Commune, 478

F

Fan Li, 218
Fang Su-jung, 410-412, 438
Feng Han-ching, 256
Feng Kuo-chang, 36, 96-99, 105-106, 184'
Fengtien (now Liaoning), 105-106, 223,
    236, 256
Fengtien army, 193
Fengtien Club, 106-107
Fengtien warlord clique, 105-108, 145,
    153-154, 179-188, 190, 192-193, 255
Feng Yu-hsiang, 108, 144-146, 152-155,
    158-159, 165, 175, 181, 185, 194, 202-203
Fifth Sister (Pu Yi's), 426-427, 429, 456,
    473-474, 476
First Allied Anti-Japanese Army, 451
First Five-Year Plan for Developing
    Production, 289, 383, 408
First World War, 111, 113, 115, 266
Five-Anti and Three-Anti Movements,
    364, 367, 370
Fokulun, 54
Foochow, 205
Forbidden City, 38, 42, 53, 56-57, 62, 67,
    75, 77-80, 82-83, 85-87, 92, 94, 96, 98-
    101, 103-105, 107-108, 114, 116, 119-120,
    122-124, 126, 128-132, 134, 141-145, 149,
    151, 153, 156-157, 161, 167, 174, 181, 183,
    207-210, 223, 239, 254, 304, 309, 355, 361,
    376, 380, 425
Fourth Brother (Pu Yi's), 426, 473-474
Fourth Section of the Kwantung Army,
    254, 262
Fourth Sister (Pu Yi's), 455, 475
Fragrance Hill, 481, 483
France, 4, 13, 191, 210, 234, 268

*From Darkness to Light* (play), 441-442
Fu, Old, 409, 416
Furumi Tadayuki, 381, 384, 431, 469
Fushun, 338-339, 344, 347-350, 352, 357, 378, 408, 410, 412-413, 417-418, 431, 472-474, 478
Fushun Open-cast Mine, 410

G

General Affairs Office of the "Manchukuo" State Council, 259-261, 274, 301, 303, 317, 379, 381, 383, 431, 469
Geneva, 267
Geneva Agreement, 431
Geneva Conference, 445
George V, King, 211
Germany, 15-16, 21, 37, 268, 444
Gloucester, Duke of, 211
Godaigo (Japanese emperor), 218-219
Gold Star Co-operative, 449-450
Goodnow, Frank J., 83
Grand Council, 44
Great Ching, 59, 82, 88, 90, 108, 115, 146, 176, 196, 200, 242, 257
Great Hall of the People, 476
Great Leap Forward, 458
Great Wall, 274, 276-277, 293-294, 311, 385
"Greater East Asian Co-Prosperity Sphere", 302, 384

H

Hall of the Northeastern Martyrs, 444, 448, 450
Han nationality, 245, 423
Hankow, 428
Hanyang, 33
Harbin, 349-351, 356, 362, 371, 444, 447-448
Harbin police headquarters, 450
Harbin prison, 354
Hart, Robert, 270
Hashimoto Toranosuke, 269, 300, 318-319
Hayashi Gonsuke, Baron, 280-281
Heaven Shining Bright Deity (Amaterasu-o-mi-Kami), 298, 300-302, 319, 329
*Hie Maru*, 280
High Consorts (Dowager Consorts), 39-40, 42-47, 49-50, 52-53, 59, 62, 65-66,

72, 74, 84-85, 87, 90, 94, 114, 116-118, 120, 125, 133, 136, 147, 150, 159, 275
Hiranuma Kiichiro, 206-207
Hirohito, 281-282, 299, 390, *see also* Japanese emperor
Hiraoka Kotaro, 205
Hiroshima, 436
Hishikari Takashi, 275-276
History Museum, Peking, 480
Ho-Umezu Agreement, 283
Hokang Reformatory, 386
Honan, 432
Hongkong, 110, 116, 188, 191, 312
Hongkong and Shanghai Banking Corporation, 191
Honjo Shigeru, 219, 223-224, 244, 247, 255-256, 260, 262-265, 290
Hopei Province, 10, 184, 194, 274, 417, 432
House of Commons, 441
Household Department, 45-46, 61-62, 68-69, 78, 82, 85, 87, 90, 95-96, 100, 110, 113-115, 119, 122, 125-126, 130-131, 133-134, 136-144, 150, 152, 154-155, 162
Hsi Hsia, 220-221, 223, 235-236, 254-256, 259-261, 324, 459
Hsiao Ping-yen, 208
Hsieh Chieh-shih, 201-202, 204, 256
Hsien, Old, 372-377, 379, 398, 433, 454, 467
Hsien Chi, 224
Hsien Feng (emperor), 4, 5, 10
Hsien Yuan, 224
*Hsin Wen Pao* of Shanghai, 99
Hsingan, 285
Hsinking ("New Capital"), 245, 270, 406, *see also* Changchun
Hsiu, Little, 336-338, 342-344, 347, 360, 389, 398, 481
Hsu Fang, 57, 59
Hsu Pao-heng, 256
Hsu Shih-chang, 80-81, 95-102, 107-108, 110, 118-120, 123
Hsu, 97, 100-101, 106, 108
Hsuan Tung (Pu Yi's title as Ching emperor), 46, 92, 94-95, 102, 120-121, 127, 137, 139, 143, 146, 199, 208, 218
Hsuchow, 89, 97

Hu Shih, 103, 127, 153, 157-158, 272, 480
Hu Sze-yuan, 178-179, 186, 192, 208, 212-213, 221, 238-239, 255-257, 259, 263-266, 276, 355
Huang, Dr., 354, 391
Huang Fu, 146, 154
Huang Yung-hung, 387
Huangkutun Railway Station, 187
Hunan, 90

### I

Imperial Maritime Customs, 270
*Imprisoned Emperor of China, The*, 437
Inner Mongolia, 97, 183, 188, 190, 274, 287
Institute of History and Literature, 475
International Military Tribunal for the Far East, 225, 328, 432, 440
Itagaki Seishiro, 220-221, 223, 225, 234-237, 240-241, 243-247, 253-254, 262-263, 269, 285, 299, 451
Italy, 268

### J

Japan, 13, 34, 37, 97, 140, 143, 167, 173-175, 177, 182-184, 186, 188-190, 197-198, 200-201, 203, 206-207, 218, 221, 225-230, 233-234, 236, 241-243, 259, 262-264, 267-268, 271-277, 279-291, 293-296, 298-303, 306, 313, 316, 319-320, 329, 348, 361-362, 366, 372, 379, 384-385, 398, 418, 430, 432, 436, 439, 448, 458-459
Japan-U.S. Security Treaty, 479
Japanese Army, 199, 223, 231, 234, 244, 259, 277, 295, 311, 313-318, 384, 390, 436, 448, 451-452, *see also* Kwantung Army
Japanese Army Cadet School, 198, 289, 294
Japanese 731 Bacteriological Unit, 444, 448
Japanese Diet, 143
Japanese emperor, 227, 276, 278, 281-282, 293-294, 298, 300-301, 313, 315, 319, 329, *see also* Hirohito
Japanese empress, 294
Japanese empress dowager, 281
Japanese Foreign Ministry, 272

Japanese Government, 272, 275
Japanese Legation in Peking, 160-173, 200, 355
Japanese press, 439
Japanese Self-Defence Force, 435
Japanese surrender, 428, 442, 451
Japanese war criminals, 398-399, 411, 431-432, 434, 437-439, 441, 443, 457, 470
Jehol, 3, 5, 274, 384
Jenchiu County, 72
Jimmu (emperor), 298, 301, 443
Johnston, Reginald Fleming, 56, 59, 103-104, 107-116, 121-131, 133, 137-143, 145, 147, 150-154, 157-161, 173, 210-211, 223, 269
Juan Chin-shou, 63-64, 69
Jui, Little, 342, 344, 346-347, 355, 357, 359-365, 370, 374, 389-390, 399-400, 423, 439, 471, 481-483
July 7th Incident, 226
Jun, Old, 440-442, 455
Jun Chi, 197-198
Jung Hui (High Consort), 118, 275
Jung Lu, 11-13, 15
Jung Yuan, 137, 139, 147, 150, 179-180, 202, 204-205, 208, 340-343, 354

### K

Kaeisumi Toshiichi, 220-221, 223-224, 227-231, 235-240, 253-254, 258
Kaiser of Germany, 15, 21
Kamakura Shogunate, 218
Kang Hsi (emperor), 60, 67, 89, 91, 135
Kang Te (title of Pu Yi as "emperor of Manchukuo"), 387, 415
Kang Yu-wei, 13, 108, 143, 175-176
Kao Shou-san, 387
Kashii Kohei, 219-221, 224, 264
Kato (Japanese consul-general in Tientsin), 201-202, 204
Kawamoto, Colonel, 187
Kawashima Yoshiko, *see* Chin Pi-hui
Kazuki Seiji, 206
Kemmu Restoration, 218
Khabarovsk, 325, 333, 339
Khasan Lake, 244
Khingan Mountains, 383
Kiangsi, 88, 109
Kiangsu, 59, 88, 184

Kirin-Heilungkiang Salt Tax Office, 257
Kirin-Meihokuo line, 318
Kirin Province, 220, 223, 310
Kishida (member of Black Dragon
    Society), 203-204, 207
Komai Tokuzo, 260-261, 269, 274
Konoe Fumimaro, 207
Korea, 349-351, 353, 357, 363, 406, 430-431,
    434, 445
Korean armistice, 445
Korean People's Army, 350-351, 431, 445
Korean War, 352-353, 357, 362, 431, 470
Koreans, 191, 245
Kou Chien, 218
Ku, Little, 340-342, 347, 358, 360-363, 374,
    389, 398, 481-482
*Ku Chin* Research Association, 425
Kuang Hsu (emperor), 3, 6, 8-9, 12-13,
    15-18, 20, 24, 33, 38-39, 43, 47, 51, 53-54,
    59-60, 68, 81, 117, 275
Kudo Tetsusaburo, 232, 274-275
Kuei Fu, 224, 256, 284
Kung, Prince (Pu Wei), 201, 425
Kung, Prince (Yi Hsin), 4-6, 9, 361
Kuo, Old, 374
Kuo Wen-lin, 474
Kuomintang, 34, 176-177, 187, 194, 196,
    201, 209, 217, 228, 267-268, 313, 325, 412,
    418, 427, 442, 444-445, 477
Kuomintang army, 314
Kuomintang government, 193, 283, 423,
    478
Kuomintang troops, 319
Kwangsi, 140
Kwangtung, 188
Kwantung Army, 129, 187, 219-222, 224-
    227, 230, 234-241, 244-247, 253, 255,
    257-262, 264-266, 269, 273-274, 276-280,
    282-295, 298-300, 302-303, 308, 311, 313-
    316, 319, 383, 451, 459
Kwantung Army Headquarters, 277-278,
    291
Kwantung Leased Territory, 266
Kyoto, 218-219


L

Labour Control Law, 385
Laohu colliery, 418

Lao Nai-hsuan, 81-82
Laotzu, 419
League Against the Favourable Treat-
    ment of the Ching House, 166
League of Nations, 221, 268, 271-273, 283
League of Nations Commission of
    Enquiry, 267-273
Legation Quarter, 14-15, 37, 108, 146, 154,
    156, 159-163
Legislative Council, "Manchukuo", 264
Li (a prison official), 374, 455, 473
Li, Big, 230, 318, 320, 328, 354-355, 359-361,
    363, 368, 370, 388-390, 398, 400, 402,
    405-408, 439, 443, 456
Li Lien-ying, 9, 11, 63, 68
Li Pan, 256
Li Shu-hsien, 481
Li Shun, 106
Li Tien-kuei, 392
Li Tien-ying, 392
Li Ying-hua, 392
Li Yuan-hung, 87, 91-93, 95, 97, 107, 119-
    120, 123, 162
Liang Chi-chao, 103
Liang Chi-chao, 13
Liang Shih-yi, 80
Liang Ting-fen, 59-60, 70, 81, 88, 90
Liaoning Province, 105, 233, 274, *see also*
    Fengtien
Liaoyang, 385
Lin Chi, 256
Lin Ting-shen, 256
Ling Sheng, 284-288
Liu (warder), 346, 358, 463
Liu Cheng-fa, 387
Liu Feng-chih, the "second Chukeh
    Liang", 189, 192-193
Liu Hsiang-yeh, 208, 219, 221, 223-224
Liu, Old, 422, 430, 443, 478
Liu Shao-chi, 467
Liulichang, 300
Liutiaokou, 234
Lloyd, Selwyn (Foreign Secretary), 440-
    442
Lo Chen-yu, 138, 142, 151-154, 159, 161,
    163, 168, 173-179, 189, 196, 200-206, 208,
    213, 217, 219-224, 227, 234-241, 246-247,
    255-256, 451

Lo Fu-pao, 256
London, 112, 269, 327
Louis XVI, 35
Loyang, 108
Lu Chung-lin, 146-148
Lu Jun-hsiang, 57, 59
Luan River, 184
Lukouchiao, 283, 290
Lung, Old, 439
Lung Yu (Empress Dowager), 20, 33-37,
   41-50, 53, 56, 64, 69, 80-82, 88, 91, 95,
   99, 108
Lungfeng mine, 417-418, 452
Lushun, 37, 86-87, 176, 188, 201-202, 205,
   223, 236-240, 253, 256, 262-263, 284-285,
   299, 311, 325, 355, 451
Lutai-Luanchou sector, 186
Lytton, Lord, 268-270

M

Ma Chan-shan, 224
Macleay (British minister), 150
Malan Valley, 194
"Manchukuo", 72, 105, 111, 129, 199, 207,
   240, 244-245, 251-320, 323-324, 333-334,
   340, 347-348, 350, 356-357, 360, 362,
   366-367, 370, 372, 378-379, 381, 383-387,
   389, 391, 397-398, 406, 409, 413-419, 424,
   426, 431, 437, 439, 443-444, 446, 449-450,
   459, 462-464, 469, 472, 474
Manchukuo Yearbook and Government
   Report, 382
Manchuria, 191, 194, 218, 221, 223, 226-227,
   242, 245, 255, 260, 266-269, 271-272, 298,
   316
Manchurian Committee of the Chinese
   Communist Party, 451
Manchurians, 240, 260, 286
Manchus, 3-5, 11, 17, 20, 36, 87, 137, 245,
   423-424, 472
Mao Tse-tung, 413, 415, 423, 430, 456,
   467, 480
Marriage Law, 427
Marunouchi Building, 448
McCoy, Frank Ross, 268-269
May Day, 401
May 4th Student Movement of 1919, 101,
   115

Mei Lan-fang, 212-213
Meihokuo, 318
Meiji (Japanese emperor), 242, 281
Mencius, 242, 473
Meng, Old, 473
Menshevik, 327
Minami Jiro, 207, 225, 275, 282, 330
Ming Dynasty, 42, 56, 62, 132
Ming Tombs Reservoir, 455-456
Ministry of Defence, "Manchukuo", 290
Mino Tomoyoshi, 205
Miyake, 255
Miyun, 274
Mizuno Katsukuni, 218
Mohism, 110
Mongolia, 191, 194, 284, see also Mon-
   golian People's Republic, Inner
   Mongolia
Mongolian People's Republic, 188, 298,
   448
Mongols, 245
Monument to the Revolutionary Heroes,
   476
Moscow, 327
Muto Nobuyoshi, 264-266, 273-274

N

Nagasaki, 434
Nanking, 34, 35-36, 88, 177, 197, 200, 217,
   228, 268, 272-273, 283
Nanking government, 273, see also Kuo-
   mintang government
Nankou, 185
Napoleon, 54
Napoleon III, 86
National Army of Feng Yu-hsiang, 38,
   108, 145, 148-149, 151-155, 157-158, 163,
   168, 175, 198, see also Feng Yu-hsiang
National Committee of the Chinese
   People's Political Consultative Con-
   ference, 423, 481
National Government, 196-197, 200, 217,
   272, see also Kuomintang government
National People's Congress, 423-424, 474,
   481
Newton, 54
"National Foundation Shrine", 293,
   300-301, 318

New Army (Peiyang Army), 12, 19
New China, 342-343, 353, 403, 419, 422, 435-436
New Fourth Army, 314
Niuhuhu (Eastern Dowager), 5
Nomanhan campaign of 1939, 314
North China, 33, 229, 274, 283-284, 313
*North China Daily Mail*, 104-105
Northeast China, 72, 86, 97, 107, 123, 129, 158, 182-184, 186-190, 193, 197-198, 209, 215, 217, 219, 220-230, 233-234, 238-240, 244-245, 253-254, 266-268, 272, 274, 284, 286, 288, 294, 297, 299-300, 304, 312, 324, 328-329, 350, 352, 354-355, 367-368, 370, 381-388, 406, 409-410, 417, 427, 432, 443, 451
Northeastern army, 416
Northern Expedition, 176, 187, 200, 217
Northeastern People's Government, 424
Northwest China, 424, 456
Notice of a Special Pardon from the Supreme People's Court of the People's Republic of China, 472

O

Ohira Kihachiro, 86
Okamura (Japanese general), 183, 293
Oki, 218
*On New Democracy*, 341
Opium Wars, 445
Organizational Law of "Manchukuo", 258
Osugi Sakae, 234
Oudendijk, W. J., 129-130, 150
Oxford University, 110, 116

P

Pacific War, 293, 312, 383
"Pagoda of the Loyal Souls", 278
Pai River, 199, 230-232
Palace Museum (Peking), 477
Panchiatai Village, 432
Pang, Old, 432
Panmunjom talks, 445
Panpitien, 6
*Pao-chia* system, 288
Pao Hsi, 150, 256, 277
Paris, 267

Payen County, 392
Peace Preservation Army, 284
Pearl Consort of Kuang Hsu, 16
Pedigree of Ching House, 249
Peihai Lake, 425
Peiyang (Northern) Army, 12, 16-17, 20, 33
Peiyang warlords, 95-101, 105, 184, 313, 423, 478-479
Peking, 3, 5, 10, 12, 14-15, 17, 34, 37, 54, 59, 73, 80, 83, 92, 97-98, 102, 105-107, 111, 119-120, 122, 125, 127, 134, 143, 145-146, 151-154, 163, 166, 168-169, 175, 178, 181, 185-186, 188, 196-197, 207-210, 212, 217, 229, 273-276, 290, 292, 300, 310-311, 328, 334, 356, 377, 425-427, 429, 435, 455, 468, 473-477, 483
Peking Botanical Gardens of the Institute of Botany, 478-479
*Peking Daily*, 166
Peking-Fengtien Railway, 187
Peking-Hankow Railway, 194
*Peking Leader* (English-language newspaper), 106
Peking Library, 480
Peking Police School, 144
Peking-Tientsin region, 196-197
People's Government, Chinese, 334-335, 352, 358, 365, 368-369, 376, 386, 388, 400, 403, 412-413, 424, 427, 436, 444, 466-467, 480, 482-483
People's Liberation Army, Chinese, 334, 336, 397, 424, 427
People's Political Council of the Kuomintang, 34
People's Republic of China, 325, 431, 444, 466, 472
Pingfangchu, 450
Pingtingshan (massacre), 409-410
Prince Regent (Pu Yi's father), 16-24, 26, 28, 31, 33-36, 147, *see also* Chun, 2nd Prince
Prison governor, 345, 355, 357-359, 366, 397, 400, 402-404, 435, 461, 465, 474
"Proclamation of the Chief Executive", 255
Proclamation of the People's Liberation Army, 424
Property Control Law, 289

Proposal of the Central Committee of the CPC to the Standing Committee of the NPC, 466
Pu Chia, 57, 113
Pu Chieh, 39-40, 57-58, 113-114, 125, 128-132, 197-198, 209, 218, 277, 287, 289-291, 294, 320, 340-342, 346, 349, 376, 397-398, 402, 422, 430, 432, 434, 439-440, 445, 478
Pu Chien, 435, 475-477
Pu Chin (also known as Pu Hsueh-chai), 425, 475
Pu Hsiu, 425
Pu Hsueh-chai, see Pu Chin
Pu Lun, 57, 84
Pu Wei, 36-37, 173, 176, 196, 201, 361

R

Red Spear Society, 193
Red Swastika Society of the Northeast, 188
Reform Movement of 1898, 12
Regulations for the Punishment of Counter-Revolutionaries, 351
Report of the Commission of Enquiry of the League of Nations, 269, 271
Republic of China, 27, 37-38, 45, 50-51, 57, 60, 77-83, 86-88, 93, 95-99, 101-104, 114-116, 119-120, 123-124, 129, 131, 140, 142, 145-148, 165-167, 200, 241, 313, 319, 376, 429
"Republic of Manchuria and Mongolia", 239
Republican Army, 99
Republicans, 34-36
Revolution of 1911, 3, 19, 21, 46, 59-60, 62, 98, 120, 141, 203, 220, 425
Revolutionary Museum, 476
"River-side Scene at the Ching Ming Festival" (Sung painting), 478
Ross (British journalist), 192
Russia, 13, 34, 417
Russo-Japanese War of 1904-05, 205

S

Saga (marquis), 290
Saga Hiro, 290
Sato Tomoyasu, 300

Schnee, Heinrich, 268
Second Opium War, 4
Second Sister (Pu Yi's), 426, 428, 455, 475
"Second Revolution" of 1913, 184
Second World War, 62, 188, 234, 267, 404, 437, 448
"Security and Rectification Law", 386
Semionov, 188-191, 206
Seoul, 351
September 18th Incident, 193, 218, 222, 234, 244, 272
Seventh Sister (Pu Yi's), 426, 475
Shaman, 6, 67
Shan Chi, 86-87
Shang Yen-ying, 139, 188, 219, 234, 236, 238, 256, 475
Shanghai, 164, 168, 184, 188, 190, 205, 276
Shanhaikuan, 145
Shansi, 59, 185
Shantung, 177, 184, 186, 417
Shao Ying, 78-79, 106, 125, 140, 142, 146-148, 150, 163
Sheng Tsu (emperor), 89, see also Kang Hsi
Sheng Yun, 189, 200, 232
Shengli colliery, 418
Shenyang, 219-220, 223, 227, 233, 235-237, 253, 318, 320, 337, 339, 342, 358, 397, 411, 431, 444, 451, 469, 473
Shenyang Machine-Tool Plant, 444
Shih Hua Pao, 325
Shih Hsu, 69, 82, 98, 100
Shinto religion, 298-299, 301
Showa Steel Works, 445
Shuifeng Reservoir, 469
Shuntien Times, 155, 158, 169
Shuntienfu, 73
Sian, 14
Siberia, 266
Singapore, 312, 315
Sino-French War (1883-85), 205
Sino-Japanese War (1894-95), 11
"Sino-Russian Anti-Bolshevik Military Convention", 189
Sino-Soviet frontier, 333
Sixth Sister (Pu Yi's), 426, 475
"Societies for the Prevention of Opium-Smoking", 384

Soong Mei-ling, 196-197
South China, 274
South Manchuria Railway, 187, 219, 233-234, 255-256, 277
South-Manchurian Anti-Japanese Volunteers, 410
Southeast Asia, 109, 226, 315
Southern Tang Dynasty (937-975), 105
Soviet Government, 323
Soviet Red Army, 188, 292, 316-317, 320, 323, 325, 379, 390, 442, 448
Soviet Union, 189, 191, 194, 267, 298, 320-334, 336-337, 340, 343, 354, 358, 361-362, 379, 406, 434, 448
Special Pardon Order, 472
Spring and Autumn Period (770-475 B.C.), 84, 218
Spring Festival, 443, 475
Standing Committee of the National People's Congress, 466-467
State Council of "Manchukuo", 259, 261, 290, 302
State Duma, 327
Su, Prince, 86-87, 97, 238, 372
Su Shun, 4-6
Suifenho, 333, 481
Summer Palace (Yi Ho Yuan), 10-12, 16, 38, 40, 73, 82, 156, 159, 361
Sun Chuan-fang, 145, 197
Sun Po-yuan, 305
Sun Tien-ying, 194-196
Sun Yat-sen, 35
Sung Dynasty, 129
Sung Hsi-lien, 477
Sung Kai-tung, 386
Sung Yu-jen, 83
Supreme People's Court, 471-472
Suzuki Kantaro, 207
Szechuan, 82

T

Tahuofang reservoir project, 444, 469-470
Tai Tsu (Nurhachi, founder of Ching Dynasty), 334
Taiping Heavenly Kingdom, 4, 90
Taishanpao, 412-413, 438

Taiyuan, 431
Takebe Rokuzo, 317, 319, 379, 383, 389-390, 431, 459
Takemoto (Colonel), 151, 153, 160-163, 239
Taku, 14, 233
Talien, 77, 86, 204, 220, 227, 237-238, 280
Talitzukou, 318, 361, 390, 451, 459
Tamama (destroyer), 280
Tan Sze-tung, 13
Tan Yu-ling, 310-311, 329
Tanaka Cabinet, 182, 194, 200
Tanaka Giichi, 182
Tang Dynasty, 56, 111
Tang Yun-lin, 256
Tangkangtzu, 234, 237-238, 451
"Tangku Agreement", 273
Tao Kuang (emperor), 3, 425, 445
Tao Yuan-ming, 473
Taoism, 110, 419
Tatung Park, 258
Te, Prince (Demchukdongrub), 287-288, 311
Te Tsung, see Kuang Hsu
Ten Thousand Men's Grave, 418, 420
Teng Chiung-lin (Pu Yi's pseudonym), 56
Third Sister (Pu Yi's), 113, 426-427, 429, 433, 475, 477
38th Parallel, 351
"Thought Rectification Law", 386
"Three All" policy, 313, 436
Three Character Classic, 483
Three Eastern Provinces (Northeast), 242
Three Kingdoms period, 192
Tibet, 468
Tien An Men Gate, 476
Tien An Men Square, 476, 479
Tientsin, 12, 14, 37, 69, 86, 97, 104, 128-129, 152-154, 168, 171-233, 238-239, 241, 261, 264, 273-274, 287, 294, 304, 310, 334, 354-355, 361, 371, 390-391, 423, 428, 446, 476
Tientsin Incident, 229
Tientsin-Pukow Railway, 185
Ting Chieh-hsiu, 256

Tojo Hidemichi, 302
Tokyo, 151, 201, 206, 218, 222, 239, 264-266, 268, 274, 281, 289-290, 319, 432, 435, 459
Toyama Mitsuru, 205, 225
Toyama Takeo, 197-198, 206
Treaty of Peking, 5
Tsai Chun, 4-5, see also Tung Chih
Tsai Feng, see Chun, 2nd Prince
Tsai Hsun (Tsai Tao's brother), 25, 150
Tsai Tao (Pu Yi's uncle), 24-25, 57, 128, 151, 422-424, 474
Tsai Tien, 8-9, see also Kuang Hsu
Tsai Tse, 20-21
Tsang Shih-yi, 255-256, 265, 282, 324
Tsao family, 180
Tsao Kun, 105-106, 108, 120, 145
Tseng Kuo-fan, 90
Tsinan, 183, 194
Tsinan massacre, 183
Tsingtao, 37, 80-81, 83, 176
Tsukuda Nobuo, 203-204, 207
Tsunhua County, 194
Tu Yu-ming, 477
Tuan Chi-jui, 37, 80, 87, 94-99, 101, 145, 153-154, 156, 162-163, 168, 175, 177, 179, 197, 479
Tuan Kang, 50-53, 107, 117-118, 147
Tuitsuike Hotel, 234-235
Tun, Prince, 425
Tung Chi-hsu, 141, 203, 208, 219, 221, 224-234, 236, 238, 256, 285, 288-291, 369
Tung Chih (emperor), 3, 6-9, 13, 23, 38, 47, 54, 59-60, 68, 117
Tung Meng Hui, 425
Tung Yuan, 105
Tunghua, 316, 426-428, 451
Tungpientao, 451
Tungshan mines, 386
Tzu An (Eastern Dowager), 5, 8, 10
Tzu Hsi (Empress Dowager), 3-18, 21-23, 25-28, 31-32, 43, 51, 59-60, 62-63, 68, 109, 137, 194-196, 211, 361, 376, 479

U

Uchida Yasuda, 219, 223, 255, 268
Ueda Kenkichi, 285-286, 298, 314
Ugaki Kazushige, 207

Umezu Yoshijiro, 298
United Nations, 445
U.S.A., 197, 267, 302, 349, 352, 435, 444, 446, see also America
U.S. imperialism, 352, 445
U.S.S.R., see Soviet Union

V

Vladivostok, 183-184

W

Wales, 116
Wan, Old (Pu Yi's brother-in-law), 357, 399-400, 426, 433, 439-441, 456, 468, 471, 474
Wan Jung (Pu Yi's empress), 27, 113, 118-119, 121, 136, 146, 148, 159, 162, 173, 212, 214, 221, 238, 254, 258, 276-277, 279, 308, 310, 320
Wan Sheng-shih, 208, 238, 256
Wan Ta-chung, 256
Wang (warder), 342, 387; (section head) 454, 463
Wang, Mrs. (Pu Yi's nurse), 71
Wang, Old, 356, 365, 367-368, 371, 389, 454
Wang Cheng-ting (C. T. Wang), 150-151
Wang Chi-lien, 256
Wang Ching-wei, 34, 222, 346, 409, 424, 439
Wang Chiu-cheng, 102
Wang Kuo-wei, 139, 164, 174
Wang Shih, 190-191
Wang Shih-chen, 93-95
Wang Ya-min, 387
Wang Yao-wu, 477
Weihaiwei, 110
Wen, Dr., 456-457, 464
Wen Hsiu (Hui Hsin), 118, 121, 148, 159, 162, 173, 210, 213-214, 310
Wen Su, 208
Weng Tung-ho, 12
Western Dowager, see Tzu Hsi
White Russians, 189-191
Whiteway, Laidlaw & Co., 211
Wu (a state), 218
Wu Pei-fu, 108, 120, 144-145, 175-176, 179, 185, 194, 197
Wuchang, 19, 176

Wuchang Rising (1911), 21, 33-34, 184
Wuhan, 293

# Y

Yalu River, 349
Yamashita Tomoyuki, 315
Yamata Otozo, 316-318
Yamato Hotel, 237, 246
Yang Ching-yu, 313, 451-453
Yang Chung-hsi, 208
Yangpai bridge, 418
Yangpai River, 418
Yangtse River, 89
Yehonala (principal wife of the first Prince Chun, sister of Tzu Hsi), 23
Yehonala (Empress Dowager Tzu Hsi), see Tzu Hsi
Yen Hsi-shan, 185, 196
Yenchi area, 313
Yenchow, 89
Yentai (Chefoo), 205
Yi Ho Tuan, 11, 13-14
Yi Huan, see Chun, 1st Prince
Yi Ko Tan, 54, 59, 138

Yi Kuang, see Ching, Prince
Yi Mo, 25
Yin Chang, 120
Yingkow, 183, 233-234
Yokohama, 280
Yonai Mitsumasa, 207
Yoshida (interpreter), 219, 222, 226-227, 229, 231
Yoshida Shigeru, 168, 207
Yoshioka Yasunori, 129, 199, 218, 284-299, 302-303, 306, 308, 310-320, 379-380, 390, 452, 470
Yoshizawa, 143, 150, 160, 163, 206
Youth Party, 209
Yu Ching-tao, 453
Yu Chung, 57-58, 84, 114
Yu Chung-han, 256
Yuan, Old, 366, 382, 398, 405, 407, 409, 416, 433, 440, 442, 467
Yuan Chin-kai, 236, 256
Yuan Ming Yuan Palace, 66
Yuan Shih-kai, 12, 16, 17-18, 20-21, 33-37, 77-88, 97, 99-100, 166, 177, 184, 479
Yueh (a state), 60, 218
Yung Cheng (emperor), 135

496

从皇帝到公民

——我的前半生——

下册

爱新觉罗·溥仪著

詹纳尔译

\*

外文出版社出版

（中国北京百万庄路24号）

外文印刷厂印刷

中国国际图书贸易总公司

（中国国际书店）发行

北京399信箱

1965年（大32开）第一版

1986年第二版第三次印刷

编号：（英）11050—32

00775

11—E—619D B